Rethinking Drug Laws

CLARENDON STUDIES IN CRIMINOLOGY

Published under the auspices of the Institute of Criminology, University of Cambridge; the Mannheim Centre, London School of Economics; and the Centre for Criminology, University of Oxford.

General Editors: Mary Bosworth and Carolyn Hoyle
(*University of Oxford*)

Editors: Alison Liebling, Paolo Campana, Loraine Gelsthorpe, and Kyle Treiber
(*University of Cambridge*)

Tim Newburn, Jill Peay, Coretta Phillips, Peter Ramsay, and Robert Reiner
(*London School of Economics*)

Ian Loader and Lucia Zedner
(*University of Oxford*)

RECENT TITLES IN THIS SERIES:

Rethinking Drug Laws: Theory, History, Politics
Seddon

A Precarious Life: Community and Conflict in a Deindustrialized Town
Willis

Exporting the UK Policing Brand 1989–2021
Sinclair

Penality in the Underground: The IRA's Pursuit of Informers
Dudai

Assessing the Harms of Crime: A New Framework for Criminal Policy
Greenfield and Paoli

Armed Robbers: Identity and Cultural Mythscapes in the Lucky Country
Taylor

Crime, Justice, and Social Order: Essays in Honour of A. E. Bottoms
Liebling, Shapland, Sparks, and Tankebe

Policing Human Rights
Martin

Rethinking Drug Laws

Theory, History, Politics

Toby Seddon

OXFORD
UNIVERSITY PRESS

OXFORD
UNIVERSITY PRESS

Great Clarendon Street, Oxford, OX2 6DP,
United Kingdom

Oxford University Press is a department of the University of Oxford.
It furthers the University's objective of excellence in research, scholarship,
and education by publishing worldwide. Oxford is a registered trade mark of
Oxford University Press in the UK and in certain other countries

© Toby Seddon 2023

The moral rights of the author have been asserted

First Edition published in 2023

Public sector information reproduced under Open Government Licence v3.0
(http://www.nationalarchives.gov.uk/doc/open-government-licence/open-government-licence.htm)

Published in the United States of America by Oxford University Press
198 Madison Avenue, New York, NY 10016, United States of America

British Library Cataloguing in Publication Data

Data available

Library of Congress Control Number: 2023936486

ISBN 978-0-19-284652-5

DOI: 10.1093/oso/9780192846525.001.0001

Printed and bound by
CPI Group (UK) Ltd, Croydon, CR0 4YY

General Editors' Introduction

The *Clarendon Studies in Criminology series* aims to provide a forum for outstanding theoretical and empirical work in all aspects of criminology and criminal justice, broadly understood. The Editors welcome submissions from established scholars, as well as manuscripts based on excellent PhD dissertations. The Series was inaugurated in 1994, with Roger Hood as its first General Editor, following discussions between Oxford University Press and Oxford's then Centre for Criminological Research. These days, it is edited under the auspices of three centres: the Centre for Criminology at the University of Oxford, the Institute of Criminology at the University of Cambridge, and the Mannheim Centre for Criminology at the London School of Economics. Each institution supplies members of the Editorial Board and, in turn, the Series General Editor or Editors.

Rethinking Drug Laws offers a fresh, interdisciplinary account of the international drug control system. Drawing on a wide range of primary and secondary sources, Toby Seddon invites us to radically rethink how we understand drugs and their control, in a bid to deal with them differently.

The book, which is organised into three parts—Theory, History, and Politics—is underpinned and connected by Seddon's exploration of the concepts and practices associated with regulation, trade, and markets. Building on work by Peter Frankopan and John Braithwaite, the book sets a wider context for the history and future of international drug production and control, with a particular focus on China.

This is a lively read, which travels far in time and space. Its main premise, that to understand drugs and their control requires an interdisciplinary and conceptually capacious approach, is persuasive. As Seddon observes in the introduction, most people will have encountered drugs in some capacity in their personal lives, whether illicit or prescribed. Yet, criminological attention to the production and official management of drugs remains an area of specialism, rather than part of mainstream debates. In this book, Toby Seddon makes clear why and how this should change. As he points out, 'the drug question' is 'inherently political'. In its ubiquity and familiarity, it thus offers what he refers to as 'the opportunity for democratic dialogue and discussion', in order to build a better politics and fairer forms of regulation. We welcome this book to the series.

Mary Bosworth and Carolyn Hoyle
General Editors
Centre for Criminology, University of Oxford
February 2023

Acknowledgements

This book is the culmination of work that has unfolded over a long period of time. It was in 2006 that I first started thinking about drug policy from a regulatory perspective and this has been a continuing intellectual project ever since. A pivotal moment early on was an invitation to a RegNet conference at ANU in Canberra in 2011. The week I spent at RegNet was genuinely inspirational. The following year, I gave a public lecture in Manchester which set out the research agenda that I would pursue for the next 10 years. Two landmarks during that decade were the publication of a pair of papers: the 'Inventing Drugs' paper in 2016 in the *Journal of Law & Society* and the 2020 paper in *Social & Legal Studies* that first introduced the *exchangespace* concept. These built important intellectual foundations for what would become the first two parts of this book. The second paper was in fact loosely based on what I had presented back in 2011 at RegNet and its later development then benefited enormously from conversations with Bronwen Morgan and David Campbell during 2018.

Direct work on this book began in the second half of 2019. In autumn 2020, I changed institutions, moving from the University of Manchester to University College London (UCL). At Manchester, I had benefited for more than a dozen years from conversations about regulation with many colleagues, including Anthony Ogus, the late Mick Moran, Graham Smith, Tom Gibbons, Dave Williamson, Carolyn Abbot, Neville Harris, and others, all of whom shaped my thinking. Some of the visitors we hosted at Manchester over the years—notably John Braithwaite, Peter Grabosky, and Clifford Shearing—were particularly influential and have continued to be supportive. Arriving at UCL in the middle of a global pandemic has meant that opportunities for intellectual exchange have been both different and more limited but it has nevertheless proved a nourishing environment for research. To return to London after 20 years away has been as exciting as it was unexpected. Special thanks to my new colleagues in the UCL Social Research Institute for the warmth and generosity of their welcome.

In addition to those already mentioned, I have accumulated several other debts during the course of writing the book. Two of the most insightful drug policy scholars on the planet—Alison Ritter and Alex Stevens—have continued to inspire and inform with their prolific output. In particular, Alison's future classic book *Drug Policy* arrived as I was reaching the final stages of completing the manuscript. The work of organisations like Transform and Release (where I have recently become a Trustee) has also been very important, especially in helping me to think through the thorny questions about the politics of drugs that are explored in the third part of the book. In addition, I would like to thank staff working in the collections at the National Archives in London and the Weston Library in Oxford, for facilitating the archival research that features in Chapter 5, and Molly Seddon for help with the index and the network diagrams in Chapter 3. Reviewers for Oxford University Press (OUP) provided constructive reviews of the very best kind and Kate Plunkett at OUP guided the project with skill and patience. Lastly, thanks to George Harrison for making *Wonderwall Music*, an album I listened to innumerable times on headphones during late-night writing sessions for this book.

Toby Seddon
London, August 2022

Contents

1
Introduction

The 'drug question'

Introduction

Drugs have become a pervasive presence in our daily lives and in our culture. They are ubiquitous in the media, in music, in films, in television. And it must be only the rarest of individuals who has not been affected by or encountered drugs at some point, either personally or within their circle of family and friends. For social scientists with broad interests, they offer a rich field of enquiry, providing a window on to almost every aspect of society today: health, crime, security, globalisation, inequalities, policing, gender, race, youth, leisure, consumerism, and many more. And so it has proved for me over the last 25 years. In an important sense, looking at the 'drug question' provides a particular way of telling the story of humanity and of human societies. Psychoactive substances have had an especially critical role in the 'making of the modern world', as the historian David Courtwright (2001) once put it.

This book is an attempt to contribute to this grand endeavour of understanding the times we live in, whilst at the same time saying something new about this thorniest of twenty-first-century policy problems. The broad rationale for the book is that whilst the tectonic plates of global drug policy appear to have been shifting in recent years, a major gap in understanding is opening up with a real dearth of serious theoretical and conceptual work to help us make sense of this changing landscape. The book therefore aims to provide a radical intellectual reappraisal of how the international drug control system functions, where it came from, and the possibilities for alternative futures, through a critical interdisciplinary analysis. The foundational premise for this analysis is that viewing this system through the lens of regulation is the best way of bringing into focus its core elements and underlying structure.

Rethinking Drug Laws. Toby Seddon, Oxford University Press. © Toby Seddon 2023.
DOI: 10.1093/oso/9780192846525.003.0001

The book is distinctive in the way that it largely abandons an attachment to any one particular discipline. It is certainly primarily based within the social sciences rather than, for example, the life sciences, but it ranges widely across law, history, sociology, criminology, economics, political science, anthropology, and elsewhere. As is explained later in the chapter, the regulation lens allows this disciplinary boundary-crossing to work in a way that is both intellectually coherent and (hopefully) illuminating. Part of the book's ambition is to use this lens to bring into focus new things and in its conclusion this is framed in terms of the Kuhnian idea of a paradigm shift. A less hubristic goal is to make a modest contribution to the much bigger project of reframing and reshaping social science that scholars like John Braithwaite have been leading for several decades. An implicit claim of the book is that the cross-cutting and cross-sectoral character of drugs as a field makes it an especially fruitful, and perhaps under-explored, place to pursue that project.

In this introductory chapter, a concise overview is presented of some of the background and context for the rest of the book by:

- presenting an overview of the 'drug problem' and its historical evolution;
- summarising the nature of the prohibition paradigm and its failures;
- outlining the principal contemporary global trends and patterns in drug supply, distribution, and consumption;
- presenting trends in drug control and the apparent fragmenting of global consensus;
- setting out the need for new analytical approaches and new intellectual resources;
- providing an outline of the rest of the book.

The drug problem: A brief history and evolution

The desire for intoxication is one of the most fundamental drivers of human behaviour, second only to the triumvirate of sex/hunger/thirst (Siegel 1989). Evidence for this goes back many thousands of years, far into 'deep history' before the written word (Smail 2008). But we have not always had 'drugs' or a 'drug problem'. Indeed, those two ideas—'drugs' and 'drug problems'—are modern creations that emerged together at the same time.

As I have previously shown (Seddon 2016), whilst the meaning of the word 'drug' as a medicine has a longer history that can be traced back to at least the late Middle Ages, the modern meaning of a 'drug' as an intoxicant is remarkably recent. It began to be assembled in the late nineteenth century but is, in essence, a twentieth-century coinage (Porter 1996). Part of the process of its assembly involved the 'problematisation' of habits like opium or morphine consumption which had previously been viewed quite differently. The idea of drugs as *problematic* lies at the heart of this modern concept of a drug.

It is not just 'drugs' and 'drug problems' that go together. The assembly of the drug concept at the turn of the twentieth century was a central element within the wider creation of the international drug control system. The drug concept is, in this sense, a regulatory construct that is inextricably bound up with the global prohibition regime (Seddon 2016). In this way, these three elements—drug, drug problem, drug control—form a triangular structure on which our entire discourse and practice relating to the 'drug question' are based. Over time, this structure has become buried by layer after layer of actions and events and it is now a rarely-questioned and largely hidden foundation. But it is neither timeless nor universal and should be understood as a formation with historical origins and a trajectory of historical development. This is essential to understand for any critical analysis of contemporary drug control laws. The conceptual terms and theoretical apparatus we use for this analysis therefore need to be 'denaturalised', that is, we must understand their basis in this historically contingent triangular structure of elements. This is, in part, also a process of decolonisation, as the origin story of that structure is deeply racialised and woven together with imperial and colonial narratives (Seddon 2016). One of the central purposes of this book is to deconstruct this origin story—theoretically, historically, politically—as part of a critical project of rethinking the 'drug question'.

The triangle of drug/drug problem/drug control offers a critical historical focus on how we have arrived at the contemporary situation. But what about the journey and the distance travelled to reach where we are at today? The evolution of the drug problem over the last 100 years or so is certainly significant and the material shifts in patterns of supply, demand, and consumption will be summarised later in this chapter. But the *idea* of the drug problem has also evolved over the last century in ways not always closely tethered to those material changes. Acknowledging this separation and distinction, it is nevertheless still productive and useful to describe this evolution as it has been so influential globally in both research and policy terms.

Painting with a broad brush, we can identify three interweaving arcs of development in the way the 'drug problem' has been viewed and constructed: *race, risk,* and *security.* The *race* arc goes back to the origins of the system in the late nineteenth century and questions of race have formed a deep seam running through the foundations of drug control. Built into the structure of the first prohibitive drug laws was a set of political choices about which substances were to be defined as 'drugs'—cannabis/opium/cocaine but not alcohol/tobacco—and these choices largely reflected Western cultural preferences (Seddon 2016). Indeed, John Marks (1990:7) once wrote of the 'looking-glass world' for visitors from the Arab world arriving in Europe 'where the products of vineyards, hop fields, and tobacco plantations are part of the hospitality', whilst the opium poppies and hemp that flourish in their own countries are viewed as targets for eradication. This has created a pattern in which 'illegality' and 'non-whiteness' are tightly connected within the socio-political imaginary of the drug laws. There are multiple examples that illustrate how this arc has shaped the way the idea of the 'drug problem' has evolved: from depictions of Chinese immigrants and opium dens in the late nineteenth century driving the initial push to prohibition (Hickman 2000), to Federal Bureau of Narcotics chief Harry Anslinger's racist campaign against cannabis in the 1930s (Musto 1972), to the racialised demonisation of crack in the 1980s and 1990s (Reinarman and Levine 2004). In the 2020s, questions of race and racial justice remain central to the debate about drug law reform, increasingly conjoined to wider societal conversations about race and policing (Loader 2021). The race arc is key to the evolution of the construction of the drug problem.

The *risk* arc has been perhaps less visible than race but has shown a similar longevity. The idea of drugs as particular vectors of risk, of (some) drug users as risk-takers, and of some types or patterns of drug use or drug-using behaviour as creating risks, are all familiar features of contemporary drug policy discourse. Indeed, arguably, the dominant paradigm for drug control has been centred around risk for the last 50 years (Seddon 2010:81–99). But the risk arc goes back far further than this. The famous Earl of Mar life insurance case in 1828 concerned whether the Earl's failure to declare his opium and laudanum habit invalidated his policy (Berridge 1977). The case hinged on actuarial expertise as to whether opium consumption increased health risks and reduced life expectancy—illustrating Ewald's (1991) classic conceptualisation of insurance as a technology of risk—and was an important element within the process of the problematisation of opium during the nineteenth century that laid part of the foundations for twentieth-century prohibition (Seddon 2010:38–55). Like race, risk is built into the foundations of that system.

The *security* arc is interwoven with both the other two but rises to the fore particularly from the 1960s. Drawing on the international relations literature, security can be understood as the political process through which states identify something as an 'existential threat, requiring emergency measures and justifying actions outside the normal bounds of political procedure' (Buzan et al 1998:24). Crick (2012) shows how the 1961 United Nations (UN) Single Convention on Narcotic Drugs, which consolidated and extended the international system, constituted a distinctive new securitisation of the drug problem, with addiction to 'narcotic drugs' represented as posing a 'serious evil' to individuals and a 'danger to mankind'. This framing of drugs as an 'existential threat' created a template that would be used repeatedly in the following decades, from Nixon's 'War on Drugs' in the 1970s to the binding together of drugs and counter-terrorism policy in post-9/11 Anglo-American politics.

These three arcs have shaped the evolving contours of the 'drug problem' as a social and political construct which has driven global prohibition policy over the last century and longer. These arcs are also of course strongly Western-centric, indeed largely Anglo-American, in their orientation and perspective. In common with knowledge production more generally, thinking about the 'drug problem' has typically been approached almost exclusively from vantage points in the Global North. Questions of economic development, the protection of agricultural livelihoods, economic justice, and so on, which might become more prominent in problematisations viewed from the vantage point of the Global South, have been mainly missing. This is partly driven by the dominance of the English language within the research literature—with the result, for example, that a scholar as important as Venezuelan criminologist Rosa del Olmo is largely unknown in the Anglophone world of drug policy, despite her extensive work on coca and cocaine in Latin America (see McMahon and West 1992)—but is also about the broader centring of Western thinking. As will be argued in the chapters that follow, seeing the drug problem differently is an essential step in creating new policy approaches and this requires a decentring of Europe and North America. It is not just that we need to decolonise global drug policy (Daniels et al 2021), we also need to decolonise how we think about it (see Bourgois 2018). Here, the book builds on the small number of earlier contributions which have occasionally disrupted our North Atlantic obsessions, perhaps most notably edited collections from Goodman et al (1995) and Coomber and South (2004).

The prohibition paradigm

Global drug prohibition, then, is a modern invention, created at the beginning of the twentieth century. This is not to say that it had no antecedents. Indeed, a more precise way of putting this is to say that before the twentieth century, prohibitions were localised. For example, one of the earliest on record occurred in the early Qing dynasty in China, when an edict was issued in 1729 by the Yongzheng emperor banning the selling of opium for smoking (Dikötter et al 2004:28–30). Similarly, in 1800, Napoleon briefly attempted to ban cannabis smoking in Egypt after the French invasion in 1798 (Bewley-Taylor et al 2014:9) and in Japan importation of opium was prohibited throughout the Meiji period from 1868 to 1912 (Kingsberg 2011). As Windle (2013a) notes, this also tells us that, contrary to much contemporary policy commentary, prohibition was not invented *de novo* by Western countries at the beginning of the twentieth century. What was novel at this time was the creation of an *international* drug control system, initially under the auspices of the League of Nations and after 1945 of the UN. What we have seen over the last few decades is a localised fragmenting of this global system, largely around the regulation of cannabis (see Seddon and Floodgate 2020). Taking the long view over the last 300 years, it may be that we will eventually see the trajectory of prohibition as local-global-local.

But what exactly is prohibition? This is a seemingly straightforward question but worth examining more closely. A dictionary definition gives the meaning as the act of forbidding or banning by authority or law. Its etymology is from the Latin *prohibere* which means to hold back, hinder, or restrain. Legal prohibition is usually understood as involving criminalisation, that is, the use of the criminal law to attempt to 'hold back' whatever undesired conduct is the target of the prohibition (Tadros 2011). Drug prohibition is, therefore, a shorthand, or an umbrella term, for the criminalisation of a set of acts or behaviours that together, if unchecked, create a viable drug trade. If intoxicant X is prohibited, this means that its production, supply, and possession are all made criminal offences. In this sense, it is perhaps more useful to think of prohibition as the use of the criminal law to hinder or restrain specified economic activity rather than as the banning of a commodity. Banning may be the policy goal but it does not give much analytical purchase on what prohibition actually is. This way of thinking also makes clear that drug laws address human action rather than inanimate objects.

The way in which these laws address human action is by criminalising transactions that would otherwise be lawful economic activity: growing a plant, selling a commodity to a willing buyer, possessing an object that you have purchased, and so on. In other words, drug laws operate as an interference with personal property rights. In common law jurisdictions, the legal position is that those rights are not extinguished but become, in effect, unenforceable in the courts by virtue of the criminal prohibitions.[1] Prohibition, then, is the use of the criminal law to interfere with personal property rights in order to restrain a particular sphere of undesired economic activity. This resonates with Foucault's novel discussion of law in his 1971–1972 lecture series at the Collège de France, *Penal Theories and Institutions*, in which he states that the 'distribution of justice forms part of the circulation of goods ... by controlling it ... (in the criminal domain) at the level of infractions, thefts, illicit commerce or appropriations' (Foucault 2019:133). This captures a core dimension of how drug laws function: controlling the circulation of goods. In Part I of the book, the theoretical understanding of this functioning is further explored and developed. As will be seen, the idea of external 'interference' or 'intervention' in markets requires some rethinking.

The impact and effectiveness of global drug prohibition has been much discussed. It is hard to make the case that it has been a success: the global trade it has sought to outlaw is estimated to be worth up to US$650 billion (May 2017) and nearly 270 million people worldwide are current or recent drug users (defined as having used drugs in the last year) (UNODC 2020a). It is, of course, possible to argue that these numbers would be bigger *without* prohibition and that is almost certainly true. But it is also evident that prohibition has come nowhere near to eliminating the drug trade, nor does the trajectory of those numbers offer grounds for optimism that elimination is likely to happen in the future. Indeed, as will be discussed in the next section, the broad pattern since the 1960s has been that the more resources have been poured into prohibition and its enforcement, the more drug use has grown. On top of this instrumental failure to achieve its overarching objective, a consistent characteristic of the prohibition system is that it has generated a significant amount of collateral damage. Commentators have

---

[1] Thanks to my former colleague Gerard McMeel for explaining this to me.

documented the various negative impacts on public health, crime, and security (e.g. Rolles et al 2016) and we can understand these secondary outcomes theoretically as the result of adaptations by market actors to prohibition interventions. For some commentators, this renders the prohibition enterprise a totally unacceptable failure; for others, it is a matter of whether this outweighs the perceived benefits of containing the overall size of the drug trade. This kind of accounting exercise is not a straightforward matter analytically, as MacCoun and Reuter (2011) have discussed.

Although much has been written about drug prohibition, as well as about other specific prohibitions (e.g. alcohol, slavery), there is surprisingly little cross-cutting scholarship that looks at prohibition as a political or governmental strategy or that examines its conceptual parameters. In this respect, Nadelmann's (1990) classic paper on 'global prohibition regimes', now more than 30 years old, repays attention. One of his central insights is that the global norms that evolve into global prohibition regimes generally reflect the interests, preoccupations, and dispositions of 'dominant members of international society' (1990:524). This is why it is important for the critical analysis of drug prohibition to historicise the power relations and dynamics between key countries, that is, to examine and understand how they evolve over time, from the initial establishment of global norms through to the continuing development of the prohibition system. Part II of the book aims to do this for a particularly significant historical moment within this process. A second important insight from Nadelmann's paper is that global prohibition regimes typically target activities that 'in one way or another transcend national borders' (1990:524). This is obvious in one sense—and the drug trade is arguably the quintessential transnational phenomenon—but it is a critical point. The current process of localised fragmentation of cannabis prohibition is no doubt being driven by multiple forces but it is plausible that it is partly related to the technology-driven restructuring of the cannabis industry which has resulted in cannabis cultivation becoming possible almost anywhere (Seddon and Floodgate 2020). As the cannabis trade has started to move to being more local rather than transnational, so the global cannabis prohibition regime has begun to crumble.

We can draw out four key points about the drug prohibition paradigm which are important for the analysis in the rest of the book:

- Prohibition is an historically and culturally contingent formation, rather than a universal or timeless phenomenon.

- Prohibition functions as a regulatory intervention in market activity, designed to slow and hinder the circulation of goods.
- Prohibition, as implemented, has a limited capacity to control economic activity, and market actors often adapt to prohibition interventions in ways that can lead to 'collateral damage'.
- Global prohibition is sustained by a complex mix of political and economic interests, dominated by more powerful nations.

Global trends in supply, distribution, and use

It is one of the most interesting features of the story of the last 100 or so years that at the time the international drug control system was first assembled, levels of consumption were actually relatively small-scale and would remain so until the 1950s. Consumption was also quite confined geographically, largely concentrated in Europe, the United States, and China (van Duyne and Levi 2005:24–28). The 'drug problem' was far from being a fully global phenomenon and, in terms of scale, was arguably not that significant. The 'big picture' since the 1950s is of two parallel developments:

- a trend of rising consumption levels and the geographical spread of the drug trade into parts of the world that had previously avoided it; and
- a hardening of the international prohibition regime, particularly after the 1961 UN Single Convention on Narcotic Drugs, encapsulated in the notion of a 'War on Drugs'.

It has been one of the recurring themes of critical accounts of drug control that these have been parallel developments: the tighter the screw is turned, the bigger the problem has got. This has been termed the 'paradox of prohibition' (Marks 1987). As we will see in Part III, this paradox has proved to be a malleable idea in the realm of drug politics. Drug law reformers have taken it as indicating the total failure of the prohibition project, whilst prohibition supporters have seen it as suggesting that the 'War on Drugs' has just not been pursued with sufficient zeal or resources. In fact, as we will see, the paradox relates to a deeper theoretical point about the relationship between markets and regulation that will be explored in Part I of the book.

The contemporary global drug situation is best described in the annual *World Drug Report* produced by the UN and readers are referred there for up-to-date and detailed data. The broad trends and patterns set out in the 2020 edition (UNODC 2020a) can be summarised as follows:

- There has been rising aggregate consumption over the last decade, from 210 million users (4.8% of the 15–64 age group of the worldwide population) in 2009 to 269 million in 2018 (5.3% of that age group), with growth fastest in developing countries.
- Cannabis remains the most popular drug (192 million users in 2018) but there has been a proliferation of new synthetic substances, as product ranges have become significantly more diverse.
- Stimulant use—mainly cocaine and methamphetamine—has been increasing in recent years in the primary regions of consumption: Europe, North America, and Southeast Asia.
- Opioids remain the most harmful drugs, in terms of mortality and morbidity, with new and newly-available synthetic opioids (e.g. tramadol, fentanyl) driving public health crises in specific regions, such as North America and parts of West, Central, and North Africa.
- More than 11 million people are drug injectors and this accounts for around 10% of HIV infections globally.
- Supply and trafficking routes continue to mutate and adapt, driven by a range of political and economic factors, as well as by enforcement action.
- Drug supply on the darknet continues to grow in importance, albeit with some volatility and fluctuations as particular sites are periodically taken down (either by enforcement action or exit scams).

To a great extent, this picture is broadly similar to the global drug situation over the course of much of the last decade and longer. Three aspects are more novel and worth briefly expanding on: the proliferation of 'new' substances; the opioid-related public health crises; and the emergence of darknet markets. The first of these began to be referred to in policy documents in around 2010 and has grown as a focus for research and policy attention since then, under the banner of 'novel psychoactive substances' (NPS). As Potter and Chatwin (2018) argue, the NPS label is in many ways unhelpful and misleading, given that many substances termed NPS are not new at all and are just newly popular or newly available. Nevertheless, the proliferation of substances, not just in availability but also in patterns of consumption, has undoubtedly been a new phenomenon that has emerged in the last decade. It has made understanding and responding to the 'drug problem' considerably more complex.

The second new feature is the opioid public health crisis. Opiate problems were, for most of the twentieth century, associated with heroin use and in the nineteenth century, it had been morphine and opium. In the last decade, however, a new problem has emerged with a wider range of opiates (natural alkaloids derived from opium e.g. morphine, heroin) and opioids (synthetic substances that have similar effects as opiates e.g. codeine, fentanyl). We might see this, at one level, as part of the wider proliferation of substances described above, although the drivers are quite different. In the United States, there have been three overlapping strands to the problem: a rise in overdose deaths associated with prescribed opioids (e.g. oxycodone); a rise in heroin-related overdose deaths; and from 2013, a very steep rise in deaths associated with synthetic opioids, primarily fentanyl and analogues. Indeed, the 'opioid crisis' has, to a great extent, become the 'fentanyl crisis' (Pardo et al 2019). Much less discussed has been what the UN *World Drug Report* terms the 'other opioid crisis': the use of tramadol in parts of West, Central, and North Africa and, to a lesser degree, parts of Asia. Although tramadol is considerably less potent than fentanyl and fentanyl analogues like carfentanil, and therefore is not causing deaths in the same way, it is nevertheless linked to health problems including psychiatric disorders. The overall significance of this development is that, after so many decades when the key challenge was to find ways of responding to heroin, the opiate problem has now multiplied in complexity and scale.

The third novel feature of the contemporary world drug situation is the emergence of online drug-selling on the darknet (Martin 2014). The first major site, *Silk Road*, came into operation in 2011 and up until 2016 there was a very strong growth rate in darknet sales, even as individual websites came and went with some rapidity. Since 2017 this has stabilised somewhat but it remains sizeable (UNODC 2020b). This has been a significant development in several respects (Seddon 2014; Martin et al 2020). It has presented new and quite different challenges for policing and law enforcement. It has also changed some of the core elements required for involvement in the drug trade, with the capacity for violence in particular diminishing in importance as a resource for doing business. Less palatable for some to recognise, it has undoubtedly provided an infrastructure with the potential to reduce harms by enhancing product safety through online ratings systems. Darknet drug markets represent perhaps the most important innovation in the global drug trade for many decades (Shortis et al 2020).

Global trends in regulation

Trends in regulation are often misunderstood or misrepresented. The first assumption that is sometimes made is that the international drug control system has a long history. In fact, as we have already noted, it is only about 100 years old. Before this, as we have also already observed, there had been local prohibitions in a variety of places—not solely Western countries—going back at least as far as the early eighteenth century. We might therefore describe prohibition as being part of the project of modernity, with some antecedents pre-dating the First Industrial Revolution but then significantly driven by the subsequent trajectory of industrial capitalism and associated colonial empires. Part II of the book explores this area in more detail and attempts to provide some new perspectives on these historical processes by decentring the Anglo-American focus that is typical within the historical literature.

In the twentieth century, as is so often the case in processes of historical development, war had a particularly significant impact on the new global control regime. The First World War drove and accelerated the first international agreements. Following the Paris Peace Conference provisions on drug control were included in Article 295 of the Versailles Treaty signed in June 1919. Article 295 committed all signatories to the obligations that had been drawn up in the 1912 International Opium Convention agreed at The Hague. This triggered a wave of national-level prohibition laws which began to form an international drug control system. The Second World War had an equally important impact, effectively ushering in the US dominance of the prohibition system which has come to be seen as a core feature of the last 50 years of the 'War on Drugs'.

A key moment of the US-dominated post-war period was the 1961 Single Convention on Narcotic Drugs which brought together and extended existing treaties and is generally viewed as putting in place the current hegemonic iteration of global drug prohibition. Lines (2017) provides a rich historical account of the Convention and its creation. It was built upon three UN Protocols adopted respectively in 1946, 1948, and 1953 which took on and then significantly extended the pre-war drug control powers under the League of Nations (Lines 2017:32–34). The idea of creating a single consolidating drug treaty to bring together and align the various instruments and agreements that had grown in the drug control sphere was first raised in 1948. The drafting of the Convention was a complex and involved process that took several years, the bulk of the work taking place between 1950 and

1958, culminating in the 51 chapters of the Single Convention adopted in March 1961 (Lines 2017:35). This process of evolution makes it clear that the Convention was, in many respects, a continuation of the existing international approach but it is nevertheless distinctive in several ways and is seen by most commentators as representing a 'break with the past' (Bewley-Taylor and Jelsma 2011:9). Article 36 is perhaps the crux of its novelty, as it mandates penal provisions to be enacted by signatories to the Convention. Further supplementary UN Conventions were adopted in 1971 and 1988 and together these three treaties form the international legal framework for global drug control today.

Despite its undoubted global significance, the apparent hegemony of the 1961 Single Convention has in practice always been less dominant than it might at first appear. As Eastwood et al (2016) have charted, there has in fact been a 'quiet revolution' taking place since the 1970s, with a number of jurisdictions around the world experimenting with decriminalisation initiatives. Indeed, examples of decriminalisation initiatives over the last 50 years—some long-lasting, some short-lived—can be found across most regions of the world (Eastwood et al 2016). To take a couple of illustrative examples, in the Czech Republic, drug possession for personal use was removed from the Penal Code in 1990, as part of the political promotion of civil liberties in the context of emergence from the Soviet bloc following the fall of communism. Modified in 1999 and 2010 to address concerns about organised crime, the Czech initiative is one of the longest running experiments with decriminalisation. In Peru, sanctions for personal possession were removed from the Criminal Code in 1991, although Eastwood et al (2016:27) state that, in practice, the policing of possession has remained relatively strict. This serves as an important reminder that understanding drug laws is not a purely doctrinal matter and, to draw on a classic trope in socio-legal scholarship, the 'law in action' is not always the same as the 'law in books' (Pound 1910).

The twenty-first century has seen the 'quiet revolution' become quite a bit noisier and more visible. In 2001, Portugal took a major step by decriminalising drug possession for all substances, a radical shift that seems to have been successful on most policy measures (Hughes and Stevens 2010; Hughes 2017). Critical to the Portuguese experiment was that law reform was accompanied by significant investment in treatment and social support. Contrary to fears expressed by some, there has been no explosion of consumption in Portugal and there have been very positive improvements on public health indicators such as rates of HIV infection

(Hughes 2017). Elsewhere in Europe, another significant development at this time was the emergence of Cannabis Social Clubs (CSCs), first in the Catalonia region of Spain (Jansseune et al 2019) and later also in Belgium (Pardal 2018). The CSC model exploits a legal 'grey area' to enable local members-only growing co-operatives, operating on a non-profit basis and usually on a small scale (Decorte et al 2017; Marks 2019; Pardal et al 2022). It is a significant model as it has the potential to allow for a form of legalised cannabis supply that is non-commercial. A further set of initiatives has seen campaigning groups deploy strategic litigation to challenge the constitutionality of laws prohibiting cultivation or possession of cannabis for personal consumption in private. This has led to rulings by the Constitutional Courts in South Africa and Georgia, and by the Supreme Court in Mexico, that those cannabis laws are in conflict with constitutional rights to privacy and personal autonomy (Marks 2019:218–221).

In the last decade, even more radical cannabis law reform has developed, in a largely unforeseen manner, and mainly concentrated in the Americas (Aaronson 2019). Rather than just decriminalising personal possession or cultivation for personal use, these new initiatives have gone a stage further in removing the entire supply chain from the criminal system. In 2013, Uruguay became the first country to establish a fully legal cannabis trade, from cultivation to consumption. Three means of obtaining cannabis were created—home cultivation, CSCs, and sales at pharmacies—and the system as a whole is state-controlled rather than commercialised. This was followed in 2018 by Canada, which became the first G7 country to legalise cannabis. The Canadian model is commercialised but under fairly strict state regulation. Meanwhile, in the United States, whilst federal prohibition has remained in place, a growing number of individual states have started to legalise cannabis for medical and/or recreational use. There are now more than 30 states with some form of legalised cannabis trade. The US approach has seen the creation of a much more liberalised commercial industry.

At the beginning of the 2020s, we have arrived at an interesting point. The world drug market is firmly established across all continents, aggregate global consumption continues to creep upwards, and local/regional markets mutate and diversify in vibrant fashion. At the same time, whilst the global prohibition framework remains in place, and indeed prohibition is still the norm in most jurisdictions, there are a growing number of localised initiatives involving decriminalisation or legalisation. Most, but not all, of these are focused on cannabis. The fundamental question now is how we should understand and make sense of this picture of vibrant markets and rapid localised change in regulation. Whilst the temptation is to look to what has been happening in the Americas as a signal that global prohibition is unravelling, there are several grounds to suggest alternative futures are equally possible. Perhaps the most fundamental—and, somewhat oddly, the least commonly voiced—is that the centre of global power is shifting eastwards, away from North America and Europe and towards Asia. What might the implications be for drug law reform if the twenty-first century turns out to be the Asian Century as many political scientists and others have predicted? This question has scarcely even been asked, let alone answered, in the resolutely Western-centric drug policy literature. A central theme of this book is to engage directly with this question by attempting to recentre China and the surrounding regions within our understanding of the dynamics of international drug control.

Understanding drug control: The need for new intellectual resources

One of the perennial challenges for the social sciences is that their object of enquiry—the social world—is continually changing. This means that it is essential that theoretical frameworks and conceptual tools are also continually revised and developed. Failure to do so can, over time, erode the capacity of social scientists to make sense of the world around them. This is one way to diagnose and explain the general sense felt by some that the social sciences have failed to deliver on the promise they were seen to hold in the optimistic times of the mid-twentieth century: they have simply not kept pace with the scale of social change in the post-war period. Braithwaite (2005, 2014) argues that in the twenty-first century, transformative social science—that is, social scientific theorising and empirical enquiry that can repeatedly generate transformative insights about the way the world works and how to make it work better—has become less likely than ever. One of the fundamental reasons for this, he suggests, is that it is constrained by the disciplinary boxes that have solidified in our universities. For Braithwaite, disciplines based on categorical objects—economics for the study of economic institutions (banks, money, markets), criminology for the study of criminal justice institutions (police, prisons), and so on—block breakthroughs in knowledge that cut across categories and constrain the ability to grasp complexity that cannot be properly seen from within a disciplinary silo. He draws a contrast with the biological sciences which restructured away from categorical disciplines—zoology (animals), botany (plants), entomology (insects)—to disciplines organised around cross-cutting theoretical themes like molecular biology and ecology. He argues that social science might benefit in a similar way from reorganising itself around theoretical ideas that cut across categories. Regulation—defined as efforts to 'steer the flow of events'—is the cross-cutting theme that Braithwaite and his collaborators have explored for approaching 40 years, with considerable success in generating transformative insights in areas as diverse as cybercrime, workplace health and safety, environmental sustainability, policing, and many others (see Drahos 2017).

The global drug problem, as sketched in this introductory chapter, is a classic example of what Rittel and Webber (1973) once called a 'wicked problem', characterised by its seeming intractability and complexity, and the impossibility of reaching definitive formulations, diagnoses, or solutions. The notion of complexity is important and will be explored further in Part I of the book but Rittel and Webber also make clear that problems rooted in 'open social systems' cannot be addressed as narrow or purely technical challenges for scientists. Another way of putting this is to say that wicked problems inevitably require expertise drawn from across multiple disciplines. They go on to argue that perhaps the 'most wicked conditions that confront us' (1973:169) are the fact that wicked problems are inherently political and therefore rooted in questions of values that, in their view, cannot ever be scientifically resolved. Part III of this book explores the political nature of the drug problem and argues that there are in fact ways of engaging constructively and productively with the political realm.

There is a strong case, then, for drug policy and drug control to be explored by adopting an approach that begins with the (wicked) problem rather than any particular disciplinary perspective. In other words, rather than seeing it as a topic for Criminology or Law or Sociology, it should be seen as an object for enquiry that can potentially be illuminated by shining lights from multiple different disciplinary boxes. Following Braithwaite, and as I have previously argued (e.g. Seddon 2010, 2020a), regulation is an especially appropriate and productive theoretical theme to shape this cross-cutting enquiry. The lens of regulation brings into focus that:

- the drug question is a market phenomenon, involving the production/distribution/retail/consumption of a particular set of commodities; and

- drug control involves attempts to steer the flow of events across different points in drug supply chains, that is, it is a form of market regulation.

It follows that prohibition is itself a particular form of regulation, rather than its absence, an idea that directly contradicts a common trope in drug law reform discourse which holds that prohibition leads to 'unregulated' drug markets. This is an important insight and an example of how the regulation concept can contribute to building new understandings of what drug control is and how it functions. Part of the rationale for this book is that there is a lack of theoretical and conceptual work in this field. The best work in this area, by scholars like Peter Reuter, Jonathan Caulkins, Alison Ritter, and many others, is undoubtedly of very high quality—empirically rich, methodologically rigorous—and has greatly advanced understanding of the effectiveness of different drug policy approaches and initiatives. But intellectual resources for moving beyond or outside the prohibition paradigm are much thinner on the ground. The capacity to generate the type of transformative insights that Braithwaite describes is limited.

The aim of Part I of this book is to undertake preliminary work to develop these resources for thinking differently about drug control. It builds on Seddon (2020a) by exploring how interdisciplinary perspectives on the market-regulation relationship can help to construct a theoretical apparatus and conceptual tools for a radical rethinking of how we understand what drug control is and how it functions. Central to this project is the shift from a control model (regulation as the application of external controls to a market) to a constitutive model (regulation as partly creating the market it seeks to control), drawing on Shearing's (1993) groundbreaking essay. From the constitutive model, the new concept of *exchangespace* is developed as a vehicle to allow light from multiple disciplines—economics, sociology, law, and others—to shine on drug control conceptualised as a specific form of market-regulation relations.

Outline of the book

The book is structured in three main parts, each consisting of two chapters. Part I of the book aims to develop the *theoretical* apparatus and intellectual resources we have available to investigate how drug control functions. As discussed in the previous section, the goal is to provide a framework that allows for a thoroughgoing reappraisal of how we understand drug control, using the new *exchangespace* concept. It provides a set of tools for reconnecting political economy, economic history, and economics, reconceptualising the relationship between markets and regulation in terms of dynamic interactions within networks of networks. This has significant implications for how we think about some core ideas and assumptions within the field of drug control and drug laws. The first chapter in this part of the book focuses on developing a detailed specification of *exchangespace*. The second chapter explores how we can understand regulatory trajectories in *exchangespace*, that is, how governance regimes change over time. Together, these two chapters provide a theoretical foundation for understanding both historical formation and change (as explored in Part II) and potential future change through reform of drug law and policy (as examined in Part III).

Part II explores the origin story of global drug prohibition in an explicitly *historical* way. Focusing on the period from the mid-nineteenth century to the beginning of the twentieth when this system was assembled, it aims to provide a new perspective by moving away from the Western-centric narratives that dominate the historiographical literature and recentring China and the wider Asian region within the story. In doing so, it draws on recent work within global history, notably by Peter Frankopan. This decolonising reorientation in focus shines a new analytical light on the economic and geopolitical underpinnings of the international drug control system. The first of the two chapters looks at the Opium Wars in the nineteenth century, as the point of origin of that system. The second chapter focuses on the first two decades of the twentieth century and the international meetings on opium control that took place in Shanghai and The Hague between 1909 and 1914, from which today's global prohibition regime was created.

In Part III, the focus is on the politics of drug control. The *political* character of the drugs issue is typically viewed as a barrier to more rational policies. Here, the contrary view is taken: the politics of drugs needs to be acknowledged and properly examined. Drawing on insights from political science, and ideas from debates on public sociology and public criminology, it attempts to set out elements for the building of a better politics of drugs, as an essential component not only for drug law reform but also for drug policy research which often deploys an unhelpfully 'thin' conception of the nature of the political in this field. The first of the two chapters argues the case for drug laws and drug control to be considered as legitimate subjects for politics, attempting to draw out more clearly what is at stake when drug control becomes a matter of political contestation. The second chapter then moves to thinking about how a 'better politics' of drugs might be achieved and how this could re-animate drug law reform.

A short concluding chapter brings together the book's argument across its three parts and considers its implications for research, law reform, and policy. What does the intellectual reappraisal developed in the book imply for how we should understand drug control and for how we might shape better law and policy in the future? By seeing the problem differently—theoretically, historically, politically—can we also start to imagine alternative and better ways of dealing with it? In the Asian Century, will it be China that becomes central to the future of the international drug control system rather than North America and what might this mean for drug law reform?

PART I
THEORY

2
Exchangespace

Introduction

The drug question is deeply fascinating and there are many puzzles and mysteries that researchers and others have explored. Much of this enquiry has revolved around two broad questions. Why do people take drugs (the consumption question)? Why do some people get into difficulties with habitual or heavy drug consumption (the addiction question)? There are very large bodies of research in both areas and we have learned a great deal over many decades. Today, there are multiple scholarly journals, conferences, and societies, all dedicated to this enterprise. Arguably, much of this research is thinly theorised, although there are, of course, many exceptions. One of the most peculiar but defining features of both these strands of work is that there exist parallel tracks of research: one in the social sciences, one in the biological and medical sciences. Whilst there are occasional borrowings and transfers of ideas, these tracks have tended to stick to their parallel paths. One avenue for future breakthroughs in knowledge about the consumption and addiction questions is likely to be through collaborative research that crosses the boundaries between the social and life sciences. Although this has occasionally been proposed (e.g. Kushner 2006, 2010; Courtwright 2005), it remains largely unexplored intellectual terrain. A highly imaginative recent paper by McLean and Rose (2021) hints at some of the potential here, arguing that the 'memory turn' in addiction neuroscience could provide the basis for a new 'critical friendship' between the biological and social sciences that better understands the lived experience of human distress caused by addiction.

The third broad set of questions is about drug policy and drug control, that is, about how we respond to and attempt to govern drug use and drug problems. This is the focus of this book. It covers a diverse span of work but in general terms has tended to be empirically driven and relatively light on theory. There has, nevertheless, been some outstanding work in this

Rethinking Drug Laws. Toby Seddon, Oxford University Press. © Toby Seddon 2023.
DOI: 10.1093/oso/9780192846525.003.0002

area in recent decades by people like Peter Reuter, Alison Ritter, Jonathan Caulkins, Rosalie Pacula, Beau Kilmer, Alex Stevens, and others. Many of the leading figures in this policy research community have been associated with the RAND Drug Policy Research Center based in California which has been immensely influential since its establishment in 1989. Characterised by rigorous methods and a resolutely analytical and data-driven approach, we have learned an enormous amount from this body of work about many aspects of drug policy. But, as I have previously argued (Seddon 2020a), although empirical research is vital, there is a need to build intellectual resources for understanding how drug laws and drug control function, as a means of broadening and deepening critical thinking about drug law reform. Part of this project involves drawing on a wider set of disciplines. The RAND community and its diaspora have always been strongly rooted in economics but less so in other fields.

The two chapters in this part of the book build on a paper that was published in the journal *Social & Legal Studies* in 2020 (hereafter, the 'SLS paper') in which I set out some parameters for this theoretical project (Seddon 2020a). The SLS paper aimed to develop a set of 'tools for thinking' about drug law reform by framing drug control laws as a form of market regulation. It examined how different disciplines have approached the question of the relationship between markets and regulation, with the aim of reviewing the cross-disciplinary state-of-the-art theoretical understandings of market-regulation interactions. This involved drawing insights from a wide range of disciplines, including economics, political economy, socio-legal studies, and economic sociology. The paper ended by proposing a new concept, *exchangespace*, as a theoretical tool for further developing this area. The central focus of this part of the book is to develop and build on that concept, as a foundation for a theoretical reappraisal of the nature and functioning of drug control.

Before turning to this task, it may be useful to set out more explicitly what is meant by theory here and precisely what questions we want to think about and answer. The type of 'theory' that is being explored comes under the broad banner of 'explanatory theory', that is, ordered and general propositions about the way that a particular aspect of the social world functions: why does phenomenon X happen in the way that it does? Our phenomenon X in this book is efforts to control the ways that prohibited intoxicants ('drugs') are produced, distributed, exchanged, and consumed: in short, 'drug control'. The conceptual foundation for this theoretical project is the notion that drug control is a form of market regulation, that is, it seeks to 'steer the flow of events' across the supply chain. The project aims to provide intellectual resources for thinking about what drug control is and how it functions. This involves considering the following set of questions:

- How should we diagnose the supply-side and demand-side drivers of drug markets?
- How should we conceptualise 'regulatory interventions' within the markets?
- How do we define, classify, and distinguish 'regulators' and 'regulatees'?
- How do regulatory interventions in the market constrain, control, limit, shape, or otherwise affect behaviour in different parts of the supply chain?
- What is the relationship between interventions and market behaviour?

In developing this theoretical project, this chapter begins by briefly restating the argument first developed in the SLS paper, tracing the critical distinction between control and constitutive conceptions of regulation, and outlining the concept of *exchangespace* first introduced in that paper. It then develops the concept by setting out a full conceptual specification, describing in turn its core elements. It ends by examining the political constitution of *exchangespace*—a theme which connects with Part III of the book—drawing on some ideas from political economy. Chapter 3 then focuses on the temporal dimension of *exchangespace*, exploring how we might theorise change and regulatory trajectories. With this theoretical and conceptual framework in place, some illustrative applications of the *exchangespace* idea to drug control are briefly discussed.

From regulation as control to constitutive regulation

The conventional way of understanding the relationship between markets and regulation is built on two premises. First, that markets are 'natural' self-ordering phenomena that come into existence when human actors wish to exchange anything with each other. This is the foundational premise of liberal economics, which can be traced all the way back to Adam Smith and his notion of the 'invisible hand'. Second, that regulation is a form of external control on those naturally-occurring markets. This premise follows logically and directly from the first. The policy discussion is then simply about when markets should be left alone and when regulatory controls are necessary. Regulation is typically seen as a 'necessary evil' only to be used when absolutely necessary, as it is a constraint on the natural efficiency of the competitive market mechanism.

Within the control paradigm, the questions of when regulatory controls become necessary, and of the form they should take, have been much debated. In the early twentieth century, building on the work of his mentor Alfred Marshall, the economist Arthur Pigou (1920) developed the concept of 'externalities'—costs which accrue to third parties—as the arbiter of when regulatory interventions might be permissible. He argued that taxes and subsidies were the best means of managing externalities. Pigouvian taxes, as they became known, came under heavy criticism from Ronald Coase, the father of Chicagoan neoliberal economics, in his 1960 paper on 'The Problem of Social Cost'. Coase (1960) argued that taxes of this kind could mostly be avoided through bargaining and negotiation and he made a forceful case that government interventions in markets should be kept to a minimum. Minimal regulation, and its close cousin deregulation, have become attractive policy and political positions for many, with the emphasis on deregulation particularly pronounced in the last 50 years as a perceived antidote to problems deemed to have come from the growth of the 'provider state' in the first half of the twentieth century. Yet, despite their disagreement, both Coase and Pigou share the shame root image of regulation as external controls on the market.

This control conception of regulation still has a strong political salience and is accepted or assumed within many strands of economics and political science. Indeed, it is the paradigm that has underpinned liberal economics for most of the last 200 years. Nevertheless, it has also come under sustained critical scrutiny. At the most basic level, it is self-evident that markets require a certain institutional infrastructure in order to function. This immediately suggests that the notion of an entirely 'free' market is, at best, an over-simplification. This point is largely acknowledged, even by the staunchest free-marketeers. Campbell and Klaes (2005:278) note, for example, that Ronald Coase explicitly recognised the need for a legal-institutional framework to be in place for economic transactions to be possible. Others have developed this idea of the foundational 'architecture' of markets, notably the American sociologist Neil Fligstein (2001) who suggests that markets are dependent upon states for their existence.

Some have taken the critique of the control model considerably further than this. Bernard Harcourt (2011) develops a radical historical perspective on the idea of 'free markets' in his book *The Illusion of Free Markets*. He argues that we can trace the historical emergence and genealogy of this idea and that it can be understood as a political construction rather than a description of observed reality. He suggests that the concept of a 'natural' order dates back to the French Enlightenment and the work of the Physiocrats in the middle of the eighteenth century. Led by François Quesnay, and as set out in his 1759 work *Tableau Economique*, the Physiocrats believed that the *ordre naturel* provided the best basis for structuring and organising the economy and society. Harcourt shows how this idea of a natural order in the economy became the notion of the 'free market' and was then applied to understanding, classifying, and designing policy relating to market organisation. At the heart of his critical analysis is the argument that as a political construction, the 'free market' label obscures rather than reveals how markets actually function. He questions whether the categories of 'free' and 'regulated' are helpful at all as ways of characterising different forms of market organisation.

In a similar vein to Harcourt, the earlier work of Shearing (1993) develops a theoretically-oriented critique of the control conception of regulation. Shearing's analysis starts from the repeated observation that regulation is rarely simply an external constraint on market activity but rather it plays a part in shaping markets. The specific form a market takes is always partly a result of the regulatory framework that is in place. Further, according to Shearing, it is clear that the way this happens can best be described as a process, in the sense that market-regulation interactions are dynamic and continually evolving over time. It is not just the case that the legal-institutional architecture of a market has significant influence on its size and shape but rather that there is an ongoing interactive process of action, reaction, and adaptation by the variety of actors in the market space. It is from these insights that he develops his constitutive conception of regulation.

Shearing (1993) provides the clearest account of the constitutive perspective in what is a foundational and important essay. His argument has its roots partly in the work of the group of German economists and legal scholars based in the Freiburg School of the 1930s who became known as the ordoliberals. It is also influenced by the Polanyian idea of the embeddedness of economic activity within social institutions and a landmark article by economic sociologist Mark Granovetter (1985). More implicitly, it is also Foucauldian, in the sense that it understands the exercise of power or authority as productive and creative, rather than simply negative or constraining. Interestingly, Foucault himself saw the significance of the ordoliberals, discussing their ideas in lectures at the Collège de France in early 1979 (Foucault 2008:78–150; see also Gane 2018). Yet, although rooted in these antecedents, Shearing's essay is strikingly original and repays careful attention.

The essay begins by situating the argument in the context of the revival at that time of the political salience and appeal of deregulation. It is worth remembering that the essay appeared in an edited volume on business regulation in Australia which had resulted from a conference held in March 1992 as part of a wider project on 'Reshaping Australia's Institutions' (for a later assessment of that project, see Braithwaite 2014:11). The regulation-deregulation debate was an important political battleground in many Western democracies in the early 1990s and Shearing's essay can be understood as an intervention in that debate. He frames what is to follow as a rethinking of the nature of regulation, designed to reveal that 'arguments for deregulation are political moves in a struggle over regulation' (1993:68). The first section in the essay sets out an exposition of the control conception, as a prelude to showing its limitations as a description of how market regulation actually operates. He argues that it is based fundamentally on the idea of markets as autonomous and self-ordering entities which will generally serve the public interest, with external regulation only required when that market ordering has failed. Built on this 'root image' of regulation, he suggests that the regulation-deregulation debate becomes a 'debate over when, whether and to what extent market ordering alone will promote the public interest' (1993:69). For some, unfettered competitive markets are almost always the best solution, whilst for others, regulatory interventions will often be required to temper undesirable outcomes of market processes. Crucially, he argues that whatever position is taken along this continuum, it is based on this shared 'root image' of what regulation is and how it functions.

In the next section of the essay, he sets out an alternative view of regulation, based on the idea that regulation, rather than being simply negative or constraining, is in fact constitutive of markets. He opens the section with the claim that 'markets are always and necessarily regulated through careful constitutive work' (1993:70). Markets are not natural phenomena that are just given or simply exist, rather they are constructions that depend on specific allocations of power and resources. To claim that a market is naturally occurring is therefore a political move that is 'essentially a discursive sleight of hand that seeks to win a political victory by denying that there is a battle to be fought' (1993:71). It follows, he argues, that there is 'no escape from the necessity of regulation' (1993:71), as there is no 'pre-regulation' market we can turn to or any form of market ordering that will remove the need to regulate. He states, in striking terms, that markets are a 'regulatory accomplishment' rather than a phenomenon that exists outside or before regulation (1993:72). In this sense, deregulation is an illusion. Drawing on Hancher and Moran (1989/1998), Shearing (1993:72) suggests that the metaphor of regulatory space is a helpful way of thinking about this: regulation takes place within a space that will have different and varying occupants but which is never empty. Occupants will include both state and private actors and their interactions will involve at different times struggle, conflict, co-operation, and interdependence.

Towards the end of the essay (1993:74–75), there is a discussion of the significance of rules and rule enforcement which highlights a fundamental difference between the control and constitutive conceptions of regulation. For the control model, rules are one of the principal means to intervene in markets and set boundaries for market ordering. Rule enforcement is then critical to ensuring that regulation can effectively serve the public interest. From a constitutive perspective, regulation is understood as the constitution of a desired 'state of affairs' and so rule-compliance and rule-following are only relevant if they enhance market constitution. Regulation, in other words, is goal- rather than rule-oriented. This implies, in a fundamental rather than trivial sense, the limits of law as a regulatory tool.

Somewhat surprisingly, given his criminological background, one issue that is not directly or explicitly addressed by Shearing in his essay is how his argument might apply to informal or illegal markets, although it is implicit that he is writing about *all* markets. If a market is based on transactions that are criminalised, does this change how the market functions? In what ways? Does it alter how we should understand market regulation? These are very under-explored questions in the general literature on markets. One of the few people to engage with this matter in a serious way is the German sociologist Jens Beckert, particularly in an important and foundational paper (Beckert and Wehinger 2013) and in an extended introductory essay in a later edited collection (Beckert and Dewey 2017). For Beckert, borrowing from Fligstein, the 'architecture' of illegal markets can be conceptualised in similar ways as for legal ones but the illegality of transactions generates distinctive co-ordination problems concerning what he terms valuation (assessing product quality), competition (struggles between market competitors), and co-operation (trust in market actors to fulfil agreements). To give an example, co-operation problems are (partially) solved in drug markets by placing greater reliance on establishing relationships of trust and also by using the threat of violence as a resource for ensuring agreements are met. Beckert does not cite Shearing but his account of how actors solve co-ordination problems through adaptive practices strongly resembles the constitutive vision of markets made up from ongoing interactive processes of action and adaptation.

The primary aim of the SLS paper was to develop a constitutive conception of drug control, building on Shearing's essay, as a necessary first step before constructing new ideas and concepts. It presents a number of challenges to thinking about drug control. Fundamentally, it decentres the state, state agencies, law, and law enforcement, all of which are conventionally viewed as being largely at the heart of the matter for drug control. The paper also argues for an understanding that drug prohibition is itself a form of market regulation, rather than its absence, a position directly counter to a common line of argument within reformist discourse which critiques prohibition for leading to 'unregulated' markets. In addition, it brings to the forefront the necessity of normative thinking about policy: what is the desired state of affairs that we are seeking to constitute? This is an under-explored question in the field of drug policy and connects partly to the often poorly conceptualised discussion of the politics of drugs, which will be the focus of Part III of this book. The paper also calls for an understanding of the challenge of drug control as a specific instance of wider debates about how to regulate capitalism in the twenty-first century. At the end of the paper, in the very final paragraph of the conclusion, the concept of *exchangespace* is introduced for the first time, with a call for further work to elaborate on and specify the concept. This is the task of the next section.

Elements of *exchangespace*: A conceptual specification

The idea for *exchangespace* first came from trying to think through what is implied by Shearing's (1993) statement that it is not possible for markets to exist without regulation and that there is no such thing as an unregulated market. As noted above, in the drug policy context, in particular, this is a strikingly heterodox position, as a standard trope in critiques of prohibition is to decry the 'unregulated' drug markets that it creates. Shearing's argument seemed to imply that this was incorrect. What if prohibition, legalisation, and decriminalisation were all just different ways of regulating drug markets?

After struggling for some time to make sense of this, a revelatory moment came to me in 2015 from encountering the various articles and documentaries celebrating the 100-year anniversary of the first publication of Einstein's General Theory of Relativity. Much of Einstein's theory was impenetrable to me but one key idea which I could not only grasp but was also fascinated by was the notion that space and time are not separate but in fact form a single spacetime continuum. This seemed to me an astonishing idea and then out of the blue I suddenly saw that perhaps this might be a way of developing Shearing's constitutive understanding of regulation: a single market-regulation continuum. I then made the link with Giddens' structuration theory, which holds similarly that structure and agency are not separate but are in fact different aspects of the same phenomenon.

The term *exchangespace* is an obvious homage to Einstein's 'spacetime', of course, and brings together the core of the notion of a market with the concept of regulatory space. The idea seeks to capture the dynamic, interactive, and constitutive relationship between regulation and markets, understanding them not as separate realms but rather as 'two sides of the same coin'. This notion that regulation and markets are in any sense 'the same thing' is in many respects an extraordinary one. But what exactly does this entail? To answer this, we must first define more precisely the two building blocks that make up the concept: markets and regulatory space.

Exchange: Bargaining transactions, markets, and economies

It will be noted, of course, that I have chosen the descriptor *exchange*space rather than *market*space. This choice has a theoretical basis. Following Harvey and Randles (2010), the rationale for emphasising *exchange* in the concept (rather than market or supply chain) is that the 'bargaining transaction' or exchange is the basic unit for the analysis of economic life from which other concepts can be built. Adam Smith of course famously claimed in *The Wealth of Nations* that 'every man ... lives by exchanging', indicating the fundamental character of exchange activity. We can define the bargaining transaction as a monetary exchange for the transfer of property rights. For example, a customer gives a shopkeeper £1 and property rights in the requested chocolate bar are transferred. Whilst an exchange is a single bilateral transaction, a market implies an aggregation of transactions. Markets can be defined in terms of a product or service (the chocolate bar market) or spatially (the UK market) and usually in combination (the UK chocolate bar market). Market definitions are constructions, that is, ways of grouping together a set of transactions. Any single transaction can, in that sense, be part of multiple markets.

The relationship between exchange and market is, however, not just a matter of aggregation of transactions. In an important sense, transactions are only possible in any stable or sustained way because of the wider framework in which they take place. As Coriat and Weinstein (2010:56) put it, 'transactions are only possible when they take place within constructed frameworks—in other words, *in markets* ... Markets are themselves organised systems founded on specific institutional arrangements.' In other words, exchanges require markets which are built upon legal-institutional arrangements that we might also term regulation. Market forms, in turn, can only be fully grasped by locating them in the wider context of the capitalist system and this involves examining the 'close ties between conditions of exchange and conditions of production' (Coriat and Weinstein 2010:56). Markets therefore need to be set in the context of the wider production and supply chain processes to which they are linked. In this way, we can build up an entire picture of the economic system from the basic unit of the exchange or bargaining transaction.

Markets are a vital part of this system as they serve as a 'co-ordinating phase between production and consumption' (Harvey 2010:4), functioning 'as institutions of exchange, and hence of coordination and integration between buyers and sellers' (Harvey 2010:12). We cannot, of course, talk about any of these actions or systems without considering the resources that circulate within these processes of exchange, that is, the goods or products. These are in effect what draw together the whole system via the bargaining transaction. As Callon et al (2002) argue, a product can best be understood not as a static or inanimate 'thing' but rather as the result of a process which involves a sequence of transformations which move from raw materials at the production end through to the purchased and consumed good at the retail end. A product, understood in this way as a sequence of transformations, describes the 'different networks co-ordinating the actors involved in its design, production, distribution and consumption' (Callon et al 2002:198). The exchange or bargaining transaction is the interaction that transfers property rights in that product. By taking the exchange as our base unit of analysis we end up being able to encompass analytically the full supply chain and connect together the concepts of the market and the economy.

Space: Regulation, organisations, and politics

To define the notion of regulatory space, it is worth going back to the original essay by Hancher and Moran (1989/1998) that was first published in 1989, as well as an important paper by legal scholar Colin Scott (2001) which elaborates on it. Hancher and Moran begin their essay by observing the centrality of regulation to modern social systems, stating that it is 'virtually a defining feature of any system of social organization' (1989/1998:148). Within this broad field, it is the regulation of economic activity which has a particular importance in what they term 'advanced capitalist' societies and it is the area of economic regulation that the rest of the essay examines. They begin by attempting to define and characterise economic regulation and in doing so argue that the conventional boundaries of the public and private realms are unhelpful in trying to grasp the reality of regulation in advanced capitalism. A large firm can have more regulatory influence than a state agency in some circumstances. In this sense, ideas like 'regulatory capture' are of limited analytical value. Instead, they suggest, the critical question is to understand the nature of the shared regulatory space (1989/1998:153).

Hancher and Moran explicitly derive this idea of 'regulatory space' from political scientist Colin Crouch's (1986) notion of 'public space' in the context of the policy process. They describe the idea as a metaphor that they use as an analytical construct to make sense of how economic regulation functions in different arenas and fields. They suggest that the basic questions the 'space' metaphor prompts are about who the occupants are. Which occupants are the major and minor participants? Who is included or excluded from the space? How do these admissions processes work? What are the competitive struggles, alliances, and interdependencies between occupants? As they observe, these questions mean that the 'play of power is at the centre' of the picture (1989/1998:154). A further set of questions concerns the scope of the regulatory space, that is, which issues are included, excluded, prioritised, or downplayed? Thinking about scope points to the importance of historical, cultural, and political perspectives in understanding economic regulation.

After these introductory and definitional considerations, Hancher and Moran then turn to looking in more detail at the five core parameters of regulatory space. The first parameter they consider is the importance of *place*, by which they mean the ways in which political culture can influence quite significantly the shape and configuration of regulatory space and its occupants. This is an important point as it reminds us that the way economic regulation happens is not timeless or purely technical, but rather reflects the history, values, and culture of a given society at a particular moment in time. The balance between public and private actors is an example of a key dimension of regulation that is very significantly shaped by specific political cultures. The second parameter they examine is *timing*. Whilst regulation is often routinised and proceduralised, it will from time to time be punctuated by crises of various kinds which then lead to change. The historical accidents of who ends up as the first movers or the dominant occupants of the regulatory space at these points of change becomes very important. These points or moments can be of great significance in understanding regulatory arrangements. The third parameter they consider is the way that economic regulation happens mainly by and through *organisations* of different kinds. Although individuals may occupy regulatory space, they do so usually as a result of their organisational role (employee, representative, delegate, etc). The organisational character of economic regulation points us to the need to understand how internal conflict or dynamics and external competitive struggles shape the regulatory enterprise. As they put it, 'the essence of regulatory politics is the pursuit of institutional advantage ... in the marketplace' (1989/1998:162). Related to this, the fourth parameter is the importance of *interdependencies* within the regulatory space. Understanding the relationships, dependencies, and linkages between actors—in short, the 'social relations between the occupants of that space' (1989/1998:166) —is a critical analytical task, for which Hancher and Moran suggest a network approach may be helpful. The fifth and last parameter concerns the defining of regulatory *issues*. Nothing is 'given' or 'obvious': what counts as a regulatory issue and how it is characterised (as 'technical' or 'political', etc) are the outcomes of processes that are steered by power, culture, and custom within the regulatory space.

The starting point for Scott's (2001) elaboration and extension of the Hancher and Moran concept is an understanding that regulatory capacity is fragmented and dispersed and is to be found far beyond official state agencies or institutions. For Scott, the regulatory space construct leads us to a conception of regulation as pluralistic, non-hierarchical, public *and* private, state *and* non-state, and deriving from interaction, negotiation, and bargaining between a diverse set of actors. It decentres both law and the state. The conventional notion of a bilateral and hierarchical relationship between regulating authority and regulatee is largely abandoned as an oversimplified and inaccurate model of how regulation actually works. If we look at concrete examples of regulation, we encounter instead multi-party relationships of negotiated interdependence.

Using the construct of regulatory space, the task of reforming or improving regulation, of developing 'better regulation', also looks different, as it can no longer be understood as achievable just through changing the rules or how they are enforced. As Scott (2001) observes, quoting Clarke (2000:25–26), Hancher and Moran's metaphor implies that regulatory reform is better conceived as a 'renegotiation of regulatory space'. In other words, as Shearing (1993:72) puts it, 'regulatory space as a whole should be made the subject of regulatory policy'. Again, this is a heterodox position in the context of drug law reform, where changing the rules is seen precisely as the core task for better regulation.

One of the implications of regulatory space is that it prompts us to acknowledge the limits of regulation or, more precisely, the limits of what we can expect it to be able to achieve. Instead of a regulator just needing to find the right lever to pull or tool to use, we have a more diffuse and complex picture, in which many of the actors cannot be directly controlled and will have their own interests and goals which may point in different directions. Taming this complexity is perhaps something that can usually only be worked towards rather than fully attained. This is a vision of regulatory strategy as non-linear and non-instrumental and also as something that travels within and through a space that continually shapes and re-shapes it. Recognising this vision, we can only begin to develop a regulatory approach in any specific context by first mapping the actual and potential occupants of the regulatory space and then attempting to understand their different motivations, interests, resources, and capacities.

Exchangespace: A four-dimensional concept

Both halves of our concept have now been defined and elaborated. In doing so, we have already begun to set out how they are tied together but the claim here, of course, is much stronger. They are not just 'inextricably linked', 'bound up together', or any other label conveying a very close relationship; the claim is that they are different aspects of the same thing. We now turn to explaining what this means and how we can specify such a concept more precisely.

Understanding this claim hinges partly on how we understand regulation. It is a notoriously slippery concept which can be defined in different ways. There are three broad definitional types. The first defines it simply as state control through legal rules backed by sanctions. This is a traditional 'command and control' definition. The second type of definition moves away from this centring of law and the state, as in Julia Black's (2002:26) well-known formulation of regulation as 'the sustained and focused attempt to alter the behaviour of others according to defined standards and purposes with the intention of producing a broadly identified outcome or outcomes, which may involve mechanisms of standard-setting, information-gathering and behaviour modification'. The third broadens the concept out even further by removing any reference to intentionality and stating that regulation encompasses all efforts to 'steer the flow of events' (Braithwaite 2008:1). Concepts like regulation are tools for thinking and therefore choices between definitions depend in part on the specific analytic purpose in hand. In the context of economic regulation, Hancher and Moran (1989/1998:150–152) argue that whilst all three types of definition may be useful in different circumstances, it is the third that best captures the complex reality of how regulation functions. This widest definition is particularly useful for thinking about drug control, as it allows us to capture the important ways in which behaviour within markets can be constitutive of local order. Drug market regulation does not just come from above.

If we understand regulation as 'steering the flow of events', this starts to unlock how market behaviour and regulation might be viewed as different aspects of the same thing. Taking the example of the consumer market for wine in the United Kingdom, this is structured around transnational supply chains, with retailers at the UK end of various kinds and sizes but increasingly dominated by large supermarkets, some of which are multinational companies. If one large supermarket decides, as part of renegotiating contracts with one of its suppliers, that it will no longer sell wines containing chemical X, then this will have a profound impact on the market, an impact that could be described as regulatory. The renegotiation and execution of that supply contract is market behaviour made up of 'bargaining transactions', yet it is also very clearly regulation which 'steers the flow of events' in a significant way. In this example, we can no longer easily answer the question of who is the regulator and who is the regulatee. Henderson (2005) provides an empirical account of exactly this type of scenario, describing how the larger British supermarket chains made decisions that had a profound impact on South African wineries.

The ability of large supermarkets to operate in this way is of course a function of their relative economic power. The extent to which any single market actor can 'steer the flow of events' across the system—that is, the extent to which their actions can have regulatory effects—can therefore be understood as a power effect. This is the 'play of power' that Hancher and Moran (1989/1998:154) see as being central to regulatory space. Thinking about this visually can help us to develop this conceptualisation. Specifically, thinking in terms of *dimensions* is productive. Below, a four-dimensional model of *exchangespace* is set out which captures its key features.

First dimension

The simplest way of conceiving market regulation is as a regulatory continuum which is typically conceptualised as a straight line, that is, in *one dimension*. Sinclair (1997), for example, discussing environmental regulation, argues that thinking of 'command and control' and 'self-regulation' as dichotomous approaches is unhelpful and suggests that they should be conceptualised as two extreme poles of a continuum. Spread along the continuum are a range of policy measures containing a different balance of the two polar approaches. The notion of a regulatory continuum is a helpful conceptual tool that has been used in a diverse set of policy areas. In the context of drug control, a continuum between, at one end, prohibition and, at the other, full commercialisation, has been a standard—and useful—description of the range of policy possibilities. But the idea of *exchangespace* requires us to multiply the number of dimensions in which regulation is conceived.

Second dimension

One of Hancher and Moran's great insights was to see regulation as happening in a space. When we do this, the straight line of the continuum becomes a plane, that is, it has *two dimensions*. We then become concerned with mapping the occupancy, occupant-positioning and inter-occupant relations within the two-dimensional space. We have moved from a line to a network. This networked character is a critically important aspect of *exchangespace*. The idea of interdependencies was one of the central parameters of economic regulation defined by Hancher and Moran and, as we will see, the networked nature of *exchangespace* is also key to unlocking its complexity. One of the most important contributions to our understanding of networked governance more generally is nodal governance theory (see Burris et al 2005, 2008). This derives from the bringing together of Manuel Castells' sociology of the network society, the Foucauldian governmentality analytic, and the regulation studies literature. Its key insight is that we should pay particular attention to understanding the nature of the nodes within a network, where nodes are understood as points at which knowledge, capacity, and resources are mobilised in order to govern within a system. The nature of the differences between nodes, and the consequent impacts on how regulation happens, leads us to think in a further dimension.

Third dimension

One way to think about the power effects described above in our supermarket wine example is simply to say that some nodes in a network are more important than others. We could represent this visually in two dimensions by drawing nodes of different sizes within the network map. But we can also think about this three-dimensionally. An analogy here is with the way Einstein rethought the idea of gravity. He imagined spacetime as a flat rubber sheet pulled taut. Objects curve spacetime in the way that a heavy object would create a depression in a flat sheet: the greater the mass of the object, the deeper the depression. It is this curvature of spacetime that we interpret as gravity. In other words, gravity is not a force, as Newton thought, it is a consequence of the way matter curves the fabric of spacetime. In *exchangespace* we can think of economically powerful nodes as objects distorting the flat sheet of the two-dimensional regulatory space—the bigger the object, the deeper the depression it causes, and the more power and resources will accumulate at that node in the network.

Fourth dimension

The importance of the dynamic adaptive character of *exchangespace* means that we need to go further and add a *fourth dimension* of time. Obviously all human action is temporal in the sense that every action has duration and actions occur sequentially in time. But the fourth dimension of *exchangespace* refers not just to this but rather to the recursivity and interactivity of action within it. The interplay of human action within the *exchangespace* is continuous and dynamic and takes place not between just two parties like a game of tennis but rather in a complex multi-party game. The key to this dimension is the idea of continuous flux or flow. This is an important distinction between how time is ordinarily considered in models of regulation. It is a standard approach to consider and evaluate changes in market behaviour between two points in time, before and after a regulatory intervention, but this is essentially a control conception of regulation. In *exchangespace*, we are concerned with the *flow* of time. We will return to this in the next chapter.

Clearly, to construct a four-dimensional working model of this kind for a specific regulatory case is not a straightforward undertaking. It would require extensive mapping, data collection, and detailed analysis to understand relationships. Social science capabilities to handle and make sense of this level of data complexity have been developing rapidly in recent years. Data science in general (e.g. Kelleher and Tierney 2018), and network science in particular (e.g. Barabási 2016), have become important interdisciplinary fields which are enabling new advances to be made. Nevertheless, the challenge in operationalising the idea of *exchangespace* is not just about data, it is also about finding ways to think about and understand complexity. This question of complexity has become an important area of study.

Complexity, complex systems science, and the micro-macro problem

One potential way of developing how we think about *exchangespace* is through engaging with complex systems science. This is a relatively new area of interdisciplinary research that seeks to transform how we understand the complexity of problems that appear to involve unpredictable and sometimes unfathomable systems. The field of complexity or complex systems science is still less than 50 years old. One of the foundational contributions was work in the 1970s by the Nobel prize-winning chemist Ilya Prigogine on road traffic but it began to take off in a significant way with the establishment in 1984 of the independent Santa Fe Institute in the United States. Complex systems science is premised on the realisation that the 'complicated and messy problems we face cannot be solved alone by any existing body of knowledge' and that these problems involve 'entangled systems of systems of systems' or 'socio-technical systems' (Johnson 2010:116). Mathematicians, scientists, and engineers were at the forefront of early developments but by the late 1990s the 'complexity turn', as Urry (2005) terms it, had arrived in the social sciences. Today, it is firmly established as an interdisciplinary field that aims to transcend the 'two cultures' of science and the humanities in a fundamental and thoroughgoing way.

Complex systems science is partly a mathematical or computational technique or methodology but, more importantly, it is also a way of thinking about problems. It has several key ideas that are relevant here: *prediction*, *connectivity, emergence,* and *irreversibility.* The ability to predict the out-comes of actions is a key aspect of science and of policy analysis. We want to know if intervention A occurs, will desired outcome B result? Even where we cannot predict this with certainty (that is, we cannot answer simply 'yes' or 'no'), we can usually formulate a response in terms of probabil-ities. Within complex systems, *prediction* of this kind—whether absolute or probabilistic—is not possible (see Johnson 2010:117–119). This is partly because complex systems are often highly sensitive to initial conditions. In other words, what appear to be very small changes to the starting state can lead to very large differences in the outputs of models. What this means is that models need to be run many times, with different starting assumptions and states, to give an idea of the span of possibilities for outcome scenarios. Johnson (2010:132) argues that the traditional concept of point prediction (that system X will be in state A at time T) is 'almost irrelevant in the science of complex systems' and goes on to state we will need not only to reformu-late the entire concept of prediction using new dynamic theories but also to create new statistical methods for testing predictions. This is a theoretical, conceptual, and technical challenge that this emerging field is still some distance away from meeting.

One of the characteristics of complex systems, a characteristic in fact which is at the heart of their complexity, is that they are based on large numbers of interactions between multiple actors. The *connectivity* between actors is an essential element of how they function. Understanding a com-plex system therefore involves understanding it as a network made up of relations of interdependence, a point noted by Hancher and Moran (1989/ 1998) in their formulation of the notion of regulatory space. Here, there is potentially a useful connection to be made with nodal governance theory (Burris et al 2005) which offers a theoretically-informed social science per-spective on how we should conceptualise networks. One of the major con-tributions of the nodal governance approach is that it focuses attention not only on connections within the network but also on the nodes. Burris and colleagues also explicitly formulate their theory as an attempt to make sense of and tame the complexity of modern systems of governance. We will re-turn to nodal governance in the next chapter, along with some other ap-proaches to understanding networks.

Perhaps the heart of the matter for complex systems science is the idea of *emergence.* This is based on the observation that at the aggregate level of a system, patterns of behaviour emerge that are the result of multiple micro-level interactions but which are not at all foreseeable or predictable from those interactions. A good example to illustrate emergence is the human brain. The brain is made up of billions of neurons which interact by transmitting electrochemical signals. From this mass of interactions, amongst many other things, a rich and complex phenomenon like consciousness emerges. Yet this could not be foreseen at all from looking at the nature of neurons and their interactions, rather it is an emergent property of a complex system. Emergence and emergent properties are the crux of what makes a system complex rather than merely complicated.

The final idea centres on the notion of system equilibrium. In a simple system, it is possible to control inputs or interventions so that it returns to a defined system equilibrium point. For example, a room-heating system with a thermostat can be set so that whenever the temperature falls below a certain level the heating switches on and will stay on until the equilibrium temperature is reached. In a complex system, it is impossible ever to return to a previous point of equilibrium and interventions are, in that sense, 'unrepeatable experiments', as Johnson (2010:122) puts it. A good example is a national economy: a policy intervention will have more or less discernible impacts but it will never be possible to 'reset' the economy and return to the original pre-intervention state in order to try an alternative intervention. A complex multi-level system is continuously dynamic and the impact of interventions is therefore, in an important sense, *irreversible*. This has implications for how we think about interventions that aim to direct or shape what happens in a complex system.

Burris et al (2005:33) make the Hayekian observation that 'complexity makes governance a challenging game'. But, contrary to Hayek's pessimism, they suggest it is not an impossible one. In many, perhaps most, contexts, *exchangespace* will function as a complex system. There will be multiple actors, large numbers of interactions and networked interdependencies, unpredictable outcomes, continuous dynamic change, and unforeseen emergent properties at the aggregate level. This means that problems of market regulation will frequently be analytically intractable to conventional social science. Engaging seriously with complex systems science will be an important part of how the concept is developed and used. This will necessitate a significantly broader approach to interdisciplinarity than is usually the case. In particular, mathematicians and computer scientists are essential to the building of models.

Modelling, of course, should not be mistaken for an analytical 'black box' that can magically solve complex regulatory problems. As has been argued here, the idea of *exchangespace* highlights the need to find ways of thinking about and managing complexity. As Burris et al (2005:54) put it, referring to an insight from political scientist Mick Moran, 'more than one line of contemporary regulatory theory has converged on the idea that complexity requires strategies that in some way change, or at least thickly engage, the internal constitutions of the regulated entities'. In other words, attempting simply to constrain or limit undesirable aggregate outcomes is a strategy doomed to fail for complex systems; instead, it is necessary to intervene at the micro-level of behaviour in order to incentivise, deter, influence, and nudge actors in ways that will tend to produce desired outcomes at the system level. *Exchangespace* provides a way of thinking about this task which acknowledges that it is neither productive nor possible to categorise these interventions and actions as 'regulation' or 'market'. Rather, they are micro interactions within a four-dimensional *exchangespace* from which macro patterns and properties emerge.

Other attempts to engage with complexity, outside of complex systems science, have also tended to centre on transcending the macro-micro divide. An interesting book by economist Richard Wagner (2020), for example, sets out to rethink the macroeconomics project in exactly this way. Wagner develops the idea of complexity within economic systems by drawing on social and economic theory which has engaged with the question of what he calls the 'systematic study of parts-to-whole relationships' (2020:3). He begins with an overview of some of the antecedents of his argument, including economist Thomas Schelling's (1978) book *Micromotives and Macrobehavior* and biologist Ludwig von Bertalanffy's (1968) pioneering development of general systems theory as an interdisciplinary approach to describing and understanding systems made up of interacting components. A critical distinction Wagner draws is between systems approaches which treat actor interactions as *mechanistic* and approaches which see them as creative or *volitional*. The former is often assumed within conventional economic theory; the latter is more typical of social theory. Wagner (2020:9) locates his project squarely in the *volitional* camp and seeks to draw on ideas of 'open-endedness, emergence, evolution, and complexity' within social theory, in order to recast macroeconomics.

In a different context, and in a rather different way, John Braithwaite (2020a) has attempted to advance understanding of patterns of crime and war by viewing them as 'cascade phenomena'. He defines these as phenomena which 'spread to multiply instances of themselves, or to spread related phenomena' (2020a:138). He notes that cascade explanations have been common in the biological and physical sciences, as well as in some areas of social science, but that criminologists have generally shown a lack of interest. This is despite the plethora of examples in that field that can be fruitfully interpreted with the cascade concept and related ideas of contagion and tipping points. He notes that there are many crime phenomena where variations in incidence rates across space and time are so large that they cannot be explained by the exogenous factors that criminologists typically enlist as explanatory variables. For example, homicide rates show such enormous historical and spatial variation that we need to find different ways of explaining the variance, beyond reaching for factors such as incomes, unemployment rates, inequalities, or demographic profiles. One alternative form of explanation, he suggests, is to look at how micro-level interactions can cascade across networks. The core of his argument is that viewing through the cascade lens brings into focus how micro-level events and processes can combine to generate macro patterns that could otherwise not be foreseen or explained. Howard Parker's detailed empirical study of local heroin outbreaks in England in the 1980s is an excellent example of a cascade explanation, as it showed how micro-level personal interactions could rapidly spread heroin use through friendship and other networks—a process he called 'microdiffusion'—to produce a full-blown localised 'heroin epidemic' (Parker et al 1988). Over time, separate heroin sites tended to join up through a process of 'macrodiffusion', spreading to neighbouring towns, resulting in a significant macro-problem. So while the initial arrival of heroin in a site was an exogenous factor driven by supply and transport routes, heroin became an endogenous cascade within some neighbourhoods through these diffusion processes.

Braithwaite takes the argument a step further. He argues that macro-criminologists have neglected cascade ideas in ways that have not only narrowed analytical accounts of crime but have also limited understanding of how crime *prevention* cascades. He gives the example of 'hot spot' policing—targeting policing resources at highly localised 'hot spots' of crime incidence—which several studies have shown not only cuts crime in the 'hot spots' but also in neighbouring areas, contrary to the hypothesised fears of displacement. Yet, Braithwaite claims, criminologists, blinded by their 'exogeneity bias', have shown little interest in building new testable theories of the cascading effects of targeted policing. Central to Braithwaite's argument is the idea that these processes of cascades and contagion, whether of crime or crime prevention, are dynamic and complex rather than static. This is a critical point to grasp as it highlights the methodological challenges involved. For example, how can we find the 'best methodologies for separating contagion effects from associations that are in fact contiguous actors being exposed to the same exogenous factor at the same time' (Braithwaite 2020a:161)? Criminology is probably not the strongest of the social sciences in terms of meeting this type of challenge. We will return to Braithwaite's work on cascades in the next chapter.

These various different ways of attempting to grapple with complexity in social systems all share several key features which can be brought together to underpin the *exchangespace* concept:

- They follow a deeply interdisciplinary approach, drawing not just on social sciences but also ideas, methods, and analytical techniques from biology, mathematics, computer science, and elsewhere.
- They cut across the micro-macro divide, understanding that macro phenomena are often emergent properties of multiple micro processes and interactions.
- They see the social order as networked and polycentric.

There is a danger that allusions to systems, modelling, and computational techniques may lead to abstractions that downplay the continuing centrality of power and inequalities within the drug control *exchangespace*. Yet, as we have seen, Hancher and Moran (1989/1998:154) were very clear in their original exposition of the idea of regulatory space that the 'play of power' lies at the heart of all forms of economic regulation. This is certainly the case for drug control and points to the importance of engaging with the political realm. In Part III of the book, the politics of drug control is explored in some detail. Here, the focus is on how we should theorise the political dimension of *exchangespace*.

The political constitution of *exchangespace*

Laurie Taylor (1971) once vividly described Robert Merton's anomie theory as viewing American society like a giant fruit machine, with rigged payouts but designed to appear fair to those playing it. But nowhere, Taylor says, does Merton explain where the machine came from, who put it there, and who is profiting from it. As Part II of this book will make clear, the search for the precursors of the international drug control system and the tracing of its genealogy is a critical intellectual task. But the notion of 'profiting' raises a related but additional set of questions that we might characterise as concerning the political constitution of the system. It asks, in other words, for the development of a political economy of the drug control *exchangespace*. How might we approach this task?

Here, my concern is not with the substantive exposition of that political economy but rather with a consideration of how it might be based theoretically and conceptually. A starting point is to understand that *exchangespace* is an analytical device that can be applied at multiple levels within the drug control system and we need to think differently about each of these levels. The historical lens applied in Part II tends to bring into focus drug control as an *international* political-economic order. A potential theoretical apparatus for analysis at this level is provided by the field of international political economy (IPE), a field largely originated by British international relations scholar Susan Strange, starting with a foundational paper in the early 1970s (Strange 1970). IPE has become a large and diverse area of intellectual endeavour over the last 50 years, with many sub-branches, characterised by as much disagreement and discord as most academic fields. Nevertheless, using Robert Gilpin's (2001) classic work *Global Political Economy* as a guide, we can draw out some common elements for a framework for thinking about the politico-economic constitution of international drug control.

Gilpin points us towards the essence of IPE: a field of enquiry concerned with global distributions of power and resources in the context of relations between states, supra-state bodies, and other powerful actors (e.g. corporations). These relations can take the form of inter-dependencies, co-operation, collaboration, conflict, and so on. Within IPE, scholars have deployed tools primarily from the disciplines of sociology, economics, political science, and international relations. This work has highlighted how these allocations and global flows of power and resources are understood as social, economic, and political phenomena. The international drug control system, as an *exchangespace* that is part of the international order, can therefore be analysed from this perspective and using these tools. This shifts us towards understanding the answer to the question of *cui bono* (who benefits)—a term often used by Strange—as rooted in an examination of the economic and political interests of key actors in that international order. This is some way from conventional accounts which typically view the prohibition regime as either an attempted technical solution to a policy problem or else as part of a moral(ising) crusade. It helps us, for example, to place actors like global pharmaceutical companies at the heart of the analysis and diagnosis of policy problems like the North American opioid crisis.

A particularly relevant sub-branch within IPE for the examination of drug policy and drug control is the Global Value Chains paradigm, developed by sociologist Gary Gereffi and colleagues (Gereffi et al 2005). This offers a set of intellectual resources for analysing the political economy of transnational supply chains and their regulation. Gereffi's work is particularly useful analytically, as it moves across and between levels from the global to the local. There are important questions about the political economy of the drug *exchangespace* at local level. In urban areas, for example, we can see how drug control functions as part of strategies for urban governance that are shaped to varying degrees by the political and economic interests of powerful groups. A recent paper by Kammersgaard (2020), presenting a study conducted in two Danish cities, illustrates this well. He shows how in one of the research sites, socially marginalised people (which included homeless people, drug users, and street drinkers) were problematised as being 'out of place' in gentrified parts of the city, leading to local businesses demanding action from the city council and the police. In the other site, in contrast, similar socially marginalised groups were constructed for a variety of reasons as being 'in place' and so less exclusionary control strategies were implemented. He charts how a complex matrix of highly localised economic, social, and cultural forces formed part of a process through which distinctive understandings of the 'problem' were constructed and then linked to specific governance strategies.

Kammersgaard's study reinforces the importance of Hancher and Moran's (1989/1998) emphasis on politics and power in their original formulation of the regulatory space construct, as already noted. The scope of the space (what is defined as an issue or problem), the processes of admission and exclusion from it, and the competitive struggles that unfold within it, are all shaped by the 'play of power' (1989/1998). *Exchangespace* is, in other words, deeply infused with politics and cannot be understood without being seen in its specific social, cultural, economic, and political context. This is not optional 'context' for descriptive colour or flavour, it is analytically essential.

Conclusion

In this chapter, the concept of *exchangespace* has been developed as a means of starting to rethink theoretically the nature and functioning of drug control. It is based on the conceptual premise that drug control can best be understood as a form of market regulation and that therefore understanding market-regulation interactions should lie at the core of any theoretical account. Its fundamental insight is that market behaviour and regulation, rather than being separate realms, are in fact two sides of the same coin. To develop the concept, intellectual resources have been drawn from a range of disciplines across law and the social sciences to create a cross-cutting theoretical idea. The notion of complexity, as a means of untangling and making sense of micro-macro relationships, is central. Bringing together the theoretical innovation of *exchangespace* with the cutting-edge analytical tools of complex systems science has the potential to lead to game-changing new insights and understandings of drug control. It was argued, finally, that *exchangespace* also needs to be understood as always situated in a political context, shaped by specific social, cultural, and economic factors. This intrinsically political character of drug control is developed further in Part III of the book.

In the next chapter, one particular aspect of the *exchangespace* concept—its temporality—is further explored. It will be recalled that this constituted the fourth dimension in the concept's specification and that it was characterised in terms of the 'flow of time'. This temporality is important because it opens up a way to think about change and the trajectory of regulation over time. In this sense, it connects together Part II (concerned with a particular period of historical development) and Part III (concerned with future regulatory possibilities), providing the theoretical foundation for the arc of the book's central argument.

3
Time and *exchangespace*

Introduction

As we saw in the previous chapter, the modal state of the drug control *exchangespace* is flow and flux, rather than stasis and stability. It is continually evolving as a diverse (and changing) set of occupants act, react, and adapt to each other, creating a dynamic multi-party complex. The focus of this chapter is to explore this temporal dimension and develop some intellectual resources for thinking about change over time. This is, of course, relevant both to histories of regulation and to explorations of possibilities for future reform. Our specific focus is on theorising economic regulatory trajectories, using the *exchangespace* concept, rather than the more general project of understanding social change. To put it another way, the aim is to understand how regulatory regimes evolve by viewing them from the perspective of market-regulation relations. If we can grasp these processes of evolution more clearly, our capacity both to understand the past and to shape the future may in turn be extended and enhanced.

A focus on change rather than stasis is important for advancing critical analysis beyond existing paradigms and conceptualisations. As political scientist Didier Bigo (2017) argues, analyses of politics and governance are typically organised around the notions of order and stability. Governance is conceived as being directed at imposing order through control. Yet historical research tells us that 'change always comes first and that order ... is a particular obsession of authorities' and, moreover, the 'priority of order over flows ... structures our thinking' in ways that create a 'central problem of misconception at the core of our logic' (2017:308). Bigo (2017:308) suggests that the focus on order is also a 'local obsession' of European and Western modernity which may not hold, for example, in China, India, or elsewhere in Asia.

The *exchangespace* concept generates theoretically an analytical requirement to examine change, flux, and flow. In the context of drug control, this

Rethinking Drug Laws. Toby Seddon, Oxford University Press. © Toby Seddon 2023.
DOI: 10.1093/oso/9780192846525.003.0003

means that rather than thinking about what type of regulatory regime or legal framework will control drug markets effectively, instead the focus must shift to devising strategies to manage and steer continuous change in desired directions. In other words, the challenge is not about the one-off design of a new regulatory system (e.g. 'state-controlled legalisation') but instead about creating frameworks within which dynamic cycles of decisions, monitoring, and review can take place to incorporate learning over time. Bennear and Wiener (2019) have termed this 'adaptive regulation' and, of course, it is a close cousin of the probably more familiar idea of 'responsive regulation' (Ayres and Braithwaite 1992).

A starting point for the chapter is Hilton Root's (2020) book *Network Origins of the Global Economy* which provides a novel attempt to marry together complexity theory, network science, and institutional economics in order to make sense of global economic history. Root's reference points—complexity, networks, institutions—articulate strongly with the specification of *exchangespace* set out in the previous chapter. The chapter also draws on important work by David Levi-Faur (2013, 2014) and John Braithwaite (2008, 2020b) on the evolution and development of regulatory capitalism. In particular, a recent paper by Braithwaite (2020b) offers a theoretical synthesis using the idea of path dependence. Like Bigo, both Root and Braithwaite directly question the Western-centrism of existing scholarship on regulatory trajectories, arguing that this is a particular weakness when we are attempting to make sense of how regulatory capitalism is evolving in the Asian Century. This provides a further point of articulation with the thesis of this book. The third starting point for the chapter is nodal governance theory, as developed by Clifford Shearing and colleagues over the last two decades (Burris et al 2005, 2008; Holley and Shearing 2017).

The first section of the chapter outlines these three theoretical contributions—as set out by Root, Braithwaite, and Shearing, respectively—in order to draw out some key ideas and concepts: network structures; path dependence; and nodes and flows. The second section then brings out these ideas in relation to thinking about the temporal dimension of drug control *exchangespaces*. The third section briefly sets out some illustrative examples of how the ideas developed across the two chapters in this part of the book provide intellectual resources that can start to be used to generate transformative insights into drug laws and drug control in ways that open up new ideas for future drug law reform. The conclusion then points towards both Part II of the book (by indicating how reframing historical change as regulatory trajectories may provide a different way of seeing familiar historical narratives) and Part III (by highlighting how these types of transformative insights require a serious engagement with the politics of drug control and the politics of reform).

Thinking about regulatory trajectories: Three perspectives

Network topology

In the first chapter of his book *Network Origins of the Global Economy*, Root (2020:5) poses what he views as a fundamental question for his thesis: 'is change best conceived in terms of mechanical or organic processes'? His answer is the latter and the rest of the book makes the case that complex systems thinking and network analysis provide the keys to unlocking our understanding of these 'natural' or organic processes of change that constitute the 'great transitions in economic history'. This, he argues, represents a new scientific 'foundation' for the political economy of global change (2020:13).

Root's analysis is built on a conceptualisation of economies as complex multilevel systems. Their complexity is rooted in an understanding of these systems as adaptive, that is, constituted by actors continually adjusting and reacting to the actions and anticipated actions of other actors. He argues that conventional economic theories that are based on equilibrium models fail to capture this dynamic adaptive character.

Drawing on complex systems science, including ideas from physical and biological sciences, Root (2020:22–23) identifies five key properties that economies share with other complex systems:

1. They are nested *hierarchies of subsystems*, made up from interconnected subsystems at different levels. Subsystems are connected through information flows and feedback loops that move up and down. System change at the level of a large complex system is an emergent property of these multiple flows.
2. They have a *macro structure that is distinct from the micro-level* and which cannot be understood as simply an aggregation of what happens microscopically with agent behaviour.

3. They are *open systems* that cannot be neatly separated from the environment in which they operate. There is no clear 'inside' and 'outside' and no sharp distinction between exogenous and endogenous forces.
4. They are *networked*: made up of networks and networks of networks. These networks tend to exhibit non-linear dynamics as they are constituted by continuous interactions. Network structure or topology is central to the functioning of complex systems.
5. They *evolve episodically*, rather than in linear ways. Change can occur in 'fits and starts', or else very abruptly. Phase transitions—when a system reaches and then crosses a critical state at which its dynamics change very rapidly and irreversibly—can lead to unanticipated extinctions, mutations, epidemics and transformations.

From this complex systems perspective, Root develops two connected concepts to underpin his theoretical account of social and economic change. He argues that within networked systems, natural scientists and mathematicians distinguish two dimensions of change: in structure (topology) and in flow (behaviour). Each of these dimensions can help us to understand how change happens. The analytical challenge is to identify the 'point at which changes occurring within a system cause it to reach a critical state, or *change threshold*' (Root 2020:43, emphasis in original). Changes in network structure are termed *percolation* and a percolation threshold occurs when connectivity first appears in large clusters that were previously unconnected (2020:43). Root (2020:44) argues that this is a necessary first stage and that 'all major social transitions require transformations of the pathways of existing connectivity'. Changes in flow are termed *cascades* and occur when new types of behaviour start to spread rapidly across a network. Percolation followed by cascades can rapidly transform an entire system—a phase transition—often in unforeseen or unexpected ways.

Root suggests that whilst the cascades tend to be most visible, and so are sometimes assumed to be driving the change, it is actually the percolation, that is, the structural change in the network(s) that is the critical precondition for major transitions. Much of his book attempts to demonstrate the centrality of network topology in making sense of economic history. The central chapters explore several episodes of social and economic transition in China and Europe, a comparison that he uses to develop his main thesis: that the very different historical trajectories of China and the West have been significantly shaped by differences in network topology within their social and economic systems. In broad-brush terms, he argues that

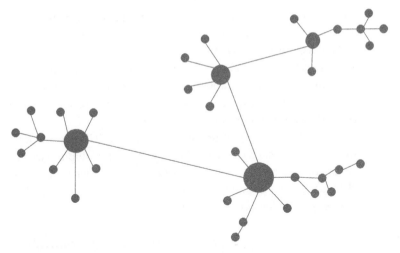

Figure 3.1 A scale-free network

differences in stability and resilience between the social and economic systems in China and Europe are driven to a great extent by structural differences in their hypernetworks (networks that cut across multiple levels within a system)—with China having a star-shaped hub-and-spoke hypernetwork and Europe a multi-hub hypernetwork. This, in turn, shapes when and how change happens.

Root (2020:33–40) describes the broad types of network structures that occur in societies (and, indeed, in nature). *Scale-free networks* (Figure 3.1) are characterised by growth patterns involving preferential attachment to a small number of nodes around which clustering occurs. Typically, these high-clustered nodes, sometimes termed hubs, are well connected with other hubs. This means that pathways from one point on the network to another will tend to be shorter than might be expected (relative to the overall size of the network). Scale-free networks have a fairly high degree of robustness to failure, as the hubs function so effectively as connectors. Hubs are also the most vulnerable part of this type of network: if too many are removed, the network will collapse. *Hub-and-spoke networks* (Figure 3.2) lack the high degree of clustering in scale-free networks, with hubs having much smaller numbers of direct connections. Highly centralised hub-and-spoke networks—with a central hub connected to several others—are sometimes described as star-shaped. They exhibit high levels of control and co-ordination. *Small-world networks* (Figure 3.3)—as famously described

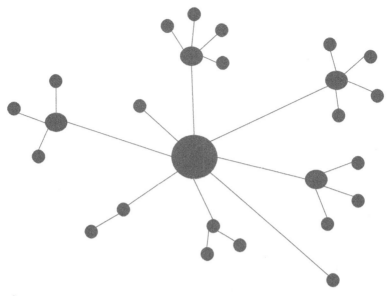

Figure 3.2 A hub-and-spoke network

in a landmark *Nature* paper (Watts and Strogatz 1998)—are characterised by a lattice structure which results in short pathways between nodes, even though they do not have the intensive hub-clustering of scale-free networks.

For Root, understanding what type of network structure exists allows us to draw certain inferences about likely patterns of behaviour, points of strength and weakness, and the dynamics of how transformations will occur. This leads to a novel approach to world economic history. The key insight is to understand economies as complex networked systems. This, in turn, points us towards an important aspect of how we might theorise change over time in drug control *exchangespaces*. Following Root, charting network topology becomes a key tool for diagnosing transformations.

Although Root argues that network topology is a critical and neglected aspect of the analysis of economic transitions, as we have noted he also identifies network cascades as the other dimension of change. Cascades— often conveyed using terms like contagion or epidemic—have been more commonly studied than structures. In the next section, we examine a particular approach to thinking about cascades using the idea of path dependence, as developed in recent years by regulation scholar John Braithwaite.

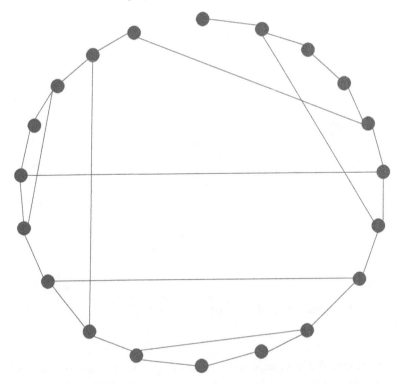

Figure 3.3 A small-world network

Path dependence

In the previous chapter, Braithwaite's (2020a) discussion of how the cascade lens might be used to bring into focus new insights for the discipline of criminology was briefly discussed as part of a consideration of how complexity thinking underpins the *exchangespace* concept. In focusing more specifically on regulatory trajectories, Braithwaite has further developed these ideas about cascades, particularly in a recent paper which uses the concept of path dependence in order to analyse 'historical sequences in the character of capitalism' (Braithwaite 2020b:33).

Although the idea of path dependence has a long history in historical research and in the field of historical sociology in particular (see Mahoney 2000), Braithwaite (2020b:32) provides his own definition of the term: 'the dependence of outcomes on the paths of previous routines, processes, and outcomes'. At one level, this might be interpreted as little more than the banal idea that what happens in the past affects the future. In fact, Braithwaite's aim is considerably more ambitious as he seeks to theorise how an understanding of *patterns* of path dependence can lead to new insights about strategies for the governance of the recurrent economic, ecological, and security crises that characterise contemporary global capitalism. In other words, path dependence is not just an analytical tool for regulation scholars, it is potentially an intellectual resource for thinking about better ways of regulating capitalism.

Braithwaite's theoretical contribution draws on Levi-Faur's (2013, 2014) earlier work on global regulatory capitalism which argued that its foundations are built on a structure of three institutional arenas: regulation, welfare, and markets. These forms or structural facets constitute the polymorphic nature of capitalism (Levi-Faur 2013). For Braithwaite (2020b), a critical step is to understand these three arenas as deeply interdependent and inter-connected. The connections between them are not the hydraulic relations often assumed (e.g. strong regulation producing weaker markets, strong markets leading to the decline of welfare, etc). Rather, there are multiple interactions and dependencies, such that it makes sense to think of an interdependent regulation-market-welfare ensemble (Braithwaite 2020b:30).

One of the key mechanisms for generating change in this ensemble, according to Braithwaite, is the creation or emergence of crises. They are an engine for change because of the way they tend to prompt those actors within the institutional arena who are primarily affected by the crisis to take problem-solving action which then, in turn, creates pressures for change across the other parts of the ensemble. He gives the example of 9/11, initially a security crisis, which led to rapid expansion of the regulatory state through investment in the homeland security function but also to a very significant increase in the markets for private security, private military corporations, and service providers to militaries like Halliburton, as well as boosting the arms industry (Braithwaite 2020b:35). A little later, welfare state growth followed, as the demand for trauma services for veterans and their families expanded. Indeed, Braithwaite (2020b:35–36) claims that the intergenerational trauma, particular on daughters of veterans, continues to create welfare demand 20 years after the initial security crisis. With only a little imagination, we can probably see how this type of pattern might apply to crisis-driven developments in the drug policy field (e.g. the North American opioid crisis).

The next stage in Braithwaite's theoretical account flows from the insight that these cascading crises—economic, security, ecological, etc—follow patterned path dependencies that tend towards growth across all three institutional arenas. This is the essence of contemporary global capitalism: more vibrant markets, more rules, more state activity. The 'myth' of neoliberalism that the state has progressively shrunk since 1980 is simply not supported by the evidence on aggregate state spending, even if welfare contraction in many Western societies has at times been stark in specific sectors (e.g. public housing) (Braithwaite 2008, 2020b:37–38). He then summarises the essence of his theory of change in terms of these twin drivers: 'path dependence and crises as mechanisms that insinuate resilience *and change* into institutions, thereby constituting polymorphous capitalism' (Braithwaite 2020b:37, emphasis in original). Path dependence here is understood in relation to the idea of an interdependent regulation-market-welfare ensemble as intrinsic to contemporary capitalism. It is those interdependencies that explain why we see recurring patterns and a systemic tendency towards expansion across all three institutional arenas.

In an important part of the paper, Braithwaite (2020b:32) argues that a 'fundamental weakness of governance scholarship in the Asian Century is that it still focuses most scholarly attention on Western states'. Drawing partly on a groundbreaking new book by Peter Drahos (2021) —which argues provocatively that China may be the world's best hope for averting the climate emergency in the twenty-first century—Braithwaite (2020b:39–42) shows how governance thinking is limited by its assumption that the West's distinctive political imaginary is universal rather than highly particular. In the context of environmental regulation, this manifests in over-reliance on price and market mechanisms to drive change that are too slow and modest in impact relative to the scale of the problem. In contrast, China's more state-centric interventionism may be more suited to dealing with the gravity of the crises facing earth systems. Theories of regulation and governance that are framed in terms of the hegemony of Western-style neoliberalism struggle to make sense of this. Braithwaite's theoretical model is able to accommodate this by showing how the different patterned path dependencies we see in, for example, China, are rooted in its distinctive historical, cultural, and political context which changes the nature of the interdependencies between regulation, markets, and welfare.

He further illustrates this argument about the importance of moving away from Western-centric perspectives by looking at path dependencies in response to the global Covid-19 crisis during 2020, where East Asian countries followed a very different track from many Western nations. He argues that the 'paths East Asia learned to take in response to the SARS epidemic created a virtuous path dependency of regulatory preparedness, welfare preparedness, and market preparedness for epidemic responsiveness' (2020b:45). In other words, the earlier experience with SARS provided very different 'initial conditions' for East Asian countries compared to Western countries which then led to different path dependencies opening up when the Covid-19 crisis emerged. This leads to his conclusion that harnessing and steering cascading crises and path dependencies may be the best and most realistic strategy to adopt in an era of globalised polymorphic capitalism. He terms this a strategy of meta governance of path dependencies.

We can draw several ideas from Braithwaite for thinking about regulatory change and trajectories in the context of the *exchangespace* concept. He emphasises the importance of understanding how the 'initial conditions' in a complex system can shape subsequent paths and outcomes in significant ways, with these pathways being particularly important, echoing Hancher and Moran's (1989/1998) identification of 'timing' as one of the core parameters of regulatory space. Histories of regulatory regimes become analytically indispensable. As well as path dependence, Braithwaite also brings to the fore the importance of crises as drivers of problem-solving, innovation, or emergency action which then leads to further reactions, adjustments, and responses. Setting this also in the context of his wider body of work on regulation, Braithwaite tells us very clearly that strategies for governance need to be framed as being about the steering and shaping of dynamic interactive spaces filled with multiple actors, rather than as technical governmental solutions to static problems.

Nodal governance

The third perspective drawn on here is nodal governance theory, a framework first developed by criminologist Clifford Shearing and various collaborators nearly 20 years ago and which built on various strands of network theory, notably sociologist Manuel Castells' influential trilogy of books on the 'Information Age' (Castells 1996, 1997, 1998). As briefly discussed in the previous chapter, nodal governance is a way of thinking about networks in which attention is focused particularly on the role and functioning of the nodes within those networks. In a much-cited early account of the approach, there is an explicit commitment to 'take complexity seriously' and to engage with the ways in which complex governance systems often go through 'rapid adaptive change' (Burris et al 2005:31–32), both of which are key aspects of the specification of the *exchangespace* concept set out in the previous chapter.

At the core of the nodal governance approach is the shift away from seeing governance as a state-centred hierarchical 'command and control' enterprise. Instead, governance is understood as polycentric, involving complex networks populated with diverse categories of actors. The distinctive insight of the approach is to understand that these nodes are much more than simply points of intersection within network flows. If networks 'help us to understand how information flows, information processing and communication take place within a social system', it is at nodes that these flows of information and communication are translated into action (Burris et al 2005:37). Paying more attention analytically to nodes is therefore critical to explaining how governance—viewed as the steering of the course of events—happens.

Focusing then on how nodes function as sites of governance, nodes are defined as sites where 'knowledge, capacity and resources are mobilised to manage a course of events' (2005:37). They are real rather than virtual, in the sense that they must take some type of institutional form with sufficient structure to enable them to marshal and mobilise information and resources and turn them into action. Examples of entities that could act as governing nodes include a street gang, a firm, a police station, or a government agency. Superstructural nodes—the 'command centers of networked governance' (2005:38)—bring together members or representatives from multiple nodes in order to concentrate their knowledge, capacity, and resources for a common goal, without fully integrating their networks (e.g. a trade association). Each of the key dimensions of nodes—knowledge, capacity, and resources—can be described empirically, in order to explain why different nodes have different levels of efficacy as sites of governance. Nodes vary greatly in their material characteristics—notably the level of resources and social capital they are able to mobilise—but share common features, including being shaped by conscious planning but also continually evolving and re-constituting themselves. In other words, although nodes and networks are typically in a perpetual state of flux and change, nodal governance is quite different from Hayekian accounts of regulation which emphasise 'spontaneous ordering' (Burris et al 2005:49).

Based on this understanding of the nodal nature of governance, the paper goes on to present a couple of case studies to illustrate the applicability of the framework both of which are relevant here. The first is the story of the Agreement on Trade-Related Aspects of Intellectual Property Rights (TRIPS), which was a World Trade Organization (WTO) agreement on intellectual property standards signed off in 1994 after several years of multi-national negotiation and development (Burris et al 2005:40–49). The authors of the paper show how the TRIPS agreement, rather than being the outcome of US hegemonic power as some commentators claimed, was in fact the end result of a complex and contingent set of nodal relations across networks. Key actors included private entities like the pharmaceutical company Pfizer, and the mobilisation of a series of different networks involving private and state actors. A central conclusion for our purposes is that accounts of TRIPS that see it primarily as a story about international negotiations between states are narrow and partial, missing out much of how TRIPS was actually agreed. Pointing to lessons that might be drawn for other arenas of governance at international level, central to the TRIPS story were processes in which nodes activated other nodes, superstructural nodes were created, and where a range of public and private actors were important.

The second case study describes innovative community work in South Africa led by Shearing, known as the 'Zwelethemba Model'. This was an experimental approach to security governance in very poor communities where state agencies were failing to provide adequate policing (for an account of the history of the model and its creation, see Shearing and Froestad 2010). Local Peace Committees were created as mechanisms to resolve disputes, serving more broadly as problem-solving deliberative forums. The Peace Committees were also given access to functioning budgets and became, in effect, nodes of security governance which mobilised local knowledge, capacity, and resources around the goal of 'creating a better tomorrow' for their community (Shearing and Froestad 2010:110).

Shearing and collaborators have further developed these ideas by focusing on the idea of security governance as the regulation of flows of people and things (Amicelle et al 2017). They argue that securing these flows embodies contemporary concerns at the heart of policing practices more closely than traditional conceptions of state-organised criminal justice agencies focused on punishing and preventing inter-personal 'hitting and taking' harms. Securing flows in ways that maximise 'goods' and minimise 'harms' is the challenge for regulators. They argue that regulating flows is inherently nodal, in the sense that it typically involves multiple and heterogeneous networks, operating at multiple levels and enlisting diverse public and private actors. This resonates strongly with the idea of drug control as operating to shape and constrain circulation through the actions of multiple actors within an *exchangespace* where the domains of 'market' and 'regulation' are fused and interconnected rather than fully distinct.

In a more recent account of nodal governance (Holley and Shearing 2017:170), it is argued that the framework can be used not only for *describing* and explaining how governance works in specific domains but also for guiding strategies for *transforming* governance in order to advance particular outcomes. The Zwelethemba work is a good example of this, where an understanding of nodal governance guided the construction of a concrete intervention at a local level. This points us towards seeing how, by viewing governance as *activity* which is continuous, multi-party, and adaptive, a range of possibilities for regulatory interventions opens up. This resonates with the constitutive foundation of the *exchangespace* concept and contrasts sharply with control conceptions of regulation. The 'obsession' with order that Bigo (2017) deprecates is transformed into a critical engagement with flux and continuous change and the opening up of new ideas about achieving governance objectives through the reshaping of nodal relations.

As a scholar who never stands still intellectually, Shearing has been breaking new ground in the last few years by transplanting and transforming his ideas about nodal governance into new areas, focused particularly around concerns for how we should deal with the novel 'harmscapes' that have emerged in the Anthropocene, notably the climate crisis. Writing with Julie Berg, he argues for an analytical approach that understands how regulatory trajectories unfold in a pluralised world in which harms, ordering practices, and governance processes intersect (Berg and Shearing 2021). It is this complex plural or polycentric character of governance which holds the key to generating ideas about how to deal with new forms of harm. Like Root and Braithwaite, Berg and Shearing (2021) also emphasise the need to expose and move beyond the Western-centric foundations of our thinking and practices.

Thinking about *exchangespace* trajectories

Looking across these three approaches or perspectives, there are some common ideas that are clearly key to unlocking explanations for regulatory trajectories over time. In this section, we bring these together to create an outline approach—perhaps best characterised as a toolkit of intellectual resources—for understanding how the drug control *exchangespace* changes and evolves over time. The toolkit has three core sets of ideas.

Origins, origin stories, and initial conditions

We know, of course, that beginnings are important. The desire to find the origins of a problem or practice or institution is powerful. Yet we perhaps sometimes mislead ourselves that these origins must always provide a clue to the deep or underlying nature of a phenomenon. As Foucault wisely warned in his famous 'Nietzsche, Genealogy, History' essay first published in 1971, faith in origins as revealing 'primordial truth' is often misplaced. When we look for the origin of things, he argued, we actually find 'not a timeless and essential secret, but the secret that they have no essence or that their essence was fabricated in a piecemeal fashion from alien forms' (Foucault 1984:78). He may overstate the point but certainly this notion of historical origins as hiding essential truth is not necessarily a very helpful perspective.

Origin stories are a little different. These are the ways in which the framing of social problems is often partly shaped by the creation of particular narratives about their origins. As I noted in the introductory chapter, part of the purpose of this book is to challenge the origin story of global drug prohibition. One persistent version of this origin story—perhaps influenced by the narrative template set in classic works by Howard Becker (1963), David Musto (1972, 1973), and Alfred Lindesmith (1965)—holds that global drug prohibition was created, and has subsequently been led, by the United States. This leads not only activists and reform advocates but also many researchers to see North America as the most significant and important place to look to see what is happening. A central theme of this book is that this Western-centrism is deeply unhelpful and that we need to recentre China and Asia within our analysis, not only historically (see Part II) but also when thinking about the politics of future drug law reform (see Part III). The latter will seem particularly challenging to many, as China and the wider Southeast Asia region are seen as favouring some of the most punitive approaches to drug use, drug addiction, and drug supply (e.g. Lunze et al 2018).

Nevertheless, there is another sense in which starting points are in fact very important analytically. As we have seen in this part of the book, one of the tenets of complex systems science is that small differences in the initial conditions in such systems can lead to very large divergences in outcomes over time. The centrality of complexity to the idea of *exchangespace* points therefore to the importance of paying attention to initial conditions when trying to make sense of regulatory trajectories. This implies that precise and careful historical excavations of origins is critical, as these initial conditions can create path-dependent trajectories with consequential impacts that are visible far into the future. This is partly because of the idea that developments in complex systems are often irreversible, as was discussed in the previous chapter.

An extremely interesting paper by management studies scholar Elizabeth Garnsey (1998) provides an excellent illustration of this, as she explores the puzzle of why high-tech districts flourish in some locations, whilst in others they never get properly off the ground. She shows how even very small differences in initial conditions can turn out to be significant for the precise reason that since 'some developments are irreversible and resources come to be committed in specific ways, the system's growth may become set along certain channels ... [T]hus, even where early conditions are similar, systems may move along different trajectories as chance occurrences set each system onto separate, successively branching paths' (1998:365). She argues that a complexity perspective allows for a reconciliation between historical analysis (which is attuned to the particularities of path dependences and the influence of chance and events in altering pathways) and social scientific perspectives (which look for regularities driven by structural factors) (1998:372–373). Interestingly, Garnsey (1998:371) draws a parallel with Giddens' structuration theory, as a way of making sense of the dynamic relations between contingent events and structural forces. It will be recalled from the previous chapter that Giddens was a reference point and inspiration in the genesis of the *exchangespace* concept (see also Farrall 2021). Here, we might also make an additional connection with historian William Sewell's (2005) classic book *Logics of History* and his notion of 'eventful history' which similarly seeks to find a theoretically coherent framework for making sense of this relationship between structure and contingency as drivers of historical change.

Crises, adaptation, and path dependence

The centrality of events within historical narratives is an area that Sewell places at the heart of his project to develop a theoretical account that brings together insights from historians and from social scientists. He notes that as individuals we intuitively understand the importance of 'happenings' in social life—getting divorced, deciding to take a new job, finding out your child has a life-threatening condition, and so on—but despite this appreciation of the 'fatefulness of time' in our personal lives, the concept of the 'event' has been significantly under-theorised (Sewell 2005:8). Sewell observes that most things that happen simply reproduce social and cultural structures and therefore do not lead to structural change. He defines 'events' as that 'relatively rare subclass of happenings that significantly transforms structures' (2005:100).

In this light, we might re-interpret Braithwaite's highlighting of crises by viewing them as a particular genre of events: happenings that are perceived or constructed as presenting serious difficulties of some kind which then precipitate actions that lead to structural change (percolation, to use Root's terminology). In *exchangespace*, we can make sense of this in terms of actors occupying the space continuously reacting and adapting to what other actors do. A crisis might be seen as a condition that emerges that prompts higher quantities of action/reaction than usual, or types of action/reaction that are in some way unusual in their nature, reach, or intensity. Again, this resonates with Hancher and Moran's (1989/1998) emphasis on the importance of timing within regulatory space—that is, the significance of contingent happenings, moments, or crises in shaping regulatory arrangements over the longer term.

In the criminological imagination, the notion of crisis has a particular salience through the classic 1970s text *Policing the Crisis* (Hall et al 1978). Readers are probably familiar with its central argument: that the British panic about 'mugging' in the early 1970s was less about a particular form of street crime and more about a wider social and political crisis at that specific historical juncture. It remains an important text for criminologists but is especially relevant here, as there is a danger that the lens of complex systems can start to separate crises from their social and political context. What counts as a crisis, how that crisis is framed, how it is responded to, are all shaped profoundly by the 'play of power' within the *exchangespace*. Crises, in other words, are often themselves social phenomena rather than merely random happenings like meteorites falling out of the sky. This insight, of course, makes crises even more important to understand within analyses of regulatory trajectories.

Hand in hand with the notion of the crisis or critical event is the idea of adaptation. Crises are only significant for the analysis or diagnosis of change because of the adaptations or reactions they trigger. Adaptation is also another concept that can bridge across historical analysis and social science. As Bennear and Wiener (2019) argue, we can distinguish between unplanned adaptation (emergency responses to crises, ad hoc measures, etc) and planned adaptation (periodic lesson-learning reviews, etc). The unplanned mode is often part of the story of historical moments and their aftermath (as we will see in the next part of the book), whilst planned adaptive regulation is a particular strategy for building learning into governance processes (as will be explored in Part III). Intrinsic to either mode is the idea that market-regulation relations are in a state of continuous flow and flux. Static models of economic regulation misrecognise the nature of *exchangespace* and are usually rooted in the type of control conceptions of regulation that Shearing (1993) so elegantly dismantled 30 years ago.

Crises and events are also closed linked with the idea of path dependence which, as we have seen, is critical for the understanding of regulatory trajectories. Paths are sequences of action and outcomes that are triggered by an initial contingent event but which then follow a pattern in which the sequence of re(actions) is dependent on that initial event. The path, in turn, has a longer-term determining influence on the regulatory trajectory. This influence derives, in part, from the irreversibility of the system. Contingent events that become historical turning points by triggering a new path-dependent sequence are sometimes termed critical junctures (see Mahoney 2000).

Network structures, nodes, and nodal relations

Change and transformation are intrinsic to the idea of networks, in the sense that networks are constituted by flows and circulation, by information and communication, and by action and reaction. Different intellectual traditions have converged on the understanding that networks are continuously dynamic and that they tend towards development over time that is non-linear. Root, for example, as we have seen, captures this through his use of the idea of phase transitions, a concept drawn originally from the natural sciences. Using a rather different vocabulary, Foucault reached some similar conclusions, by arguing for an approach to the historical analysis of power networks that emphasises discontinuities, thresholds of transformation, and events (see Foucault 1991a, 1991b).

By placing networks at the analytical centre, we can certainly utilise a distinctive set of conceptual tools for thinking about historical change in market-regulation relations. Mapping network topology and diagnosing the network singularities that constitute moments of transition both become critical elements in the analysis of social change. Further, by thinking in terms of *exchangespace*, we are pushed towards a very broad conception of what constitutes the network. Instead of focusing solely on actors directly involved in drug transactions, the requirement is to look at the entirety of actors who have any role or function in contributing to 'steering the flow of events' across the drug supply chain. This leads to a much larger cast of characters than we see in, for example, studies that have looked at drug markets and drug trafficking using social network analysis (e.g. Bichler et al 2017).

The networked character of *exchangespace* also helps us in thinking about social action and reform. We have already seen how nodal governance theory guided community safety work in South Africa in the Zwelethemba model (Shearing and Froestad 2010). This type of local security governance, based on intervening to reshape nodal relations within a network, has considerable potential for generating innovative community-led action. Extending the network idea, the Zwelethemba work was scaled up under the auspices of the Community Peace Programme (CPP) based at the University of the Western Cape, spreading to over 200 community sites across the Western Cape and then to other countries, notably Argentina. CPP provided a range of materials and resources—Codes of Good Practice, guidelines, pro formas for recording activity, evaluation tools—to support the implementation of the model. We will return to microgovernance strategies of this kind in Part III of the book.

Another example of how network thinking can shape social action is highlighted in an interesting recent paper by August (2022). He observes how Foucault's radical prison reform activism in the early 1970s in the *Groupe d'Information sur les Prisons* (GIP) was built on a theoretical understanding of power functioning in the social system in a networked way. The GIP manifesto, issued in 1971, emphasised the importance of generating and disseminating information about prisons, with the GIP conceptualised as a relay in a communication circuit. Again, the significance of *faire savoir* (making known) information as a way of intervening within a social system will be examined further in Part III.

Thinking about regulatory trajectories through the lens of *exchangespace* is therefore considerably sharpened by foregrounding how market-regulation relations are networked. It enables us both to add to our analysis of historical change and to extend our repertoire of strategies for social change and social transformation. In this respect, network thinking and analysis is critical to Parts II and III of the book. It is especially useful when considering digital technology which is increasingly part of drug markets and their regulation (see Seddon 2014; Shortis et al 2020). Recent work by Shearing and colleagues has argued exactly this point in relation to how nodal governance theory can be adapted to think about the new security challenges and harms presented by technologies of cyberspace (Holley et al 2020).

Applying the *exchangespace* concept

In this first part of the book, across this chapter and the previous one, the argument has been developed that the *exchangespace* concept is an analytical game-changer, that is, a theoretical tool that can generate new transformative insights about drug control, drug laws, and drug law reform. The strength of this claim will be explored across the two remaining main parts of the book. In this section, the articulation of the claim will be anticipated, in very brief outline, by, first, summarising the novel features of the concept and, second, presenting a sketch of a couple of illustrative examples of its application to key policy issues.

What is new about *exchangespace*?

Recall that *exchangespace* is a shorthand for market-regulation relations. It captures the two foundational ideas that: a) these relations consist of economic transactions taking place within a regulatory space; and b) when regulation is understood as a constitutive phenomenon, markets and regulation emerge as 'two sides of the same coin' rather than as separate or independent realms. This is *exchangespace*.

What new ideas, perspectives, or insights potentially flow from using this concept in the field of drug law and policy? We can summarise the distinctive elements as follows:

- *Decentring state action.* In much of the existing literature and discourse on drug policy and drug law reform, states and supra-state bodies are the key actors. The targets for groups advocating reform are primarily national governments, state bodies, and various organs of the UN. *Exchangespace* directs us to consider a much wider set of actors. State agents are simply one node amongst many within a market-regulatory network and it is an entirely empirical question whether they are of prime importance or not. In some instances they will be, in others not.
- *Moving from law to regulation.* A common way of thinking about drug control is that it consists of bodies of legal rules and their enforcement. From this perspective, changing drug control therefore requires law reform and/or shifts in strategies or practices of law enforcement. Calls, for example, for the decriminalisation of drug possession for personal use take precisely this form: *de jure* decriminalisation involves changing the rules; *de facto* decriminalisation involves changing law enforcement practice. *Exchangespace* points to a different perspective: seeing drug control as a continuously evolving state of affairs produced through the actions and reactions of multiple actors at multiple levels. The reform challenge then is not about designing (and then enforcing) the optimal system of rules, rather it is about creating adaptive systems to steer the flow of events towards preferred states. Engaging with the normative (and political) question of what is the most desired state of affairs becomes critical. This normative task is also ongoing rather than a one-time activity.
- *Focusing on temporal explanations.* Related to the move from law to regulation is the introduction of time as a critical analytical dimension. As soon as we move from thinking about largely static rule-systems to complex adaptive networks shaped by flow and flux, we have to take the temporal dimension more seriously. Understanding how and why change happens becomes a central analytical task. This applies across the full spectrum of scales of change, from the short-term (why did intervention X lead to outcome Y in context Z?) to the long-term (why did situation X come to evolve into situation Y a century later?). A theoretical account of change over time is necessary not just for historical work but also for evaluating the impact of policy/practice interventions and, in fact, even for thinking about policy reform (which is, in effect, a mode of hypothesis-making about future change).
- *Foregrounding markets.* Drug control can be seen as being about health, politics, morality, and many other things—and it is all of

these—but *exchangespace* highlights the centrality of markets. Drugs are commodities that flow through supply chains—from production to consumption—and drug control is about the regulation of those supply chains. Drug control is therefore, in a fundamental sense, about regulating markets. This implies a need to amplify the voices of economic sociologists and economists and turn down the volume a little on criminologists and health researchers.

• *Systems thinking*. *Exchangespace* requires us to see drug control as a complex system. This is not just a descriptive shift, it represents a different way of thinking about the problem. Systems thinking points to the importance of seeing disparate activities as part of an interconnected whole. It tells us that policy change or reform must involve paying attention to system design principles. Complexity thinking adds the additional insight that macro phenomena are emergent properties constituted by multiple micro-level interactions across networks. Seeing systems as networked opens up a further set of analytical insights about structure, flow, and change, reinforcing *inter alia* the importance of introducing temporal explanations.

Together these ideas present a radically different picture of how drug control works and what drug laws are. Changing legal frameworks—drug law reform—and shifting law enforcement practices move from being the central task for reformers to a small part of a rather different strategy. To begin to illustrate what this might mean, we now turn to a couple of examples of policy initiatives that have been seen as important elements within drug policy reform: Cannabis Social Clubs and Heroin Assisted Treatment. Through the very briefest of sketches, the potential of the *exchangespace* concept to illuminate new contours of familiar ground is illustrated. Its potential to reveal entirely new terrain will be explored later in the book's conclusion.

Example 1: Cannabis Social Clubs

The origins of Cannabis Social Clubs (CSCs) lie in the work of cannabis activists in the Catalonia region of Spain in the early 1990s (Jansseune et al 2019). From 2001, CSCs began to spread more significantly across Catalonia and elsewhere in Spain, as well as emerging in several other European countries (Pardal et al 2022). In their European form, CSCs have been largely user-driven grassroots initiatives. In Uruguay, CSCs have formed one part of the pioneering national approach to cannabis regulation, initiated in 2013 (Queirolo et al 2016).

The essence of the CSC model is of small, local associations of cannabis users which collectively organise the cultivation and distribution of cannabis to their members on a non-profit basis. They are viewed as a middle ground between a fully commercialised industry and a state-controlled system. As the name suggests, CSCs can serve additional social support functions for members and typically function as community co-operatives. Some CSCs are also involved in cannabis activism and campaigning. In the Spanish context, CSCs operate in a legal 'grey area'; in other European countries, the legal position is even less clear (Marks 2019).

The appeal of CSCs to reform advocates is obvious. They provide a means of supplying cannabis in which the spectre of profit-seeking large corporations being in charge is avoided and cannabis users are empowered to control their own access to cannabis. As research expands in this area, we are also learning more about the diversity of CSCs and in practice there is considerable variation (Pardal 2023). Although the norm is small non-profit self-organising collectives, there are some CSCs that are large, some that make profits, and some that are run by employed professionals rather than member-volunteers (Jansseune et al 2019; Pardal et al 2022). Most people involved in drug law reform debates see a role for CSCs in the regulation of cannabis (e.g. Seddon and Floodgate 2020).

What if we think of CSCs as a form of intervention or action within the *exchangespace* of cannabis market-regulation relations? There are at least two new sets of insights that become visible. The first is to understand each CSC as a newly-created node within the network of market-regulation relations that shape the cannabis supply chain. In the language of nodal governance theory, CSCs are governing nodes, that is, sites where knowledge, capacity, and resources are mobilised in order to steer the flow of events. In this sense, CSCs very much resemble the Peace Committees in the South African Zwelethemba model. Federations or associations of CSCs are potentially 'superstructural nodes' with significantly enhanced governance capacity. This perspective opens up a different empirical research agenda in which, in order to understand how CSCs function, we would want to be able to describe in detail and specificity those three components—knowledge, capacity, resources—and to investigate the mechanisms through which these translate into action. We also see very clearly here how the lines are blurred between who are regulators and who are regulatees and between what counts as 'market' behaviour and what as 'regulation'. Quite simply, a conventional control conception of regulation does not take us very far in understanding how CSCs function.

The second set of insights flows from the understanding of *exchangespace* as always being in a state of flux and change. If we think about regulatory trajectories, it is evident that CSCs emerged in a particular time and place—Catalonia in Spain in the early to mid-1990s—and that this was in response to (or an adaptation to) a specific situation there. There is then a story to be told of how and why they later spread to some places but not to others. These are perhaps relatively conventional questions for policy research. But we might also reflect on whether, within the bigger picture of the trajectory of regulation, CSCs ought to be understood as a transitional mechanism or phase, bridging from cannabis prohibition to different non-penal forms of regulation. CSCs are often proposed as a potential post-prohibition model of regulation—attractive to reformers because they are non-profit and community-led—but when we think in terms of regulatory trajectories it may be more plausible to see them as transitional regulatory forms. They have emerged and grown precisely because prohibition still exists. The question to ask is whether, in a post-prohibition situation, CSCs would still exist in any significant number if cannabis could be readily bought from retail outlets. What would be the drivers to sustain them? For reformers, thinking strategically about CSCs as potential stepping stones to a new regulatory future, rather than a destination in themselves, provides an altogether different perspective.

Example 2: Heroin Assisted Treatment

The term 'Heroin Assisted Treatment' or HAT is a contemporary euphemism. It refers to the prescribing of heroin by medical clinicians to individuals assessed as addicted to heroin bought in 'illicit markets'. It has been positioned as a clinical intervention, delivered by doctors in medical settings and evaluated by clinical trials. Over the last three decades, substantial trials have taken place in Switzerland, Canada, Spain, the Netherlands, Germany, and the United Kingdom (see Strang et al 2015), as well as in Belgium (Demaret et al 2015). HAT has been defined as suitable only for so-called refractory patients (i.e. people who have 'failed' with other treatments), with the model based on medically supervised on-site consumption. The accumulated evidence from the trials is positive, showing strong levels of effectiveness in terms of treatment retention, reductions in use of illicit heroin, and improved outcomes in various health and social domains (Strang et al 2015).

So what do I mean by saying HAT is a euphemism? The requirement for supervised consumption is not therapeutically-based but rather is primarily to prevent diversion of heroin to the illicit market. The focus on refractory patients is not based on studies of what works best with which patients but instead is shaped by the perceived need to limit a politically unpalatable intervention to where it is most necessary. The need for it to be a doctor-led clinical intervention is driven more by its clinical framing than any actually required expertise. It does not cure the condition of heroin addiction, it simply manages some of the negative consequences of that condition. The HAT label obscures much of this. Arguably, it serves—quite effectively—as a presentational device more than as a precise description of the intervention.

There is also something rather curious about the politics of HAT. One of the oddities is that support for this very narrow version of heroin prescribing in the form of HAT is seen as a touchstone for a progressive policy outlook. Drug law reform non-governmental organizations (NGOs) like the UK-based Transform and the US-based Drug Policy Alliance strongly promote HAT. Even stranger is the way that despite long-established evidence as to effectiveness, it continues to be considered as an experimental intervention. In the United Kingdom, for example, new heroin prescribing services that launched in Glasgow and Middlesborough in 2019 were both described as pilots, even though the UK RIOTT randomised trial had reported its main findings back in 2010 (Strang et al 2010). The RIOTT study was itself closely based on earlier trials in several other countries, the first of which had started in Switzerland in 1994. The Swiss trials were, in turn, influenced in part by the work of John Marks in England in the 1980s and early 1990s (Seddon 2020b) and a much-cited clinical trial was conducted in English treatment clinics in the 1970s (Hartnoll et al 1980). Marks also saw his work as guided by long-established practice—the so-called 'British System' traceable back to the 1920s and the famous Rolleston Report (see Berridge 1980). So why, after 100 years of prior experience, are we still running heroin-prescribing interventions as pilots?

A different perspective emerges if we think of heroin prescribing in terms of *exchangespace*. Viewed through the prism of market-regulation relations, HAT most resembles a supply-side intervention. There is a network of actors involved in a supply chain, each of which can be seen as engaged in economic transactions which also have regulatory effects by steering the flow of events. In the United Kingdom, manufacture of the product is by a private company (under a licence provided by the state) which then sells the product to a state agency (the National Health Service (NHS)). Distribution within the NHS to licensed state outlets at local levels (treatment services) is achieved through a complex set of procurement arrangements. Local prescribing doctors then provide the product at no cost to the consumer. The particular ways they set up their service further alter the nature of that regulatory impact. Imagine, for example, a version of HAT which was not targeted at a small sub-group of 'refractory' patients but instead was low-threshold and accessible to anyone using 'street' heroin. Provision of heroin would be more akin to licensed shop-keeping rather than clinical prescribing. There would be a de facto legal local heroin supply. And it is at this point that the support of those reformist NGOs and the curious politics of HAT begin to make a little more sense. Indeed, this imaginary version closely resembles the radical model John Marks developed 30 years ago and this perspective helps us to understand both the extraordinary political heat that his work attracted at the time and its continuing interest to reform groups (Seddon 2020b).

It is worth emphasising quite how different the HAT terrain looks when illuminated by the *exchangespace* concept. Instead of seeing a clinical intervention managed by doctors, we see a market intervention with potential regulatory impact. Again, as with the example of CSCs, the distinction between regulatory and market action becomes almost impossible to draw clearly and it is more productive to see them as two sides of the same coin. What, for example, was John Marks doing in his local clinics in the 1980s when he prescribed injectable or smokeable heroin for take-home use? Providing medical treatment? Keeping heroin users alive? Undercutting prices in the local illicit heroin market by providing free products? Reducing profits for local organised crime? Reducing the size of the illicit heroin market? Making heroin use safer? Prolonging heroin-using careers? Tackling heroin-related crime? There is only limited overlap between these questions and those asked in clinical trials of HAT. Marks was doing individual clinical work *and* making a market intervention *and* having a regulatory impact.

Conclusion

What these two examples (CSCs and HAT) crystallise is the central thesis of this part of the book: that the lens of regulation and the conceptual apparatus of *exchangespace* shift the analytical gaze in a fundamental way. Instead of debates centred on law reform, morality, or even health, we can start to see that the heart of the matter of drug policy is actually regulation, economics, and politics. To put it another way, when we study drug policy, we are engaged in analysing the political economy of regulatory regimes for psychoactive commerce. Prohibition is simply a particular form of regulatory regime, rather than a unique type of policy. Questions of health, social and racial justice, civil liberties and human rights, individual freedom, economic development, and so on, provide a menu of criteria for guiding and evaluating different regulatory regimes. To select from that menu we have to bring our values to the surface, through explicit and open political deliberation, and this process of selection is an obligation that cannot be evaded simply by appeals to 'science' or 'evidence'. We explore this further in Part III of the book. *Exchangespace* offers a novel conceptual toolkit that enables us to bring together explanatory and normative theory, in ways that can help make sense of a) historical trajectories, b) contemporary drug control policies and interventions, and c) future possibilities for drug law and policy.

The next part of the book focuses on historical trajectories. More specifically, it examines two key moments in the history of international drug control and drug laws. In Chapter 4, we look at the two Sino-Western conflicts of the nineteenth century that have become known as the Opium Wars. The premise is that these are the origin or starting point for what would evolve into the twentieth-century global drug prohibition model. The argument in this chapter is that by re-examining these 'initial conditions', we gain new perspectives not only on the regulatory trajectory of the twentieth century but also on our contemporary situation. In brief, the chapter will argue that there are at least two novel insights that emerge from this approach. First, the chapter directly challenges the conventional origin story of prohibition as a US-driven Western phenomenon, recentring China and the wider Asian region in the historical narrative. As will be seen, this is fundamental to the book's overarching thesis. Second, using the *exchangespace* concept brings to the surface the ways in which the Opium Wars were, at heart, about the contentious and mobile boundaries between what counted as licit and illicit trade. Boundary work of this kind is, of course, deeply influenced by the 'play of power' that always shapes market-regulation relations. This notion of boundary work remains a fruitful way of understanding a key part of what is at stake in drug policy today.

In Chapter 5, we move forward to the first two decades of the twentieth century which is the period which saw the assembly of the international drug control system. The most significant episodes during this period were two sets of international meetings in Shanghai in 1909 and at The Hague between 1911 and 1914, as well as the post-war Paris Peace Conference that concluded at the beginning of 1920. In this chapter, the focus is primarily on the 1909 Shanghai meetings, partly because they are relatively neglected in the literature but also as they particularly highlight critical aspects of this phase of the regulatory trajectory. Specifically, it is argued in this chapter that it was in Shanghai that the centrality of China to this part of the story was most visible. This thread has been lost, or at least submerged, in the tendency to focus on the meetings at The Hague and on the Paris Peace Conference.

This pair of chapters in Part II will, taken together, provide a distinctive account of the 'initial conditions' and very early trajectory of contemporary drug prohibition. The analytical claim is that this generates insights that are relevant to our contemporary understanding of prohibition, as well as informing thinking about post-prohibition futures, the latter being the focus of Part III of the book. It allows us to set debates about drug law re-form in a long-term historical perspective. Taking a long view in this way is critical for the study of social problems and social policy, as so often the contours of today and the apparent limits of possibility for tomorrow that we take for granted are in fact historically contingent. Understanding this contingency opens up a wider space for thinking about the future but, at the same time, also reminds us of the truth of Stan Cohen's (1981) famous observation about criminology that often when we think we are studying a 'strange creation' we eventually come to realise that the 'footprints in the sand' we have observed so keenly for clues are in fact our own. As we will see, there is much about the 'drug question' that may seem at first sight to be 'naturally occurring' features of the phenomenon but which turn out to be the product of political and policy choices in the past that could have been different. And it is to the past that we now turn.

PART II
HISTORY

4
China and the Opium Wars

Introduction

Understanding the contemporary world is impossible without knowledge of its historical development. We cannot fully grasp where we are without seeing the paths that have brought us here. As Hancher and Moran (1989/ 1998:160) put it, 'understanding regulatory arrangements in the present depends on understanding the historical configuration out of which they developed'. In other words, no serious examination of drug laws and policy can ignore the central analytical importance of historicising the 'drug question' and 'drug control', particularly when we are considering alternative scenarios for future reform. And when we start to take historical perspectives seriously, the apparently obvious starts to look a little less familiar or clear. For example, we might imagine that modern societies have always banned 'dangerous drugs', yet the global drug prohibition system is in fact a relatively recent invention of the twentieth century. Even the concept of a 'drug', which might be thought to be a self-evident or timeless category, is less than 150 years old (see Seddon 2016). As we saw in the previous two chapters, the *exchangespace* concept provides a theoretical rationale for the necessity for historical analysis to our full understanding of drug control.

Historical scholarship on drug policy has grown significantly in recent decades and we know considerably more today about the origins and development of prohibition than was the case 30 or 40 years ago. An early pioneer was David Musto, especially his groundbreaking 1973 book *The American Disease*, and this was followed by important research in the 1980s and 1990s by historians like David Courtwright, Virginia Berridge, Terry Parssinen, and others. Third and fourth waves of historical scholarship have followed, including key books by Bewley-Taylor (1999) and McAllister (2000) and, more recently, Lines (2017). Much of this literature looks out from the West and a reasonably well-established narrative has been created about the birth and subsequent development of global drug prohibition.

Rethinking Drug Laws. Toby Seddon, Oxford University Press. © Toby Seddon 2023.
DOI: 10.1093/oso/9780192846525.003.0004

As the balance shifts from origins to evolution, the United States comes to the fore in the story as the pre-eminent driver of increasingly penal measures of drug control, notably in the post-1945 period (see Lines 2017). This narrative does of course capture many of the central features of this area of history but, like all stories, it emphasises some elements over others. The premise of this part of the book is that a reappraisal and reassessment of this history is overdue and that the key to taking a fresh look is to recentre China. It builds, in this respect, on work by Trocki (1999) and Dikötter et al (2004) which are rare examples in the English-language literature of histories focused on East Asia and China.

In moving the vantage point to China, this part of the book also draws on, and situates itself within, new work on global history which seeks to change the centre of focus away from Europe and the West and back towards Asia. Historian Peter Frankopan's two *Silk Roads* books are outstanding examples of this. He provides a radical reassessment of world history by placing Asia at the heart of the story. In the first of his books, *The Silk Roads* (Frankopan 2015), he argues that the rise of Europe was a temporary shift in the world's centre of gravity, away from where it had been for thousands of years before. In his second book, *The New Silk Roads* (Frankopan 2018), he explores how this may now be moving back in the twenty-first century, with a new world order forming around China and Asia, as Europe and the United States experience a prolonged period of crises and decline.

The long history of drugs is ripe for re-telling in this way, set in the context of global history as it has unfolded over millennia. The goal of this part of the book is more modest: it seeks to recover the initial conditions for the historical emergence of the international drug control regime. As we saw in Part I, initial conditions can be critical for shaping subsequent regulatory trajectories and therefore a focus on origins repays attention. The distinctive perspective it aims to provide is generated by viewing the historical narrative through the prism of China and, in particular, of Sino-Western relations. By recentring China in the story, the economic and geopolitical underpinnings of the historical emergence of international drug prohibition are more clearly highlighted. Indeed, the central dynamic that comes into focus is the evolution of trade and power relations between Western nations and China from the mid-nineteenth century to the beginning of the twentieth. This, in turn, provides a clearer understanding of the prohibition paradigm as a distinctive form of market regulation, an idea that was developed theoretically in Part I of the book.

This chapter begins by presenting on overview of Frankopan's work on global history and briefly considers how we might situate our existing understandings of the long view of the drug question within this picture. It then moves to a focus on the nineteenth century and the development of Sino-British relations. It synthesises the existing historiographical litera- ture on the Opium Wars in the middle of that century but its centrepiece is a careful analysis of Mao Haijian's important revisionist monograph *The Qing Empire and the Opium War*, first published in Chinese in 1995 and in a new English translation in 2016. The next chapter will turn to an examin- ation of the international meetings about opium control that took place be- tween 1909 and 1914 in Shanghai and The Hague, with a particular focus on the 1909 Shanghai meeting. Here, as well as the existing literature, the ana- lysis will draw on primary archival research on material held in the Weston Library in Oxford and the National Archives in London.

Global history, the long view, and the Silk Roads

Frankopan's long view of global history helps to set a wider context for what is usually a mainly twentieth-century story about international drug prohibition. He begins the first of his pair of 'Silk Roads' books with the rise of Persia in the sixth century BCE, as one of the most remarkable and important of the early civilizations. The expansion of trading and ex- change through the region was accelerated by the growing ambitions and expanding horizons of China under the Han dynasty (206BCE–220AD) which served to 'link Asia together' (Frankopan 2015:9). He describes how, over time, the ancient world became interlinked right across the Pacific, Central Asia, India, the Persian Gulf, and the Mediterranean. These links and connections were built on trade, of course, but the 'ancient Silk Roads of antiquity were coursing with life' in all its richness, and intellectual, reli- gious, and cultural exchange were just as significant as trading (Frankopan 2015:25–28). Indeed, the history of the birth and spread of world religions can be written through this lens and Frankopan provides a fascinating and detailed interpretation of those stories. Another familiar historical narra- tive that becomes transformed through viewing from this different vantage point is the story of slave trades. Whilst we already know much from the historical literature about slavery in the Roman Empire, Frankopan tells a less familiar story about the scale of the slave trade across Arabic-speaking lands 1000 years ago (2015:117–135). We are given an overall picture of how, for at least 1500 years, the centre of the world—economically, culturally, intellectually—radiated out from Asia and the East.

It was with the Crusades 900 years ago that Europe began to shift closer to the heart of things. The Crusades started the stimulation of the economies and societies of Western Europe but, even then, in the 1200s and 1300s it was the Mongols from Asia that dominated globally, through their spreading strands of empire. The Mongol conquests further served to 'transform the economies of Europe', partly by fuelling interest in the 'exotic' lands they came from (2015:181). In the fourteenth century, merchants from Europe increasingly travelled east in search of spices, silks, fabrics, and other luxury goods that they could bring back home. As well as goods, they also brought back diseases, carried along the same trade and travel routes. In the middle of that century, in the 1340s, Europe was afflicted by a devastating plague of the Black Death which had an enormous death toll. This had a radical impact on European societies, but instead of simply damaging them, it became a transformative catalyst for profound social and economic change (2015:175–201). Indeed, Frankopan (2015:193) argues that the 'transformations triggered by the Black Death laid foundations that were to prove crucial for the long-term rise of north-west Europe'. The roots that would eventually create Western dominance were laid down in this post-plague world.

The fifteenth century saw the opening up of new trade routes, connecting for the first time the Americas to Africa and Europe and Asia. This was significant, as Europe was no longer just an end point for one of the Silk Roads coming out of Asia. This began the shift that would move Europe closer to the new centre of the world. Human and material resources discovered in Africa and in the New World across the Atlantic became vital to the emergence of the new European powers of Spain and Portugal. For the next 500 years, the centre of European power would shift several times—from the Iberian countries, to the Ottoman Empire, to the Dutch and the British—but Europe remained in its new position at the heart of global power.

In the nineteenth century, with the British Empire at its zenith, the rise of Russia as a major force proved significant geopolitically for the way it connected East with West. Russia became central to the story of the tumultuous twentieth century, partly because of its position at the crossroads of East and West. Frankopan (2015:345) quotes Trotsky, writing in the aftermath of the 1917 Russian revolutions, that in cultivating the international revolutionary project, the 'route to Paris and London is through the cities of Afghanistan, the Punjab and Bengal'. As that century unfolded, the United States gradually rose to dominance, after 1947 locked in cold warfare with the resurgent Soviet Union. From the 1950s, control over the Middle East, and especially its oil, became a key dynamic within the Cold War. Even as it ended in 1991, apparently in victory for the West, the ongoing, and indeed worsening, instability in the Middle East would continue to sap the strength of the United States.

The late twentieth and early twenty-first centuries have seen the former modern sites of power, Europe and the United States, experience a chastening fall from grace, at the same time as power and influence has inexorably grown in China. It is now widely proclaimed that the twenty-first century will be the 'Asian Century'. This is the story that Frankopan picks up in his second book. Its core argument is that the 500-year 'blip' in which Western countries were closest to the centre of global power is passing, and the region that lies between the east Mediterranean and the Pacific is once again becoming the dominant part of the world.

Frankopan (2018:7) begins *The New Silk Roads* with the claim that the 'decisions being made in today's world that really matter are not being made in Paris, London, Berlin or Rome ... but in Beijing and Moscow, in Tehran and Riyadh, in Delhi and Islamabad'. He charts the ways in which the major centres of power in the West are increasingly isolated, inward-looking, and fragmenting, whilst to the East there is growing collaboration and co-operation. Large-scale investments in infrastructure—from travel to energy—are tying countries together. He gives the example of the TAPI pipeline being developed to bring gas from the Galkynysh field in Turkmenistan to Pakistan and India, via Afghanistan, connecting Central and South Asia (2018:67–71).

At the heart of the shift to the East is, of course, China. The 'One Belt, One Road' policy, launched by President Xi Jinping in 2013, is designed to connect China with neighbouring countries and regions through an enormous investment in transportation, infrastructure, and energy (2018:89–108). The scale of the Belt and Road programme is astonishing: it involves over 80 countries, with a combined population of more than 4 billion people, representing over 60% of the global population (2018:91). Frankopan describes how many of the countries involved expressly refer back to the ancient Silk Roads, linking to the past as a way of emphasising the long history of cultural ties in the region. Alongside the Belt and Road initiative are a whole series of other blueprints for growth and development across the region, including 'Saudi Arabia's Vision 2030 plan, the Eurasian Economic Union of Russia, Belarus, Kazakhstan, Armenia and Kyrgyzstan, the Bright Road initiative of Kazakhstan, the Two Corridors One Economic Circle initiative of Vietnam, the Middle Corridor initiative of Turkey, the Development Road initiative of Mongolia ... alongside regional masterplans, such as the Asean Community Vision 2025, formulated and adopted by the nations of South East Asia' (Frankopan 2018:220–221). The countries along the Silk Roads clearly understand how the world is changing and are positioning themselves to prepare for the future. For Frankopan, the absence of anything comparable in the European Union (EU) is a telling indicator of where power is growing and where it is receding in the world.

Global history and the histories of drugs and drug control

The relevance of global history, and in particular of Frankopan's thesis about the importance of the Silk Roads region, to thinking about drug control has several strands. The story of the interconnectedness of cultures across the region from the Eastern Mediterranean to the Pacific Ocean, of how trade and exchange flourished along the Silk Roads that linked this vast region together, is also the story of how psychoactive commerce spread across the globe. In his magisterial history of 'drugs and the making of the modern world', David Courtwright (2001) focuses on the last 500 years and tells the stories of what he calls the 'Big Three' (alcohol, tobacco, coffee) and the 'Little Three' (cannabis, opium, cocaine). His broad thesis is that there was a 'confluence of the world's principal psychoactive resources', with those six commodities all entering the stream of global commerce at some point (2001:3) and that the twentieth century then saw, in effect, a selective 'psychoactive counterrevolution' in which access to some of them was legally restricted. This is an important analysis but we can also take a longer view, drawing on Frankopan's historical narrative.

To illustrate this, we can take the example of cannabis. The cannabis plant has a very long history, so long in fact that we cannot be entirely sure or precise about its origins. We do know that it originated at least 10,000 years ago in central Asia, most probably in what are known today as Tajikistan, Kyrgyzstan, and the Xinjiang region in Western China, but perhaps also in parts of Mongolia and Kazakhstan (Russo 2007). It has been suggested that it was one of the very earliest plants cultivated by humans (Abel 1980). It was used extensively for its fibrous stem, to make cloth and twine, and cannabis seeds became one of the staple grains in many parts of ancient China. The psychoactive and medicinal properties of the flowers, leaves and resin of the plant were probably discovered a little later but have certainly been known for thousands of years. The slow diffusion of cannabis from central Asia—to the East across China and into Japan, to the South into India and then later the Eastern side of Africa, to the West through the Middle East and eventually into Europe—was a long process of the kind Frankopan describes in *The Silk Roads*. Cannabis was one of the many things transported and exchanged along the ancient trading routes that radiated out from the East. Its versatility no doubt made it an attractive new discovery as it spread to new places.

After this long and slow process of diffusion, the very rapid acceleration of the global travel of cannabis over the last 400 or so years was shaped by the rise of Europe during this period. In short, cannabis became an important commodity within the colonial empires of the major European powers. Both the Spanish and the Portuguese, for example, introduced cannabis to parts of Latin America in the sixteenth and seventeenth centuries (Warf 2014:425–426) and historian James Mills (2003) provides a detailed and insightful account of the British imperial entanglement with cannabis in India. Even into the twentieth century, the fading colonial interests of European states still shaped the landscape of cannabis. For example, between 1912 and 1956, cannabis cultivation was permitted by the Spanish protectorate in the mountainous Rif region in northern Morocco, as a means of extracting economic value from the land (Joseph 1975). As it was not permitted in the rest of the country, then controlled by the French, a vibrant smuggling trade was created. This had a lasting impact on the cannabis trade, as Moroccan cannabis resin later dominated the European market from the 1970s to the 1990s (EMCDDA 2017). Recent moves to establish a legal cannabis industry in Morocco—with a decree passed in March 2022 to license cultivation in three provinces for medical and industrial purposes—are arguably being shaped by path dependence in ways that can only be properly understood in the historical context of cannabis cultivation in the country. Indeed, Chouvy (2020) suggests that this history has potentially given Morocco competitive advantages in any future regional or global legal cannabis markets.

Turning to the question of cannabis *control*, a global history perspective is also illuminating. One of the first points that comes into focus when taking the long global view of events is that across its multi-millennial history, the idea that the cultivation, trade, and use of the cannabis plant might need to be controlled is extremely recent and novel. It was only at the start of the nineteenth century that we first see it surfacing, as Napoleon attempted to ban hashish consumption during the short-lived French occupation of Egypt (1798–1801) (Kozma 2011). Across the nineteenth century, many of the localised prohibitions of cannabis that started to appear in diverse locations followed this template of being driven by European imperial activities and interests. As Mills (2003) argues, it was in part the financial exigencies of running their empire that led the British to focus on generating income from the cannabis economy in India, which at the time was the world's largest cannabis marketplace. The British created a complex system of licences and taxation, designed to extract profits from the cannabis trade (Mills 2003:47–66). One notable consequence of this system was that it led to a flourishing illegal cannabis market within India, as producers attempted to evade the various levies and duties imposed by the British (2003:66–68).

The reverberations from the imperial concerns of the nineteenth century would be felt into the following century. The Indian Hemp Drugs Commission Report published in 1894 was an important landmark that would still be cited by cannabis law reformers in the 1960s. The Report concluded that the moderate use of cannabis was not injurious mentally, physically, or morally and that it could even be therapeutically beneficial. It essentially made a case for regulating and taxing the cannabis trade in India rather than attempting to prohibit it, on the grounds that regulatory restrictions and controls were the most appropriate and effective way of managing and suppressing excessive or problematic use (see Shamir and Hacker 2001). Cannabis first entered international discussions about control in 1911, at the instigation of the Italians who were concerned about cannabis smuggling in their newly-acquired North African colonies (Bewley-Taylor et al 2014:13). It would not be until 1923 that cannabis was brought back to the international table, this time by South Africa. As Mills (2003:160–172) discusses, this initially aroused little interest amongst other nations, until the following year when the representative for Egypt, supported by counterparts from Turkey and Greece, pressed for it to be added at a meeting in Geneva. Mills (2003:177–187) suggests that Egypt was motivated by a complex tangle of issues partly shaped by British imperial involvement there. It was from this point that cannabis became part of the international drug control system.

We can tell similar long stories about opium, coca, tobacco, and so on. Each has their own narrative, their own geography. But they also share features in common: ancient origins; a slow process of diffusion along ancient trading routes; accelerated diffusion with the rise of Europe post-1600; entanglement with European empires; transformation by industrialisation; increasing regulatory controls of different kinds in the twentieth century. An understanding of the long trajectory of global history allows us to zoom out and see these common patterns, before focusing back in on the details of specific stories. We now turn to one such story that unfolded over the course of around 60 or so years in the nineteenth century but which has had a pivotal influence in shaping our present.

The Opium Wars

The wars fought over opium in the nineteenth century between China, Britain, and other Western countries have been extensively studied, although arguably, in Britain at least, they remain surprisingly little known in the public sphere. My experience over many years of teaching in English universities, for example, is that European students are generally very surprised—and often shocked—to hear about the Opium Wars. Yet, as economist Jeffrey Sachs (1999) argues, they were the first wars of modern capitalism and so have a significance that goes far beyond the drug question. They have also had a profound influence in shaping China and its place in the world in the twentieth and twenty-first centuries. The English-language scholarship on these conflicts is built around a small number of important monographs, including classics by Fay (1975), Beeching (1975), and Inglis (1976), and more recent work by Wong (1998), Lovell (2011), Gao (2020), and others. These works are quite different in many respects but in this chapter I attempt to synthesise what we know from across this body of work. As noted in the introduction, particular attention will be paid to Mao Haijian's landmark revisionist monograph on the first of the two conflicts.

Before the wars: From Macartney to Napier

As always, it is important and illuminating to consider what was going on in the period before a momentous or major event. We can take long-, medium-, and short-range views. Zheng (2003) takes a long view by looking back to the fifteenth century and tracing the historical development of opium in

Chinese life over a 500-year period up to the end of the twentieth century. Her rich and detailed account tells us that opium was a multi-faceted and polysemic social and cultural phenomenon throughout this period but above all it was *important*. By placing opium in its historical context within social and cultural life in China, Zheng opens up a way of engaging with the question of the nature of the *demand* side of the opium economy in the nineteenth century. The *supply* side situation was much clearer: by the late eighteenth century, the British tea addiction was causing a serious trade deficit with China which was only solved for the British when they began selling opium (grown in India) to the Chinese from the early 1800s onwards (Lovell 2011:2). The opium trade became an economic necessity for Britain.

It is worth noting that until the Treaty of Peking in 1860, this trade would remain prohibited within China, as it had been since 1729. A peculiar system for trading in this contraband had developed in the first part of the nineteenth century. The East India Company managed the cultivation of the opium poppy in plantations in British-controlled India, its processing and packing, and then its shipping to Calcutta. From this point, it was sold to private merchants who sailed the opium chests up to the Chinese coast, anchoring at Whampoa, 12 miles outside the port of Canton, and later on when this was restricted, further away off Lintin Island in the Pearl River estuary. Smaller Chinese junks and rowing boats then carried the chests into Canton. Under the Qing Canton system, this was the only place where Western merchants were allowed to trade.

An interesting recent book by historian Hao Gao (2020) takes a medium-range view of the precursors to the conflict. He attempts to set the outbreak of the First Opium War in the broader context of Sino-British relations during the half-century that preceded the first conflict. He begins the story with an examination of the Macartney embassy of 1792–1794 which was the first official contact between the countries during this period. This was a trade mission led by the British diplomat Lord George Macartney and has generally been viewed in the historical literature as an outright failure. An alleged 'diplomatic incident'—the failure by Macartney to perform 'kowtow' at an audience with the Qianlong Emperor—led to the premature end of the mission before it had properly begun (2020:22). Gao (2020:24–46) argues that although it undoubtedly failed to achieve its trade and diplomatic objectives, nevertheless it 'provided the British with an unprecedented opportunity to have direct contact with the Chinese government and people, as well as to observe China's conditions at this time' (2020:45).

This would shape how relations with China were viewed and developed by British officials in the following years.

In 1816, 22 years after the Macartney embassy, a second official trade mission, the Amherst embassy, was formed. Lord Amherst, leading the mission, found himself embroiled in another 'kowtow' diplomatic incident and the prevailing evaluation in the literature has been that this was an even starker failure than the Macartney embassy. Gao (2020:51–85), again, argues for a partial re-appraisal of Amherst. One of its most significant aspects is that its formation was initiated not by the British government but by the East India Company. Legislation in 1813 had renewed the East India Company's commercial charter for another 20 years but had also ended its commercial monopoly in India, with the important exceptions of the tea trade and trade with China. The latter immediately became much more significant and the Company's Court of Directors made strong representations to the British government to send another ambassadorial trade mission to the Qing court, with the aim of preserving and strengthening its trade with China (Gao 2020:54). This meant that Amherst's team included East India Company employees who had direct experience of living and working in China. However, rather than sharpening the mission's ability to negotiate the complex diplomatic obstacle course, this appeared to multiply the differences of view within the team and, in the end, proved unhelpful. Indeed, Amherst failed even to get an audience with the emperor in Beijing which, on the face of it, was a step backwards from the Macartney mission. Yet Gao's careful analysis of primary sources shows that the Amherst embassy nevertheless had a profound influence on Sino-British relations in several ways and that it led to Britain's 'previously deferential posture ... [giving] way to a more hard-line approach in the decades to come' (2020:85).

During the 1820s, Gao (2020:95–118) argues that a key part of the story was not diplomatic or military but economic, driven by the supply-side forces already alluded to. Whilst the East India Company had an official monopoly on trade with China, in reality there was a growing number of private 'foreign' traders doing business with unlicensed Chinese merchants. The private traders pushed their case for the removal of the Company's commercial privileges by making arguments under the banner of 'free trade'. Downs (1968) makes a similar point, arguing that American merchants played a significant role in expanding the opium trade and opening up new sources of supply. This helped to ratchet up pressure on the monopolistic British East India Company. Significantly, the free trade advocates had a much more antagonistic stance towards China, believing that the laws and governing authorities were acting against the interests of Chinese people and were therefore unworthy of respect. Pressure to take a more forceful stance towards China began to build, driven by free trade advocacy.

In 1833, the free trade movement achieved its goal, as the East India Company's monopoly in China was finally removed by the British government. From this point, representing British merchants became the direct responsibility of the government, and a new trade commission was established in 1834, led by Lord Napier. The 'Napier fizzle', as it became known, was a brief, tragic, but ultimately politically significant incident. In a nutshell, Napier took a forceful approach from the start, with even his arrival into Chinese territory in the Whampoa harbour being without formal permission (Gao 2020:122). He proceeded to ignore diplomatic protocols and very rapidly the local authorities in Canton ordered his departure. Napier responded with a 'show of force', using two British frigates to force a passage to Canton. However, ill health quickly forced his withdrawal and he died in Macau soon afterwards. Clearly, this incident was, to an extent, a prelude to the later conflict but, as Gao (2020:124–137) suggests, even after Napier British views in the mid-1830s still varied quite considerably about the most appropriate line to take with China. Whilst 'force' was generally agreed on, direct military conflict was not and many thought it would be precisely the wrong action to take.

An analysis that looks at both the short range and the long range is offered by Japanese scholar Inoue Hiromasa. In a very interesting paper, Hiromasa (1986) explores the role of Cantonese intellectual Wu Lanxiu in shaping local attitudes to opium and the opium trade in the 1820s and 1830s before the first conflict began in 1839. Hiromasa describes how Wu was part of the Guangzhou intelligentsia and was involved in debates and discussions about the opium problem. Wu strongly influenced Xu Naiji's 1836 *shijin* memorial to the emperor, advocating the legalisation of the opium trade, a memorial which Hiromasa (1986:104) claims was the 'fuse leading directly to the war'. Hiromasa's (2004) later book develops this analysis by stepping back and setting the events in the 1820s and 1830s in a longer perspective that he traces back to the 1720s. He argues that heated internal debates within China about how to deal with the opium trade did not just start in the decades immediately before 1839 and were in fact part of a long conversation about opium.[1] In a complementary analysis, Melancon (1999,

---

[1] Hiromasa's 1986 paper is translated into English but the 2004 book is published in Japanese. I have relied on Joshua Fogel's (2006) extended English-language summary of the latter.

2003) argues that the reasons underlying the declaration of war at the start of the 1839–1842 conflict were not solely economic and in fact reflected a wider set of social, cultural, and political drivers.

We can draw a number of lessons from this. First, relations between Britain and China in the period before the first conflict were fundamentally structured around, and driven by, trade and economic interests. Britain's position at this time as probably the dominant global power shaped the dynamic between the two countries. Second, opium was no ordinary commodity for China. It occupied a complex but important place in China's social and cultural life that went back centuries and internal debates about opium and the opium trade were not something that only began in the 1830s. It follows, third, that any trade war centred on opium would have the potential to have profound and long-lasting impacts, not just on China but also on Sino-British relations and wider distributions of global power. As we will see, these impacts can still be felt two decades into the twenty-first century.

The First Opium War: 1839–1842

The story of the first conflict is a long and complicated one. As already noted, there are many book-length attempts to tell it. One of the best, in my view, is Lovell's (2011) and this would be a good place to start for those wanting to know and understand what happened during this episode. An alternative is Fay's (1975) classic book which remains a compelling and insightful read. My goal here is different, as the aim is not to re-state this narrative but rather to analyse it as a critical moment in which some of the initial conditions out of which international drug control later emerged started to be set. As we saw in Part I, initial conditions are theoretically important for understanding regulatory regimes as complex systems. My focus is on an analysis of Mao Haijian's work, as it is not only exceptionally comprehensive and insightful but is also particularly focused on trying to recentre China and Chinese perspectives which is a theme of this book.

Mao Haijian's 1995 study of the First Opium War is an astonishing work of modern Chinese history. Published in a new English translation in 2016, it repays detailed attention and close reading. At a technical level, it is a work of rare historiographical virtuosity, weaving together Chinese, Japanese, and English language sources and material of very different kinds. The idea of 'revisionist' history has often been quite loosely applied, including to histories which are broadly orthodox in their positions, but Mao Hijian's history is genuinely original and presents a distinctive heterodox thesis. The established orthodox position is that the First Opium War marked the beginning of China's 'century of humiliation' at the hands of Western powers, which lasted until the founding of the People's Republic of China in 1949. Mao upended this narrative by focusing on the agency of China, Chinese authorities, and Chinese people in the events leading up to and during the conflict.

He begins with a detailed account of the state of Qing military power before the war began, as part of an evaluation of whether or not a Chinese victory was even possible (2016:27–73). His conclusion is stark: 'on the eve of the Opium War the Qing armed forces were in an extremely dire state and it is difficult to state anything positive about them at all' (2016:70). He also notes that pre-war knowledge about the strength of the British military was very limited indeed, even at the most senior levels of government (2016:74). This was obviously not a recipe for success. Mao (2016:74–129) goes on to describe a series of miscalculations and misjudgements made by Lin Zexu, the Imperial Commissioner to Canton who had been sent in 1839 to deal with the problem of the opium trade. As a result, Lin failed to see the war coming—Mao calls it the 'unexpected war'—and did not prepare properly for it.

In military terms, the war went badly for the Chinese side during 1840. Mao (2016:136–148) shows how a combination of the concentration of decision-making power (to an emperor with only 'ordinary' qualities and poor advisors), a lack of timely and accurate information about what was going on, and a largely unknown enemy, led to a sequence of bad calls and wrong decisions. Nevertheless, he emphasises that the difference in strength between the two sides' military forces was the most decisive factor in shaping the trajectory of the conflict (2016:212). The British military was simply more powerful. When Lin was replaced by a new Imperial Commissioner, Kišan, in autumn 1840, there seemed to be some recognition of this and the last few months of the year were occupied with conciliation talks and negotiations (2016:154–176, 184–197).

By the start of 1841, however, tensions were rising, as talks began to break down (2016:190–197). In February, fighting began again and Kišan was replaced by new commanders, Yishan and Yang Fang (2016:205–214). A bloody battle in Guangzhou took place in May, in which the British incurred their worst losses since the start of the war but still emerged as clear victors (2016:236–244). After the battle, popular resistance by locals in

Sanyuanli inflicted further casualties on the British, triggered by anger at the behaviour of the British (including accusations of looting, desecration of the dead, and rape) (2016:250–270). Mao resists the orthodox representation of the Sanyuanli resistance as a heroic show of patriotism, arguing that the evidence points to it being driven more by local grievances about British misconduct.

The resistance made little difference, however, to the continuing trajectory of the conflict during the autumn and winter of 1841, with British forces gradually progressing up the east coast from Guangzhou to Xiamen and then Ningpo, just south of Shanghai. A Chinese counter-offensive in East Zhejiang in March 1842 marshalled together a very significant number of soldiers and civilians but was rapidly defeated (2016:324–341) and this ushered in the final stages of the conflict. From May, the British began what would turn out to be the last part of the campaign, working up the Yangtze River until they reached Nanjing in August. This final push up the Yangtze would turn out to be one of bloodiest of the whole war, a fact which no doubt accelerated the beginning of the end. Negotiating the peace had in fact been underway since the end of May but came to a head when the British arrived in Nanjing. With the British poised to open fire on the city, intense negotiations took place and eventually on 29 August a treaty was signed aboard HMS *Cornwallis* on the river, bringing the war to an end (2016:392–414).

The terms of the Treaty of Nanjing are instructive and Mao provides a brilliantly insightful analysis of their significance to the Chinese and the response to them. The Treaty consisted of 13 articles but it contained three basic components:

1. Paying an indemnity of 21 million dollars to the British;
2. Ceding Hong Kong Island to the British 'in perpetuity';
3. Opening up four new Treaty Ports (in addition to Canton/ Guangzhou) in Xiamen, Foochow, Ningpo, and Shanghai, and abolishing the restrictive *cohong* system that had controlled trade in Canton.

Mao describes the feelings of humiliation and anxiety expressed by many officials in correspondence at the time. In one of these letters, from the Governor of Zhejiang, Liu Yunke, a prescient note is struck as Liu observes 'I feel very worried that the settlement will not resolve the situation permanently' (2016:420). Anxieties about implementing the new trading systems in ways that would not lead to new tensions rapidly developed. Cutting through the detailed points made in these various letters, Mao (2016:432) identifies what lay at the heart of these disparate concerns:

> In the West, commercial activities were [not] ... subject to specific governmental control. Merchants simply had to follow the laws. But in traditional Chinese society ... everyone operated within the network of governmental administration.

He describes this as being rooted in 'social and cultural differences between China and the West' but it could also be seen as based on fundamentally different conceptions of the *exchangespace* for Sino-British trade on Chinese soil. The *cohong* system in Canton had arguably provided a mediating mechanism which allowed these two very different systems of market-regulation relations to co-exist and interact in tightly delimited ways. In brief, it had meant that under Qing regulations, foreign merchants could only trade in Canton and only with merchants licensed by local authorities (*hong* merchants), to whom they had to pay various taxes and fees. They could also only communicate with Qing officials through the *hong* merchants. The *cohong* system was administratively complex and, for foreign merchants, no doubt frustratingly restrictive and controlled, but it provided a relatively stable and effective system for trading. The Treaty was now removing that mechanism and forcing the systems to interact without any mediating mechanism to facilitate exchange. In effect, the *exchangespace* was being radically reconfigured overnight, through a high-level agreement (signed 'at gunpoint'), without any detailed plans of how the new system would work.

In the months after the Treaty was signed, discussions continued about further agreements that would be necessary to provide some of these details. These took place against a backdrop of some continuing tensions between the Chinese and the British. A further Treaty was eventually signed on 8 October 1843 (the 'Supplementary Treaty on the Five Open Ports', known as the Treaty of the Bogue or the Treaty of Humen), with provisions on import and export tariffs, judicial authority, and dispute resolution, 'favoured nation' status for Britain, and the right to anchor British warships in the five Treaty Ports (Mao 2016:433–455). These two Treaties paved the way for other foreign powers to take advantage of the commercial opportunities offered by the new Treaty Ports. The French were granted certain rights to trade shortly after the signing of the Treaty of the Bogue (2016:455) and the Americans would negotiate their own agreement with China, which resulted in the Treaty of Wanghia being signed on 3 July 1844 (2016:455–469). The French, in turn, also achieved a formal agreement, the Treaty of Whampoa, signed on 24 October 1844 (2016:469–479).

These settlements between China, Britain, and other Western powers would prove to be unstable, and certainly insufficient to prevent the outbreak of a second war the following decade, as will be discussed in the next section. Indeed, as we will see, even after that, relations remained tense, troubled, and far from stable. Before we turn to consideration of this second conflict and its aftermath, what does Mao's analysis have to tell us about the 1839–1842 war and its place in the pre-history of the international drug control system? We can draw out four key points.

First, Mao clearly argues that British imperial aggression was a primary driver of the conflict and that Britain's superior military force was the main reason for their eventual victory. Nevertheless, he is at pains to identify and highlight the numerous points at which the beliefs, mind-set, and actions of Chinese actors contributed to the worsening or prolonging of parts of the conflict. This attempt to re-introduce Chinese agency and responsibility into accounts of the war was a radical move, particularly for a scholar based in China. As Lovell put it in her introduction to the 2016 English edition:

> While tough on British behavior during the war, the book was also trenchant in its criticisms of the ruling Qing dynasty's response, and subsequent Chinese myth-making. In the cultural context of 1990s China, the publication … —a serious, audaciously heterodox account of one of the key crises of modern Chinese history—was an extraordinary intellectual event. (Mao 2016:xv)

The 'audacity' is the implication that China's 'century of humiliation' was partly self-inflicted rather than entirely caused by Western imperialism. This leads to the *second* point, concerning the longer-term impact of the Treaty of Nanjing. As Mao (2016:417–418) observes:

> The West crashed over China's old systems like a great wave. The production and the livelihood of the masses suffered greatly, especially in the coastal areas. From this tragedy the sprouts of all kinds of unprecedented socio-economic phenomena began to appear in China. Britain's main goals in this war … reflected its desire for China to be brought into

the system of world trade ... In some ways, this was disadvantageous to China, but objectively it also offered China a new path to escape from the cycles of its history. In the short term, the negative effects outweighed the positive ... In the twentieth century, the positive effects surpassed the negative.

In other words, the First Opium War can be read as a first step towards a long process of economic development for China which now, from the vantage point of the twenty-first century, looks remarkably positive. It certainly signalled the beginning of the end for the Qing dynasty which, from the 1850s onwards experienced a series of internal rebellions, civil unrest, and conflict. The Qing dynasty eventually came to an end with the 1911 revolution. As we will see in the next chapter, the collapse of China in 1911 has been neglected in histories of the emergence of international drug control but is in fact an important part of the picture. An interesting review essay by Bracken (2019:175–176) argues that the 'semi-colonial' Treaty Ports established in 1842 would come to be the 'instruments that forced China to open to the world' and that they had a long-term influence on Chinese economic development and modernisation into and throughout the twentieth century. In short, he claims 'their legacy is China's place in the world today' (2019:175).

The *third* issue Mao makes clear, as indeed have other histories of the First Opium War, is that the question of the legality of the opium trade was left unresolved. Indeed, opium was not explicitly mentioned in the Treaty of Nanjing. Mao (2016:434–435) observes that after the Treaty had been signed, Lord Pottinger, the British plenipotentiary who had led the negotiations and would become the first Governor of Hong Kong, sought to persuade the Chinese to abandon its prohibition of opium. This point was not pressed, however, and the ambiguous status of opium continued. Zheng (2018:18) notes that a year after the Treaty 'the opium trade exploded along the south-eastern seabord ... [and] Shanghai overtook Guangzhou to become the centre of trade and consumption'. In the 10 years after this, opium shipments from India to China doubled in quantity (Morse 1910, cited in Zheng 2018:19). The failure to resolve the opium question created an ongoing instability in Sino-British relations that would not be resolved until 1860, and only after a further armed conflict, the so-called *Arrow* war that will be discussed shortly in the next section in this chapter.

The *fourth* point we can take from Mao (2016:513) is made explicit in the final lines on the final page of the book:

It is commonly said that the nineteenth century was the British century, while the twentieth century belonged to the Americans. What about the twenty-first? Some ... people declare that the twenty-first century will belong to the Chinese people. But the really critical question is ... [how] can the Chinese people make it so this really is 'the Chinese people's century'? No matter what choices are made, in my view the most important question left to us by the Opium War is this: has the gap between China and the West shrunk in the last 150 years, or grown?

The challenging question of what this might mean for the future of drug law reform is engaged with later in this book. What Mao's dazzling historiographical achievement provides is a detailed and rigorous account of the roots of this question in the First Opium War, but from within an account which also centres China and Chinese actors at the heart of the story. It is for this reason that Mao's history is so important and relevant for the development of the thesis of this book, as it is arguably one of the most powerful contributions to date to the project of decolonising knowledge and discourse about global drug policy and drug law reform.

The Second Opium War: 1856–1860

The Second Opium War, sometimes called the *Arrow* War, has been significantly less well studied than the First and John Wong's (1998) detailed and exemplary monograph remains the principal work. But it is arguably of nearly equal importance to the First Opium War in shaping our understanding of the making of the twentieth-century drug prohibition experiment. The second conflict was longer, lasting from 1856 to 1860, more fragmented, and more complex than the first. It involved an alliance between the British and the French against China, and the United States also had minor involvements in the war in 1856 and 1859 whilst remaining neutral for most of the time. Russia also had an interest but did not join the Franco-British alliance. Given the number of major powers involved, it was probably one of the most serious wars of the nineteenth century. Indeed, Wong (1998:1) describes it as a 'world war', making its relative neglect by historians all the more puzzling. There were multiple battles in different locations, diplomatic incidents, lootings, the burning of palaces, and even a brief pause in hostilities in 1858 as a number of Treaties were signed. The full story of the war that Wong (1998) tells at length and with immense skill is fascinating in its complexity. Space precludes a recounting here and interested readers are referred to Wong's book. Instead, we focus here on how we should make sense of the *Arrow* War in the context of the broader narrative of this part of the book.

The immediate trigger for the conflict was an 'incident' in October 1856 on a lorcha (a type of boat used in Chinese waters) named the *Arrow*, whilst it was anchored at Canton. This led, first of all, to some unauthorised hostilities that later turned into full-blown conflict. By drawing on multiple archival sources, Wong is able to go through in great detail each of the incidents, episodes, and actions that shaped the unfolding events during the war. These details need not detain us here. Wong's central argument, however, based on his archival research, is that, contrary to the conventional narrative, in fact the *Arrow* incident was not the cause of the war but rather was the public justification for a conflict that had been planned for some time before that. He argues that the actual cause was the desire to force revisions to the Treaty of Nanjing. The rejection in June 1856 of an official British request to revise the Treaty was, in that sense, the real trigger for war (Wong 1998:28–29).

So what Treaty revisions did the British want? In brief, the objective was to open up the whole of the interior of China for the purpose of trade, including fully legalising the trade in opium. As Wong (1998:31) puts it, the 'pivotal origins of the *Arrow* War … [were] the expansion of British economic interests in China and thereby globally'. Opium was central to those interests. By presenting detailed statistics on trading between Britain, China, and other countries, Wong is able to flesh out, with some precision, the nature and scale of those interests and how they shaped the relationships between the countries that became involved in the war. The flows of opium, tea, silk, cotton, and silver, between China, India, Britain, the United States, France, and others, created a complex set of transnational economic interdependencies (see also Deming 2011). Trading on Chinese soil operated within an equally complex set of regulatory arrangements covering activities within Canton and the other Treaty Ports that had been created in 1842. Just as the Treaty signed in 1842 had started a major reconfiguration of the *exchangespace* for the opium trade in China, so now the British wanted a further reshaping and were prepared to use military force to make this happen.

The first phase of the conflict—fought initially by Britain alone and then joined by France in 1857—came to a pause in the spring of 1858, as negotiations took place leading to the signing of the Treaty of Tientsin in

June. Unlike the Treaty of Nanjing, signed 16 years earlier, this Treaty had five signatories—China, Britain, France, the United States, and Russia—illustrating how even though only the first three were formally engaged in military conflict, this was a broader international affair. The pause in hostilities did not last long and the second phase of the conflict began with further fighting taking place into 1859, including a brief military involvement by the United States during a failed attempt to take the Taku Forts in Tientsin. The concluding stage of the war came in 1860, as the Anglo-French forces proceeded to Beijing, entering the city in October. The looting and then burning down of the Summer Palaces in Beijing finally ended the conflict and negotiations for peace started.

The formal ratification of the earlier Treaty of Tientsin was incorporated in a new and wider-ranging treaty, the Convention of Peking, which was signed on 18 October. This very significantly shifted the relationship between China and some of the key European powers. The 'opening up' of China that had been the underlying driver of the First Opium War was now considerably extended and the opium trade was legalised. Under a supplementary treaty signed a couple of weeks later, Russia acquired new territory where they shortly after founded the city of Vladivostok.

The significance of the *Arrow* War, as a prelude to twentieth-century developments in drug control, is manifold. First, and most obviously, the legal status of the opium trade, which had been left unresolved in 1842, was now settled (for the time being) and the prohibition/legalisation dynamic was established as a major animating force in regulatory regimes for opium. Second, it marked a shift away from British imperialism to a more multinational imperialism, paving the way for the international meetings that would characterise the assembly of international drug control in the first few decades of the next century. Third, it further accelerated the decline of the Qing dynasty, after a second humiliating defeat at the hands of Western powers in the space of a couple of decades. Fourth, and relatedly, Zheng (2018:32) suggests that despite the 'defeat and humiliation' of the *Arrow* War, it may also have helped to propel China 'onto the path of reform' and contributed to her 'long-term commitment to modernisation'.

After the *Arrow* War, a new type of commercial order for Sino-Western trade in China had to be built. This immediate aftermath of the Opium Wars has been little studied, with economic historian Eiichi Motono's (2000) excellent monograph a rare exception. Motono's research shows that in the period from the Convention of Peking in 1860 up until the 1911 revolution, Sino-British business was characterised by a mix of co-operation and conflict. He describes, as an illustrative example, the conflict that took place between 1885 and 1887 over the imposition of a tax on imported Indian opium stored in Shanghai. The Swatow Opium Guild in Shanghai (*Shanghai Chaohui Huiguan*), a Chinese merchants' group, wanted to retain the right to collect the *Lijin* tax in exchange for granting the right to sell opium, whilst British merchants wanted to break this system in favour of 'free trade' (2000:92–94). Disagreement over this proved hard to manage and the dispute rumbled on through 1885 and 1886 without resolution. It effectively ended with an Additional Agreement in March 1887 which removed the Swatow Opium Guild's control over the opium trade. But this left merchants in an unsatisfactory and unclear situation (2000:109–114). Eventually, the merchant-control system would completely collapse, leading to the drafting of a new Chinese commercial law code in the first decade of the twentieth century (2000:143–165). Again, the impact of the opium trade on the later modernisation of China cannot be overstated. There is considerable future scope for more research on the period after 1860, building on Motono's research, as well as on the *Arrow* War itself. As Zheng (2018:31) notes, research on the *Arrow* War will demand language skills, to dig further into the French, Russian, and Chinese sources, but there will no doubt be considerable new knowledge and insights to be gained from serious historical scholarship on this. Some companions for Wong's lonely monograph are long overdue.

Conclusion

The purpose of this second part of the book is to identify some of the initial conditions out of which the international drug control system was forged at the beginning of the twentieth century. One of the premises for the pair of chapters that make up this part is that a reappraisal and reassessment of the historical emergence of this system is analytically important. A further premise is that by recentring Asia in general, and China in particular, in this story, we can gain a different perspective on these origins of global drug prohibition. The claim is that this new perspective brings to the surface and makes visible some aspects of drug control which are essential for a critical reappraisal of the contemporary situation and for thinking about future directions for law and policy. This chapter has focused on the nineteenth century and the two military conflicts with China that have become known as the Opium Wars. An attempt has also been made to set this in the broader context of global history and the need it highlights to move away from the Western-centrism which is rife in this field of study, as it is also in many others.

So what have we learned? There are four main insights we can draw from this chapter which help us to understand some of the elements that formed the early foundations on which the global prohibition system would be built in the early twentieth century. *First*, the Opium Wars represented a military contestation of the boundaries between legal and illegal trade. In a fundamental sense, this contestation lies at the very heart of drug control. The British wanted to make the opium trade fully legal, operating on the same basis as the trade in other commodities (and 'at home' opium was still controlled as a matter of business regulation, even after the 1868 Pharmacy Act). The Chinese, on the other hand, wanted to maintain strict controls on a prohibited trade. Part of the complexities of this legal/illegal boundary for opium was that the Chinese also had strong economic interests in trading with Britain, as well as considerable demand for opium within their population. The *cohong* system that existed until 1842 was, in effect, a way of managing these complexities, providing some control without entirely eliminating or displacing the trade. This boundary work can be usefully theorised using the *exchangespace* concept.

This links to the *second* insight which is that the Opium Wars marked the point at which one of the core dynamics came to be viewed as the dichotomy of prohibition versus legalisation. This is a good example of long-term path dependence, as this dichotomy continues to pervade drug law reform discourse today. As discussed in Part I, the dichotomy dissolves theoretically when we use the intellectual resources offered by the notion of *exchangespace*, as 'prohibition' and 'legalisation' become merely labels for particular configurations of market-regulation relations. In other words, they simply represent different regulatory regimes rather than dichotomous systems or approaches. Nevertheless, the dichotomy retains a discursive significance.

The *third* insight is that the *Arrow* War was the first clear moment when opium control became a multinational affair. This international character has come to be one of the defining features of drug control. From this point, it is possible to tell the story of the drug control system through an account of the succession of international meetings that have taken place and the international treaties that have been agreed over the course of the last 160 years. Today, of course, drug control operates under the auspices of the United Nations (UN) and within the legal framework of three UN

Treaties. Given this, it is somewhat surprising that there is a dearth of serious international law scholarship in this area and that drug law reform is rarely framed as, in part, an international law project (for a couple of exceptions, see Thomas 2003; d'Aspremont and Zhang 2021).

This leads to the *fourth* and final insight from the chapter which is that we can draw a direct line from the Opium Wars to the events that constituted the emergence of global drug prohibition half a century later. These are sometimes narrated as if they are largely separate matters: the Opium Wars as distant events of historical interest but largely unconnected with the birth of prohibition in the twentieth century. To the contrary, and as will be further shown in the next chapter, the links and connections are very clear (see also Berridge and Edwards 1981:173–205). The materials from which prohibition was assembled were laid down in the events in China in the middle of the nineteenth century that have been described here. Indeed, taking a longer view, we might observe in addition that the prohibition of opium that China (with others) would press for in, for example, Shanghai in 1909 was no more than the reinstatement, and internationalisation, of a prohibition it had first put in place in 1729 (see Windle 2013a). The notion of global drug prohibition as an American project is an ahistorical distortion that can only stand if we ignore pre-1945 events.

The next chapter moves forward to the first decade of the twentieth century and focuses on a series of linked events that have often been underplayed in accounts of the birth of drug prohibition: the 1906 Chinese imperial edict on opium; the 1907 British-Chinese-Indian Ten-Year Agreement; and the 1909 International Opium Commission meetings in Shanghai. The chapter will explore how these events were critical elements for the assembly of the international drug control system in the following two decades. Making visible, and understanding, the ways in which today's prohibition system only makes full sense when we view its origins through the lens of China is a central part of this book's thesis. As will be explored later in the book, this dimension of prohibition's past potentially has major implications for its future.

5

The birth of prohibition

Introduction

In this chapter, we continue the story of the origins of prohibition, focusing primarily on events in the first decade of the twentieth century. This period has arguably been under-researched and there is much to learn from examining it carefully. As we will see, it further highlights the centrality of Asia and China to the creation of the initial conditions from which international prohibition emerged. Part of this book's thesis is that this aspect of those initial conditions is not just relevant to an understanding of prohibition's past but also has significance for the future possibilities for global drug regulatory regimes, as will be explored in Part III and the concluding chapter.

This first decade of the twentieth century is in fact often skipped over rapidly in histories of prohibition, in a hurry to get to the Opium Convention in 1912, the impact of the First World War, the Treaty of Versailles in 1920, the creation of the League of Nations and then the Geneva Opium Convention in 1925. Sometimes it is almost as if nothing of note happened between the end of the Opium Wars and the 1920s, or even as if the two are minimally connected. This chapter is a corrective to this and attempts to show the continuities across the nineteenth and twentieth centuries. The claim is that these continuities move into the sharpest focus when we view events through the lens of China and recentre Asia in the story. In the absence of this understanding and historical perspective, we risk viewing matters almost entirely from the vantage point of the Global North and with an extremely limited sense of how we have ended up where we are today. Braithwaite (2003) has criticised this tendency in Western scholarship to saw off the genealogical branches that are in the periphery of the world system from the history of the (North Atlantic) present. As he puts it: 'we can learn a lot from a history of jazz that does not mention Africa; we can learn more from one that does' (2003:9). For the history of drug control, as we saw in the last chapter, re-tracing these more forgotten branches of

Rethinking Drug Laws. Toby Seddon, Oxford University Press. © Toby Seddon 2023.
DOI: 10.1093/oso/9780192846525.003.0005

the genealogy also reconnects the present with the branches growing out of the business regulatory trunk not just those from the criminal law trunk as is usually the case. As will be explored later in the book, this is also critical for thinking about the future and potential pathways for drug law reform (e.g. see Seddon and Floodgate 2020:85–118).

The chapter draws partly on a synthesis of the historical literature. Unlike for the Opium Wars explored in the previous chapter, there is not the same spread of major English-language monographs directly covering this period. The literature is primarily dispersed across several articles and essays by different scholars and there is less sense of the 'bigger picture'. The chapter is also based on primary archival research conducted at the Weston Library in Oxford between January and March 2020 and then at the National Archives in London between June and July 2021. It is organised in three principal parts. The first scene-setting section examines the Imperial Edict of 1906 and the Ten-Year Agreement signed at the end of 1907. These are neglected but important events to understand as they not only go to the heart of China's position on opium in this decade but they also ushered in policies and action that would have long-term effects. The second, and main, part of the chapter explores the International Opium Commission meetings that took place in Shanghai in February 1909. The Shanghai Commission was a pivotal moment in the creation of the international drug control system but is often overlooked in favour of the meetings in The Hague between 1911 and 1914. The third part then briefly looks at the period after the Shanghai Commission, including a consideration of the importance of the 1911 revolution in China which, again, is almost entirely absent from the historical literature. The concluding section of the chapter brings together what has been learned in this part of the book and introduces Part III by considering the potential relevance of this analysis of the past for thinking about the possibilities for the future.

The Imperial Edict and the Ten-Year Agreement

In the two decades after the end of the *Arrow* War in 1860, the export of opium from British India to China remained at a very high level. In an important essay on the late Qing period, the economic historian of China, Albert Feuerwerker (1980:9), notes that opium was China's single largest import by value up until the mid-1880s. By the end of the century, however, the quantity of imported opium had significantly decreased. As he notes, 'the principal reason for the fall in the quantity of opium imports was the steady spread of domestic opium cultivation' (1980:9). This is important context for the events at the start of the twentieth century, for at least three reasons. First, the opium trade was becoming of declining economic importance to the British. This was not only because of China's growing domestic cultivation but also, as Newman (1989:530) notes, as a result of increasing competition from Persian and Turkish imports. This opened up a space for the British to take a different stance than it had for most of the nineteenth century. Second, demand for opium within China was not reducing and may even have been growing. Third, with the rise of domestic cultivation, responsibility for controlling the opium supply was shifting partly to China, becoming also an internal matter rather than just a question of foreign affairs. As we will see, these were all significant factors in what would unfold in the next few years.

Another important part of the shifting context at the end of the nineteenth century was also centred in Asia. The short Spanish-American War fought between April and August 1898 in the Caribbean and the Pacific led to the United States acquiring the Philippines from the Spanish as part of the post-war peace settlement. Smith (1994) argues that this conflict had an important impact on America's place in global politics in the twentieth century, signalling the arrival of the United States as a key player in world affairs. It also gave America new responsibility for a major site of Asian opium cultivation which would fundamentally shape its perspective on the question of opium control (see Wertz 2013). As Reins (1991) argues, this put the United States in the position of having a strong interest in attempting to suppress opium cultivation and consumption. The appointment in 1902 of the Canadian-American Charles Brent as Episcopal Bishop to the Philippines would prove to be highly significant. He was part of the Philippine Opium Committee of 1903–1904, which was set up to make recommendations about how best to deal with opium, and, as we will see, he also went on to lead the American delegation at the Shanghai meetings in 1909.

The Philippine Committee was an interesting episode (see Taylor 1967; Wertz 2013). When the Americans had first taken control of the Philippines, they abolished the 'opium farming out' system that had been established by the Spanish in the 1840s to regulate the trade. This was in effect an outsourcing model, in which responsibility for wholesale and retail was contracted out. Opium could only be sold to Chinese inhabitants of the islands and purchase or use by Filipinos was prohibited. The system allowed the Philippines administration to generate revenue without having responsibility for the operational running of the system, whilst at the same time protecting the indigenous population from the perceived harms of opium. Following its abolition, the Americans imposed an import duty, created a licensing system for retailers and prohibited opium dens. However, the new model was quickly seen to be a failure, as levels of opium consumption increased significantly and spread into the Filipino population where use had previously been almost non-existent. The opium question had now become highly controversial and many called for a return to the Spanish system. To try to find a way forward, the Committee was set up to investigate how the opium trade was being handled elsewhere in southeast Asia and to make recommendations for the Philippines. Led by Brent, it worked quickly, visiting Japan, China, Burma, Singapore, and other areas in the region, before returning to Manila. The Committee recommended establishing a strict government monopoly on import, wholesale and retail, for a transitional three-year period, working towards a complete prohibition by 1908 except for legitimate medical use. The Philippine administration accepted the general thrust of the recommendations but implemented a licensing system for the three-year transitional period rather than a government monopoly. From 1908 until the Second World War, the Philippines served as an example of a Western-controlled area operating a strict opium prohibition model.

Although these developments in the Philippines, and the involvement of the Americans through their imperial interests, were critical elements within the unfolding events of the decade, China remained the most important player. China's approach was about to shift in an unexpected direction. As Reins (1991:101) argues, out of all the many reforms of the late Qing period, 'perhaps none is more surprising than the opium suppression movement' which took off in 1906. Prior to this, China had seemed resigned to its opium situation, although, in fact, a number of trade agreements made between 1900 and 1905—with Britain, the United States, Germany, and Portugal—had already sought to limit imports of opium and morphine into China (Reins 1991:104–105). The game-changing moment, however, was the issuing of an Imperial Edict in September 1906 which stated that 'it is hereby commanded that within a period of 10 years the evils arising from foreign and native opium be equally and completely eradicated'.[1] By

---

[1] National Archives. FO 415/418. Reproduced in Memorandum on Opium from China, Appendix A, Proceedings of the International Opium Commission Shanghai 1909.

referring also to foreign opium, it was clear that this Edict could not be ful-filled without engaging foreign powers. In other words, this was not an ex-clusively internal policy decree, it was also a declaration of a new foreign policy goal.

The 1906 Edict explicitly framed the problem as the negative impact of opium consumption on Chinese people, referring to the 'poison of this drug' permeating the 'whole of China'. This impact is vividly described— 'the opium smoker wastes time and neglects work, ruins his health, and impoverishes his family'—and then linked to problems of national decline by referring to opium's contribution to the 'poverty and weakness which for the past few decades have been daily increasing amongst us'. This, in turn, is linked to the nationalist cause, as the opium problem is described as arousing 'Our indignation ... at a moment when We are striving to strengthen the Empire'.[2]

The Edict emerged at this point for a number of reasons, as Reins' (1991) careful analysis explains. The association between opium and Western im-perialism made it an obvious space for China to seek to assert its status in the world and its sense of nationalism. The growing internal disorder within China, which would lead to the entire collapse of the dynasty in 1911, pro-vided fertile ground for a variety of 'reforms' of this kind. But probably the most significant driver for the Edict was that China became aware in 1905 that the British might be willing to change their stance on opium and give up their export trade (1991:107–108). As we have already noted, Britain had become less economically dependent on this trade and was also ex-periencing pressures from a growing anti-opium movement back at home, a movement which, as Berridge and Edwards (1981:173–174) note, had been created partly as a result of disquiet about the Opium Wars. The American experience in the Philippines added further Western impetus be-hind Britain's new position. The only proviso to the British offer was that China would need to commit at the same time to eradicating its domestic cultivation. This mutual commitment would crystallise after a period of negotiation into a formal agreement signed by the British and Chinese in December 1907 and known as the Ten-Year Agreement.

The Ten-Year Agreement did not have formal binding status and was more an informal understanding but constituted, nevertheless, a pro-foundly important step. In many respects, it is a key moment in the origin

---

[2] Ibid.

story for prohibition, connecting together the Sino-British beginnings in the nineteenth century to the international meetings that would follow in the next 20 years, starting in Shanghai just over a year later. At the heart of the agreement was the commitment to implement the Imperial Edict's command to eliminate the opium trade over a 10-year period. Given the bloodshed less than 50 years earlier, precisely to maintain and expand that trade, this was quite remarkable. As Newman (1989) describes, after a prolonged period of negotiation, the informal agreement of 1907 would be placed on a more formal footing with the signing of a full Sino-British Treaty in May 1911. As we will see, events in China later in that year would have a major impact on its implementation.

If we step back to assess the regulatory trajectory in this 50-year period after the end of the *Arrow* War, one of the most striking features is that Asia remains at the centre of developments in opium regulation but with a widening set of international actors becoming involved. We can read this as a continuing multinationalism which, as noted in the previous chapter, was something that gathered pace during the *Arrow* War itself. But we can also see it as the increasingly multi-level nature of opium control. As may be recalled from Chapter 3, the *exchangespace* concept, and specifically the conceptualisation of market-regulation relations as constituted by networks of networks, is a way of making sense theoretically of multi-level governance in the drug sphere. Opium control, for example, was partly located in international agreements between states but it was also to be found in the detailed regulations and practices that governed trading activities in the Treaty Ports in China, and in the policing of opium dens in Manila. But from a complex systems perspective, such as underpins *exchangespace*, these are not separate phenomena; they are interconnected subsystems connected through information flows and feedback loops that move up and down levels. The evolution of the overall system is an emergent property of these multiple flows.

The Imperial Edict and the Ten-Year Agreement provided the foundation for the momentous events of February 1909 in Shanghai that will be explored in the next section. If the Shanghai meeting is the neglected part of the story of the birth of prohibition, the events that immediately preceded Shanghai are even more forgotten. Yet, as we have seen, they are critical parts of the narrative as they help to explain how the nineteenth-century Opium Wars and the twentieth-century creation of international prohibition are deeply connected within a single arc of historical development. Recognising these connections is central to the book's thesis that, in the twenty-first century, we need to recentre China in our analyses of drug policy and drug control if we are to understand fully both where we have come from but also, crucially, the possibilities for the future.

The Shanghai International Opium Commission

The convening of an international meeting in Shanghai in early 1909 was undoubtedly a critical moment in the modern history of drug control. It has been relatively neglected in the historiographical literature, certainly compared to the meetings at The Hague just a couple of years later, with perhaps the best work remaining the early sections of Peter Lowes' (1966) somewhat forgotten book on *The Genesis of International Narcotics Control* and contributions by historian Thomas Reins (1981). Indeed, the focus of Lowes' study on the Shanghai and Hague meetings, and its centring of Asia rather than North America within the narrative, remains unusual and is perhaps what lies behind its semi-forgotten status in the literature. Readers looking for more detail on the period examined in this chapter are recommended to track down a copy. In addition to this work, this section also draws on new archival research, from two sources. The first is the collection of the papers of Cecil Clementi held in the Weston Library in Oxford.[3] Clementi was a British colonial administrator, India-born and Oxford-educated, who had a long career of service. He participated in the Shanghai Commission meetings at the age of only 33. His papers include a contemporaneous journal written during January and February 1909 which paints an extraordinary 'inside' picture of the Shanghai meetings. Reading Clementi's handwritten account in his small notebook provided an unusual sense of peering directly into the past. The second source is the report and associated papers on the Shanghai Commission held at the National Archives in London.[4]

It is clear that the Shanghai Commission followed on directly from the developments of the previous few years described above, which had culminated in the agreement signed in December 1907. For example, in his welcoming address on 1 February 1909 at the Palace Hotel in Shanghai, His Excellency Tuan Fang, Viceroy of the Liangkiang Provinces, alluded to the

---

[3] Clementi Papers. MSS. Ind. Ocn. s.352/45/2 and MSS. Brit. Emp. s.600/32.
[4] National Archives. FO 405/418: China: International Opium Commission, Shanghai, February 1909; reports of the proceedings and delegations.

1906 Imperial Edict in his very first sentence.[5] Indeed, the idea for an international meeting had first been raised by Bishop Brent, prompted by his experience of leading the Philippines committee in 1903–1904, in a letter to President Roosevelt in the summer of 1906 (Barop 2015:127). Roosevelt was persuaded and this eventually led to the convening of the Shanghai meetings. Being clear about this chain of events is important as it helps us to see both the continuing centrality of China and Asia and also the longer connections back to the previous century's Opium Wars.

There were 13 nations represented at the Commission: Austria-Hungary, China, France, Germany, Great Britain, Italy, Japan, the Netherlands, Persia, Portugal, Russia, Siam, and the United States. Not all countries had the same number of delegates, with Austria-Hungary, Italy, Persia, and Russia only having one each, and China having the most with six.[6] The United States had only three delegates but at the first session on the morning of 1 February it was Bishop Brent who was unanimously elected as President of the Commission, proposed by one of the Chinese delegates and seconded by one of the British.

There were 14 days of sessions between 1 and 26 February. Clementi was a junior member of the British delegation with a specific responsibility to represent Hong Kong. His uncle, Sir Cecil Clementi Smith, was one of the lead British delegates and Clementi's journal contains frequent references to 'Uncle Cecil', reinforcing the sense, captured nearly 50 years ago by Kettil Bruun and colleagues, that international drug control was largely the product of discussions amongst a small circle of 'elite' officials (Bruun et al 1975). On his arrival at the Palace Hotel on 25 January, the week before the sessions began, Clementi observed that outside the front entrance was a large board proclaiming 'American Opium Commission' and a more modest one indicating 'Office of the Chinese Opium Delegates'.[7] The British delegation was on the 4th floor, with the Americans on the 5th floor next to the main conference room.[8] He describes in his journal discussions taking place in this week over who would chair proceedings, with the Chinese wanting to do so and trying to gather support.[9] It became clear during the course of the week, however, that Brent was the best compromise candidate, although Clementi himself was somewhat sceptical about his abilities,

---

[5] FO 405/418, Report of the Proceedings, pages 9–10.
[6] Ibid, pages 3–16.
[7] Clementi Papers. MSS Brit Emp s. 600/32. Notebook 1, entry for 25 January.
[8] Ibid, entry for 26 January.
[9] Ibid, entry for 25 January.

commenting that he 'does not appear to me to be the type of man who is likely to be able to keep order among the delegates if they become at all unruly'.[10]

In the week before the Commission formally began, both the Chinese and the Americans were busy. Clementi described calling into the American delegates' office on the 5th floor to 'find them each at a desk in their room labelled with their names and with the stars and stripes hung up over the wall: also a long table down the centre of the room filled with opium papers'.[11] The British delegates, on the other hand, had been 'instructed that HM government does not wish to take a prominent part in the Conference' and that they were therefore to support Brent as Chairman.[12] This was in many respects quite an extraordinary position to take. With only China having more delegates, Britain was clearly understood to be one of the principal players in Shanghai, yet the British government was seemingly content to let others take the lead.

In his opening address at the first session on 1 February, Brent made clear that the 'opium question in the Far East' was the animating concern for the Commission but indicated that there had also been a widening of the scope of the inquiry to include countries that 'have not the problem in its more acute form'. The goal was for a genuinely international Commission.[13] After acknowledging the complexity of the problem and the need for full co-operation between delegates, Brent expressed the desire that they would be able to reach 'certain unanimous resolutions and, perhaps, some recommendations of a practical, broad and wise character in connection with those resolutions'. He went on to suggest that 'it would be extremely wise if we were to rule out of our deliberations what might be termed useless historical questions beneath which a great deal of controversy lies hidden, and which would only tend to fog the issue'.[14] This was as clear a statement as there could be that the deep rancour caused by the Opium Wars and their aftermath was not to be allowed to derail the discussions and negotiations in Shanghai. He ended by declaring that delegates were assembled 'to do such work as will bring ... the utmost benefit possible to mankind' and announced that the Commission was now 'ready for business'.[15] Lowes

---

[10] Ibid, entry for 27 January.
[11] Ibid.
[12] Ibid, entry for 25 January.
[13] FO 405/418, Report of the Proceedings, page 11.
[14] Ibid, page 12.
[15] Ibid.

(1966:1) describes this day as 'marking the official beginning of international narcotics control'.

At sessions two and three, held on 2 and 5 February, delegates discussed, negotiated, and agreed various formal aspects of how the Commission would function. Substantive discussions then began after the weekend at the fourth session on 8 February. The Chinese delegation presented a report on the opium situation in China, followed by reports from Germany, the Netherlands, and Siam. At the following sessions, further country reports were presented.[16] At the 6th session on 12 February, Sir Alexander Hosie, part of the British delegation, spoke at some length, in Clementi's words 'attacking the Chinese report'.[17] The core of his criticism was the failure to provide accurate figures on the acreage of land under poppy cultivation, the number of opium smokers, and the extent of opium production in China.[18] Given the tone of much of his speech, Hosie's assertion in conclusion that 'I have made these remarks in no carping spirit'[19] should perhaps be interpreted with a degree of scepticism.

In the 7th session on 15 February, further country reports were presented and discussed, before T'ang Kuo-an from the Chinese delegation responded to Hosie's remarks at the previous session. He stated that he was sure that the criticisms of the Chinese report 'were made in no fault-finding spirit' and acknowledged with appreciation the recognition of the seriousness of the opium problem in China which he hoped the Commission would expressly reinforce.[20] It reads as a diplomatic response to a provocative intervention but it also highlights how, for the Chinese, their core objective seemed to be to reach agreement about the severity of the problem and a collective commitment from Commission members to address it.

After adjourning for lunch, the session continued into the afternoon with further presentation and discussion of country reports. At the end of the session, a discussion took place about the scope of the Commission after Mr de Jongh from the Netherlands delegation queried a request for a report on the opium situation within his country on the grounds that 'he had understood that the object of the Commission was to deal with the opium question in the Far East only'. The Portuguese and French delegations supported de Jongh's view, offering an early sighting of the tendency

---

[16] Ibid, pages 21–26.
[17] Clementi Papers. MSS Brit Emp s. 600/32. Notebook 1, entry for 12 February.
[18] FO 405/418, Report of the Proceedings, pages 27–28.
[19] Ibid, page 30.
[20] Ibid, page 32.

throughout the proceedings for the old European colonial powers to stick together. The Chair curtailed the debate by proposing a compromise.[21] This was an interesting moment, as it foreshadowed the widening out of the question that would start to happen a couple of years later at the meetings at The Hague between 1911 and 1914. As we have seen, up to this point the principal focus had been on East Asia and, specifically, China. The Shanghai meeting was an important bridging event in this sense.

At the 8th and 9th sessions on 18 and 19 February, at the instigation of the Chinese delegation a discussion took place about a proposal to set up a sub-committee to consider the issue of 'cures' for the opium habit but with the express exclusion of methods which involved opium itself or its derivatives. A similar resolution had been rejected at the 6th session but T'Ang Kuo-an now sought to press the argument again. Sir Cecil Clementi Smith argued against the proposal, on the grounds that although a highly important question, there was insufficient medical or scientific expertise within the Commission to address it properly. His counter-proposal—effectively asking members to take the issue back to their respective governments for consideration—was narrowly passed by 7 votes to 6. Interestingly, amongst those joining China in voting against the counter-proposal were the United States and Japan.[22] The unspoken context here was that the British had long been involved in sending very large quantities of morphine to China, some directly and some via Japanese smugglers, as Parssinen and Kerner (1981) describe in a fascinating and detailed analysis. The British suppliers were pharmaceutical manufacturers like Macfarlan and whilst much of the trade was ostensibly for legitimate medical purposes, in practice there was very considerable diversion to the illicit market. The emphasis the Chinese delegation placed on the control of opium derivatives, and the support they received from Japan for their proposal, was partly driven by their concerns about the illicit morphine market. We also see here the intertwining of licit and illicit trade and importance of seeing business regulation as part of the picture.

After the weekend, the Commission reconvened on the morning of 22 February for its 10th session. There were some questions and answers relating to various matters deriving from earlier discussions of country reports, before Brent, speaking as Chair, gave a speech declaring the fact-finding part of the Commission's work complete and proposing that they

---

[21] Ibid, page 34.
[22] Ibid, pages 36–38.

should now move towards discussing and agreeing resolutions and actions. The session concluded at lunchtime, with an agreement to adjourn until the following morning. When they recommenced on 23 February, after a brief procedural discussion it was agreed to take draft resolutions in alphabetical order as the delegations appeared on the official list of participants, which meant that 'America, United States of' was first. Dr Hamilton Wright gave a lengthy speech before presenting the American resolutions. Much of the speech was filled with standard diplomatic rhetoric but in the second half he shifted to more substantive and more challenging ground, beginning with a striking statement:[23]

> We have concluded that the traffic in opium for other than necessary uses ought not much longer to continue, or, there will yet loom between the East and West a problem that in its magnitude and potentialities for strife will outstrip the magnitude and forces of that long since, and happily settled, slavery question.

This frames the opium question as a geopolitical concern that constituted a profound fault line between East and West. The seven American resolutions that were then presented were strongly worded and amounted to full-throated support for international action on opium and opiates. Specifically, they called for the restriction of opium use to 'legitimate medical practice', targeted action on opium smoking, prevention of diversion of opium and derivatives to other countries, controls on the morphine trade, commitment to international co-operation, and a call for an International Conference on opium.[24]

The second American resolution—that any revenue problems for governments that might be raised by tightening up opium controls needed to be settled as soon as possible—was a direct challenge for the British in particular and it was unsurprising that Sir Cecil Clementi Smith spoke first, and at length, in response to Hamilton Wright. Clementi Smith in fact opposed not only the resolution on revenue but also the first, which sought to restrict opium use to 'legitimate medical practice', citing the example of India as indicating the impossibility of ensuring compliance.[25]

---

[23] Ibid, page 44.
[24] Ibid, pages 46–48.
[25] Ibid, pages 48–51.

After further discussions in which various members suggested relatively minor amendments to resolutions three to six, the Commission reached the final American resolution on the calling for an International Conference. Clementi Smith argued he was not empowered to agree to this as it went beyond the instructions he had been given and the resolution was withdrawn with an agreement to reconsider it at a future date. At this point, an intervention by a member of the American delegation, Charles Tenney, brought some tensions to the surface as, in effect, he called for Britain to be prepared to accelerate progress in eliminating the opium trade under the Ten-Year Agreement if China were able to meet her side of the agreement more rapidly. When T'Ang Kuo-an spoke in support of Tenney's proposal, Clementi Smith responded in unusually strong terms, describing it as an 'absurdity' which would have the effect of an 'entire abrogation of Treaties'. T'Ang Kuo-an was measured but firm in response, arguing that they respected the Ten-Year Agreement but that 'China did not have in mind never to bring up the subject for discussion' and that 'notwithstanding this agreement, we believe that we are not precluded from requesting the Powers whose Representatives are here assembled, and especially the British Delegation, to take our case into further sympathetic consideration'. Clementi Smith declared himself 'astounded at the words which have fallen from Mr T'Ang'. The Japanese delegation then attempted to move a resolution to the effect that this was a diplomatic matter between Britain and China and therefore out of scope of submission to the Commission—a move that Tenney protested was a 'subterfuge'—which was eventually passed by 8 votes to 3.[26] The session concluded with some more minor skirmishes but it was evident that the temperature of debate had risen several degrees.

The 12th session got underway at 2.30pm on the following afternoon, as the morning had been taken up with informal discussions between the British and American delegations. After some discussion of resolutions put forward by the Netherlands delegation, the rest of the afternoon was taken up by a long speech by T'Ang Kuo-an and the presentation of four resolutions from the Chinese. Together, the speech and resolutions set out China's core position and objectives. It is a fascinating and important passage of text that repays close attention.[27] T'Ang began by asserting that China was 'more deeply interested in the outcome of this Commission than any other Power', with the opium question representing 'one of the most acute moral

---

[26] Ibid, pages 53–57.
[27] Ibid, pages 65–71. The speech is on pages 65–70 and the resolutions on pages 70–71.

and economic questions which as a nation we have to face'. This positioned China at the heart of the Commission's purpose and proceedings. By referencing the 'economic' dimension, it also placed trade at the centre of the issues and this would be elaborated on at some length later in the speech. T'Ang went on to state that China understood 'we must work out our own salvation' and that there was no expectation that other nations either could or should solve the problem for them. He then identified Britain as the other country with the most at stake in the opium question—implicitly referencing the previous century's Opium Wars which, it should be recalled, had concluded less than 50 years earlier—before praising several of the other members of the Commission (Germany, the United States, Japan, France, and Russia) for their support. He referred to the 'many and such far-reaching relationships' with these other nations.

The opium question, then, was framed by T'Ang as bearing most heavily on China, as being about both morality and trade, and as being embedded in a set of international relations particularly with Western powers, with Britain singled out as a particular protagonist. Developing the idea of China embracing its own responsibility to deal with opium, T'Ang referenced first of all the 1906 Imperial Edict and the way this had galvanised the Chinese people to work hard over the following two years to reduce levels of opium cultivation and consumption. He then argued that such 'intensity' of effort would be hard to sustain over an extended period and that therefore speedy responses and action were essential. This linked, of course, back to the previous day's heated discussions about accelerating progress towards the commitments made in the Ten-Year Agreement, to which Clementi Smith had taken such exception. T'Ang was revisiting and reasserting China's desire to speed up the elimination of the opium trade.

His speech then turned to the impact of opium on the Chinese people (despite beginning this section with the claim that 'I shall not yield to the temptation to describe the effects of opium in China'!). After a short passage with some standard rhetorical flourishes ('dismal and wretched hovels', 'abject poverty', 'emaciated, depraved . . . victims'), he began an extended description of what he called the 'economic burden imposed on China by the use of opium'. T'Ang set out at some length calculations and estimates for the aggregate expenditure on opium, the economic loss from land being used for opium cultivation rather than other crops, and the loss of earning capacity from 'victims of the opium habit'. He then developed an argument that this drain on the economic strength of China was damaging for other nations as it placed a brake on its capacity to buy foreign goods. He described it as 'commercial folly' to place retaining the opium market (by then worth less than 10% of its total foreign trade) above the 'almost infinite expansion' in trade that would be possible if the opium 'evil' could be eradicated. In this sense, he argued, the 'opium traffic is *economically*, as well as morally, indefensible' (emphasis in original). This is an important part of the debate, as a reminder and reiteration of the centrality of transnational trade to the conflicts and arguments between China and other nations about opium, going back at least 100 years before the gathering in Shanghai.

In the final part of his speech, T'Ang connected the opium question with the broader matter of the modernisation of China, suggesting that the continuation of the opium trade was compromising her ability to re-form and become a 'modern and progressive' nation. Although he circles around the question of what precisely is meant by this, it is these three ideas—reform, modernity, progress—that he repeatedly references in this passage. The modernity question is one of the central concerns within the extensive scholarship on the history of modern China, as Mitter's (2005) review of the historiographical literature demonstrates. It is part of the dynamic of China's history during the late nineteenth and early twentieth centuries. T'Ang's tone of urgency on this matter is perhaps best understood in the context of his words being spoken just a little over two years before the 1911 Revolution. As historian William Kirby (1997:437) observes of the Qing Empire at this time, the 'first decade of the 20th century was full of portends of its dissolution'. Against the backdrop of domestic turmoil, the Chinese delegation that arrived in 1909 in Shanghai, that most international of Chinese cities, was understandably keen therefore to highlight China's strong desire to play a full part in international society and to press home the importance of international co-operation to help her address the problem of opium. As if to underline this point, T'Ang closed his speech with a reference to the anti-opium movements in Western countries and the 'mighty force' of the 'Christian conscience'. With the time now at 5pm, it was agreed to defer consideration of the four resolutions submitted by China to the following morning.

In his journal, Cecil Clementi noted that on the next day, 25 February, which would turn out to be the penultimate day of proceedings, the Commission members gathered for a photograph on the roof of the Palace Hotel,[28] from where they would have been able to look down on the city

---

[28] Clementi Papers. MSS Brit Emp s. 600/32. Notebook 1, entry for 25 February.

and the Huangpu River. Posing for the photograph, they were no doubt unaware of quite how significant their work over the previous few weeks would prove to be. As had been agreed, the session began in the morning with a discussion of the Chinese resolutions. The first resolution, which called for delegates to urge their governments to help China expedite her progress with opium control by agreeing to co-operate with reducing opium imports into China at the same time as opium cultivation within China, drew an immediate response from Clementi Smith. He reiterated his position from a couple of days earlier on 23 February that he did not have the authority to speak on a matter on which China and Britain had already had formal diplomatic negotiations (i.e. the Ten-Year Agreement).[29] This makes clear that this first resolution was in effect a request by China to speed up progress towards the 10-year target of eliminating the opium trade. In response to Clementi Smith's objection, T'Ang agreed to withdraw the resolution but expressed a desire to 'have it put on record that it is the desire of the Government and people of China to have the abolition of the opium evil effected as quickly as possible'.[30]

The second Chinese resolution called for governments with 'Concessions or Settlements in China' to take action to close opium divans and opium shops in those places. This was very directly addressed to those Western countries with imperial interests in China. Monsieur Ratard, on behalf of the French delegation, immediately expressed concerns about the position in Kuangchowwan (a small enclave on the south coast of China that had been ceded to the French as a leased territory in 1898). Ratard noted that the French government had a contract with opium farmers that ran until the end of 1911 and that it would not be able to breach that agreement. There then followed some manoeuvrings by the French and Chinese, involving amendments and counter-amendments, and eventually a version of the resolution was approved and adopted.[31]

The third resolution, again targeted at governments with 'Concessions or Settlements' in China, called for an end to the use of anti-opium medicines that were opium- or opiate-based, unless on qualified medical advice. The resolution was primarily but not solely concerned with morphine. Interventions from the Japanese and French delegations expressed some reservations—with Ratard for the French asserting that 'we cannot

---

[29] FO 405/418, Report of the Proceedings, pages 71–72.
[30] Ibid, page 72.
[31] Ibid, pages 72–74.

interfere with legitimate trade in foreign concessions'—but an amended version of the resolution was adopted.[32] Following discussions between the Chinese, American, and German delegations during the mid-day recess, an amended version of the fourth and final resolution (on applying domestic pharmacy laws to activities in Concessions and Settlements in China) was very quickly adopted without further discussion. After some discussion about arrangements for printing the Commission's proceedings, Clementi Smith 'expressed the hope' that they might be able to complete their work the following day.[33]

At 2.30pm on 26 February, the 14th and final session began. It was largely taken up with formalities and proceedings came to an end just over two hours later at 4.40pm, with nine resolutions adopted. The significance of the Commission extended far beyond the text of those resolutions and is hard to overstate. It marked the beginning of international co-operation in drug control, effectively ushered in the creation of the global prohibition system, and saw the first stirrings of what would eventually become the American dominance of that system post-1945. As Barop (2015:127) argues, it was the moment when opium moved beyond being just a 'matter of colonial politics' and 'entered international politics as a global problem'. It has remained in that state ever since (Su 2020). Nevertheless, as Barop (2015:134) notes, the European colonial powers stuck together in Shanghai, in quiet mutual support, with France, Portugal, and the Netherlands never voting against Britain in any of the 14 sessions. The Shanghai Commission can be understood in this sense as a pivotal moment: looking back to the Opium Wars and the trading relations between China and European empires; looking forward to a century of international co-operation on drug control with America increasingly at the helm.

The further significance of the Shanghai meetings lies in two features that, as we have seen, were fundamental to the purpose, remit, and parameters of the Commission. First, it was resolutely China-centric: as hosts, with the largest delegation, and as the focus of the proceedings (the opium question in the 'Far East'). Rather than China fading from importance in the story after the Opium Wars, it was at the heart of this most critical of moments in the origins of global drug prohibition. Second, although as Barop (2015) correctly argues, part of what the Commission accomplished was an international consensus about the immorality of the 'opium evil', at

---

[32] Ibid, pages 74–77.
[33] Ibid, page 78.

the same time it was also very clearly concerned with the economics of the opium trade. Perhaps the most heated session—the 11th on 23 February—sprang into life on the question of the revenue consequences of accelerating efforts to eradicate the trade and this underpinned discussions at most of the sessions. Both these features are critical elements within the 'initial conditions' for the creation of the international drug control system. Core to this book's thesis is that they have continued to shape and steer the development of the *exchangespace* for the global drug trade over the course of the century that has followed since that momentous month of discussions in Shanghai in early 1909.

After Shanghai

Almost as soon as the Shanghai report had been published, moves to set up a new international forum on opium, this time with the power to making binding resolutions, started to be made. In September 1909, the Americans wrote to all the Shanghai participants inviting them to an International Opium Conference (Eyffinger 2019:1690). The Netherlands offered to host the Conference at The Hague with a provisional opening date of 1 December that year. There followed a protracted series of preliminary talks about the scope and remit of the Conference, which went through 1910 and into 1911, leading to it being postponed twice, with the first meeting not taking place until 1 December 1911, exactly two years later than originally planned (Eyffinger 2019:1691–1692).

At the same time, the 1907 Anglo-Chinese Agreement also came up for renewal and this was the subject of negotiations between the parties in the second half of 1910, working towards a deadline of the end of the year. The negotiations were complex, however, and over-ran considerably, eventually concluding in May 1911 with the signing of a formal treaty. Newman (1989:544–551) provides an excellent account of the details of those negotiations. Perhaps two points are worth emphasising here. First, the question of how to ensure an orderly contraction of foreign imports of opium into China was a preoccupation for the British and the Indian administration throughout the talks. Whilst accepting the trade was scheduled to end by 1917, nevertheless they wanted to try to make the reductions leading up to eradication as predictable and phased as possible. This was, in essence, a matter of revenue planning and the Indian administration remained concerned about this even after agreement was reached, with the Viceroy complaining that 'we shall be in a nice financial mess in two or three years unless we find some new means to meet the deficit of our opium revenue' (quoted in Newman 1989:551). Second, it was also clear that the Chinese were still interested in exploring whether progress towards eradicating the opium trade could be further accelerated, just as they had been at the Shanghai Commission. Although they ended up sticking with the 1917 target, the continuing desire to get there as quickly as possible was notable, as was Britain's continuing reluctance to speed up.

One important aspect of the immediate backdrop, both to the preliminary talks about the meetings planned for The Hague and the renewal negotiations over the Ten-Year Agreement, was the very significant internal unrest within China at this time. In October 1911, sandwiched between the signing of the renewal treaty in May and the start of the first Opium Conference at The Hague in December, the situation reached a tipping point as the Qing Dynasty collapsed in what became known as the Xinhai Revolution. Historian Joseph Esherick (2012) provides an insightful evaluation of the significance of 1911, arguing that it launched China on a revolutionary course in the twentieth century. This course would eventually lay the foundations that would lead in the twenty-first century to China becoming the dominant power in the world system.

The significance of the 1911 revolution for the history of modern drug control has been significantly understated (for a partial exception, see Lowes 1966:9–10). The effective collapse of China, just a couple of years after it had been one of the major players in hosting the Shanghai Commission, fundamentally changed the dynamic of the international diplomacy that was shaping the nascent drug prohibition regime. It also had more direct impacts within China. Newman (1989:552) notes, for example, that whilst the new republican government expressed a desire to continue the opium reforms, it became difficult to enforce opium controls in some provinces as 'political insubordination' was increasingly common (see also Madancy 2000:240–243). There were also new flows of people to and from different parts of the republic, displaced by, or fleeing from, the continuing internal conflicts and these further compromised and complicated the capacity to control the opium trade in a consistent or sustained way. Collins (2018) argues that 'China's imperial collapse in 1911 served as the spark that ignited the drive towards a global regulatory system' (see also Windle 2013b). There was a widespread view within China that opium had weakened the country and hastened the collapse of Qing rule. Opium suppression was therefore an important priority for the new post-1911 republic.

Despite this, the continuing internal strife in China gradually eroded the capacity of the central government to control domestic opium cultivation in the provinces so that by 1917, when eradication was meant to be complete, it was growing again. This hardened the resolve of other countries to take steps to tighten controls on opium through international co-operation. By the 1930s, China would once again be at the centre of the global trade and in a fragile state of warlordism and civil war. On top of all this, the continuing decline of British imperial power and America's rise was shifting the balance on the international stage in favour of global regulatory controls.

So when the delegates from 12 countries sat down for the first meeting of the Opium Conference at The Hague on 1 December 1911, China was in a state of turmoil and entering an uncertain new phase that would provide an additional force propelling the establishment of a global drug control system. Over the course of the next two months, delegates met 26 times, with the concluding session taking place on 23 January 1912.[34] The scope of discussions extended beyond opium and morphine to include, for the first time, heroin and cocaine. The eventual recommendations sought to create a comprehensive system for controlling the manufacture, import, export, distribution, and retail of those substances (Eyffinger 2019:1692–1696). The Convention agreed at the Conference would prove to be highly influential and significant in the years to come.

Delegates reconvened at The Hague for a second Conference at the beginning of July 1913, on this occasion for a little over a week. This time there were delegates from 22 countries, illustrating the growing internationalisation of the drug control project. As Eyffinger (2019:1697–1702) explains in an insightful overview of the Hague meetings, little was achieved this time around, as the complexities of international diplomacy and of technical issues associated with the 'inverse ratification' process that had been created and agreed at the first Conference, dominated discussions. With matters still unresolved, it was agreed to hold a third Conference.

Delegates returned to The Hague for a third time in the middle of June 1914. There were now 27 powers represented at the Conference. They met six times over the course of just over a week and largely resolved the technical matters and other disagreements that had proved so difficult the previous summer (Eyffinger 2019:1708–1709). The final session took place on Thursday 25 June, concluding in the afternoon, with delegates generally

---

[34] National Archives. FO 405/419: China: International Opium Conference, The Hague, December 1911–January 1912; summary of the minutes; acts and documents.

optimistic about the progress that had finally been made. On the Sunday morning, 28 June, Archduke Franz Ferdinand was shot dead in Sarajevo, triggering the outbreak of the First World War. This would prove to be the driver that accelerated the establishment of the international drug control system. Signatories to the Paris Peace Treaties agreed in 1919 and 1920 also committed to implementing the substantive terms of the Opium Convention agreed in 1912 at the first Hague Conference. The newly-created League of Nations was tasked with co-ordinating the new international system. By the mid-1920s, there were nearly 60 parties signed up and in 1925 further international meetings on drug control took place in Geneva, for the first time including cannabis in their discussions. The global prohibition system we still have 100 years later in the 2020s was now largely in place.

As we have seen, then, the Shanghai meeting can be understood, in retrospect, as the pivotal moment in this story, as it connected the nineteenth-century conflicts over the opium trade in China with the agreements and commitments made at The Hague between 1911 and 1914 which would provide the template for the first iteration of the international drug control system. Contrary to what Collins (2022) calls the orthodox narrative, even at this most critical moment in the creation of drug prohibition, the Americans were in fact on the sidelines rather than at the centre and they remained so into the 1920s. They refused, for example, to join the League of Nations, based on concerns about loss of sovereignty, effectively absenting themselves from the principal international body in the field. They also walked out of the Geneva meetings, at which cannabis controls were discussed, and it would not be until 1937 that federal prohibition of cannabis would arrive in the United States. It is by viewing the origins of the international drug control system through the lens of China and Asia that we can most clearly see the initial conditions from which global prohibition was assembled.

It is also important to situate this key moment in our story of the origins of drug prohibition within the wider context of global history. As historian Adam Tooze (2014) argues in his book *The Deluge*, the First World War, and the decade that followed it, saw a fundamental remaking of the global order which has profoundly shaped the world we live in now in the 2020s. The assembly of an international system of drug control was in this sense one small part of this remaking, and so was shaped by the bigger picture of war and peace in the first three decades of the century. Central to Tooze's argument is the understanding that the world system is dynamic and inter-connected, meaning that we can only fully understand the trajectory of global historical development if we study that system as a whole. Western-centric perspectives will lead to partial and limited understanding. Indeed, as will be explored in this book's concluding chapter, seeing new possibilities for the future of drug control depends, in part, on understanding in historical context the changing place of key global actors like China within international society. To put it more sharply, in the Asian Century, work that focuses on China within the fields of international relations and world politics (e.g. Kaufman 2010, 2013) and global history (e.g. Frankopan 2015, 2018) is essential to any serious exploration of drug law reform that seeks to go beyond the limitations of ideas that frame North America as the heart of the matter. In other words, we must engage with what China scholar Rana Mitter (2021:161) has called the 'most important question in geopolitics today': what kind of global order does China want to create? And what implications could this have for the remaking of existing areas of international co-operation and co-ordination like global drug control? We will return to this question in the final chapter of the book.

Conclusion

It is perhaps the strangest, yet also most persistent, misinterpretation of the origins of today's global drug prohibition system to claim that prohibition was a Western, and especially American, invention. The pair of chapters in this part of the book have aimed to demonstrate that, from an historical perspective, this is a deeply flawed idea (see also Windle 2013a). The first opium prohibition was in China in 1729 and, as we have seen, in the nineteenth century it was Britain and other Western imperial powers who fought wars to sustain their ability to trade opium in China. The Peking Convention signed in 1860 at the end of the *Arrow* War in effect overturned China's prohibition and legalised the trade. It was then Asian countries, not only China, who were attempting to prohibit opium at the tail end of that century. In Japan, for example, the importation of opium was prohibited throughout the Meiji period (1868–1912). At the Shanghai meetings in 1909, the strongest pressure to ban the opium trade came from China, with full support from the Americans but more mixed and equivocal backing from European colonial powers like Britain, the Netherlands, and France. Although the Americans were undoubtedly important players both in Shanghai and at The Hague, it was arguably not until the post-1945 period that global prohibition truly became an American-led project (see Collins 2022). Interestingly, so far in the twenty-first century, the epicentre for the fragmentation of consensus on cannabis prohibition has also been North America (see Seddon and Floodgate 2020).

The historical analysis presented in this part of the book has some important implications for how we might understand prohibition's origin story. It requires us, first of all, to reject what Collins (2022:10) describes as the orthodox thesis of the international drug control system as a US-created global prohibition regime (e.g. Bewley-Taylor 1999). This means framing the story in a longer time-frame than is usual, that is, as a narrative arc that has developed over the course of closer to 200 years than 100. It also involves widening out the geographical perspective and, more specifically, recentring China and Asia in the story. Extending the ambit of the historical narrative in time and space in this way, opens up an alternative vista in which international trade and commerce, economic regulation, European colonial power, and the modernisation of China become the central driving forces in the dynamic that shaped the emergence of the global drug control apparatus that we see today.

We can make sense of this dynamic partly by understanding it as a complex networked system of the kind envisaged in Part I of the book. The *exchangespace* concept provides a set of intellectual resources for this analytical task. It will be recalled that one of the key ideas explored in Chapter 3 was that the initial conditions in a system could have very long-term impacts through the creation of path-dependent trajectories, as the system's development becomes set along certain channels. This explains how, for example, the colonial origins of drug prohibition have continued to manifest in contemporary drug policy, often in ways that are otherwise hard to explain (see Daniels et al 2021). Perhaps less visibly, but equally significantly, the nineteenth-century debates about trade and the need to protect revenue streams have echoes today in debates on cannabis regulation which revolve around the potential for job creation and economic growth (as well as the need to temper corporate power) (see Seddon and Floodgate 2020). Part of this book's thesis is that the centrality of China and Asia in those initial conditions has been largely forgotten, a branch of the genealogy that has simply been removed, and that this has limited our understanding both of where we are today and of the possibilities for the future. Although you would not know it from the drug policy research literature, for international drug law reformers in the 2020s it is arguable that China's Belt and Road initiative is at least as important to understand as, say, cannabis regulation in Canada.

What is also evident from the historical analysis in this part of the book is that this evolving *exchangespace* was continually shaped by the 'play of power' that Hancher and Moran (1989/1998) referred to in their classic essay on 'regulatory space', as discussed in Chapters 2 and 3. Power and politics are everywhere in the origin story of prohibition, from the brute military force of the Opium Wars, to the diplomatic 'battles' at the international meetings in Shanghai and at The Hague. In the next part of the book, the focus shifts to this political realm. Just as Part I attempted to deconstruct prevailing theoretical approaches to drug policy and Part II the same for historical orthodoxies, Part III seeks to develop new ways of thinking about the politics of drugs and drug control. The argument developed in the first chapter of Part III is that rather than politics being a distraction from or impediment to drug policy reform, something to be evaded or neutralised, in fact the drug question needs to be understood as being inherently political. Embracing this political dimension, through a serious and rigorous engagement with the intellectual tools of political science, is a critical and essential foundation for any programme of reform. Having established the need to embrace rather than deny the politics of drug policy, in the second of the chapters, the focus turns to exploring what a 'better politics' of drugs might look like and how it might be built. In other words, how can we create a genuinely deliberative drug politics that is informed and inclusive? As we will see, this is a difficult challenge which requires the drawing of intellectual resources not only from political science but also law, regulation studies, criminology, and sociology.

PART III

POLITICS

6

The politics of drug control

Introduction

Drug policy is a deeply political arena. It tends to attract more heat than light and mainstream politicians usually steer away from engaging too closely or directly with debates about moving from the policy status quo. The political climate for the drug question is undoubtedly hot! In the face of this heat, academics and reform advocates typically decry politicisation and press for more scientific and evidence-based policy-making. Indeed, calls to move away from 'ideologically-driven' drug policy have become a key trope in reform discourse. In one sense, this seems like a reasonable and rational line to take. Why would it be appropriate or conducive to good policy-making to allow ideological considerations to have any influence? This part of the book, however, takes a very different view by arguing that this position is fundamentally misguided and involves a serious misrecognition of what is going on within the politics of drug control and drug law reform.

It has already been shown theoretically, in Part I of the book, how drug policy-making is about regulatory choices that are always also choices about political ends and values. In Part II, we have seen how power and politics are embedded in the historical foundations of international drug control. In Part III, the argument will now be developed that it is through embracing (rather than denying or lamenting) the intertwining of politics and drug policy that more productive ways forward will be found. This chapter focuses on exploring and elaborating on the question of what exactly is at stake when drug laws and drug policy become a matter of political contestation. The next chapter then moves to considering what a 'better politics' of the drug question might look like and how it could be achieved. The overarching goal of this part of the book, building on Parts I and II, is to re-animate the project of drug law reform with some new intellectual resources and fresh ideas. Continuing a thread running through

Rethinking Drug Laws. Toby Seddon, Oxford University Press. © Toby Seddon 2023.
DOI: 10.1093/oso/9780192846525.003.0006

the whole book, a key dimension of this re-animation is a decolonising impulse, moving away from viewing Europe and North America as the centre of the drug policy world and shifting our gaze eastwards towards China and Asia.

The chapter proceeds as follows. It begins by providing a brief summary overview of some relevant social science work on the concept of ideology and on ideological contestation. This sets out an important conceptual and theoretical context for the rest of the chapter, as well as providing the basis for a sharp counter to the commonly-expressed notion in the drug policy field that 'ideology' is a barrier to progressive reform, a barrier which should be stripped out from policy discourse. It focuses in particular on Michael Freeden's influential work and on its creative extension and development by Loader and Sparks in the context of questions of crime and security. Loader and Sparks provide an especially productive framework for thinking through how we should understand the political contestation of drug policy. In conclusion, it is argued that the call for a non-ideological scientific approach to drug policy is itself an ideological position and one which is, arguably, conservative, in the sense that it seeks to remove the space for the democratic deliberation of policy by making it a matter for 'experts'. This points towards Chapter 7 which explores this question of how we might create a 'better politics' of drug control, as a precursor to drug law and policy reform.

Ideology and ideological contestation

There is a rich, broad, and deep body of social science scholarship exploring the concept of ideology. Gerring's (1997) dizzyingly detailed and comprehensive tour of the field makes at least one point abundantly clear: ideology is a capacious and malleable concept. A more recent mapping by Maynard (2013) reiterates this point but provides a slightly more secure purchase on it. Perhaps the most useful part of Maynard's map is his very clear demarcation of different methodological approaches to ideology, which he divides into three broad categories: conceptual, discursive, and quantitative. All three, of course, have their uses but for this project the category of conceptual approaches provides the most productive framing. So what does Maynard mean by this?

Fundamentally, for Maynard (2013:301), conceptual approaches view ideologies as 'systems of ideas', meaning they can be studied for their ideational content. In other words, ideologies are about political thinking as an underpinning for political behaviour (2013:302). He notes the connections between conceptual approaches to ideology and some approaches to intellectual history, notably the 'Cambridge School' associated with Quentin Skinner and the *Begriffsgeschichte* tradition of conceptual history first developed by German historian Reinhart Koselleck. These connections are important as they show how politics is inextricably linked with processes of historical change in society, a theme that was explored at length across the two chapters in Part II of the book. Skinner, in particular, is interested in how sets of ideas, concepts, and conventions are central to the various dynamics of socio-political contestation, challenge, and legitimation that influence social change.

An extremely interesting paper by Maynard and a cross-disciplinary group of collaborators makes a further important theoretical connection by framing ideologies as complex systems (Homer-Dixon et al 2013). The question they explore is how we can unpick the causal mechanisms through which ideologies 'shape social and political behavior' (2013:338). They argue that the key to this puzzle is to understand the 'systems of ideas' studied in conceptual approaches to ideology as complex systems. They define ideologies as systems of ideas constituted by networks of concepts embedded in networks of people, and characterised by all the distinctive features associated with complex systems (non-linearity, emergence, path dependence, and so on) (2013:342–343). It will be recalled that the *exchangespace* concept developed in Part I was also rooted in ideas about complexity and complex systems, including the emphasis on market-regulation relations as based on networks of networks.

Maynard's way of thinking about ideology thus provides a theoretical basis for seeing the three foundational parts of this book—theory, history, politics—as woven tightly together. This is a fundamental insight which underpins the structure of the book's argument. In the context of this chapter and the next, in particular, it explains why the political dimension of drug control is not a superficial or distracting side-show—to be overcome by rationality and science—but rather a core element for any fully comprehensive and coherent analysis.

The final strand of conceptual approaches to ideology that Maynard (2013) describes in his mapping exercise is the work of political scientist Michael Freeden, which he argues has been amongst the most influential in this large and diverse body of social science work on ideology. Freeden is also a key reference point for Loader and Sparks in their important analyses of the politics of crime and security (e.g. Loader and Sparks 2016). It is therefore worth looking at Freeden's work in some detail, particularly what he describes as the morphological analysis of ideology.

Freeden's contributions to the field span several decades, going back to the 1980s. His 1996 book, *Ideologies and Political Theory*, is a major statement of his distinctive approach to the question of what is meant by the concept of ideology and how it relates to the social and political world (Freeden 1996). Another landmark contribution that is drawn on here is his 2013 essay on 'The Morphological Analysis of Ideology' (Freeden 2013). A starting point for Freeden is that rather than viewing ideology in a pejorative light as a tool for domination, he sees it more neutrally as simply a standard or typical feature of politics and society. It is part of how we make sense of the world, how we act within it, and how we seek to influence others to behave. Ideological contestation is the continuing competition over the ideational content of this political thinking.

It follows from this that, as Loader and Sparks (2016:319) put it, 'there is something profoundly impossible in the idea that it is possible to inhabit the world outside of political categories'. In other words, there is no such thing as a non-ideological position in the social world and one cannot stand outside ideology by claiming an exclusive allegiance to 'evidence' or 'pragmatism' or 'science'. This means that one of the most important analytical tasks is to uncover and examine the ideological positions that underpin different approaches to thinking, talking, and acting in relation to the drug question. Loader and Sparks (2016:320) term this a 'political mode of evaluation' of different approaches to policy. We will return to the question of how this type of evaluation might proceed shortly.

This gives us a good initial flavour of the approach. In his 2013 essay, Freeden sets out seven features of the morphological analysis of ideology that are worth briefly summarising here, in order to flesh this out and develop a fuller understanding of his approach. The *first* feature, as we have already noted, is that ideology is considered as a 'ubiquitous and permanent form of political thinking' (2013:116), rather than something exceptional, occasional, or extreme. The *second* is that ideology emerges 'at all levels of social articulation', cutting 'across the distinction between elite, professional, and vernacular political thinking' (2013:116). This is a critical point, as many traditional forms of political analysis proceed as if ideology is almost exclusively a matter to be studied by looking at what elites say or think. The *third* feature is that it sees the political concept as the 'fundamental building block of political thought' (2013:116), so that ideologies are constituted by particular patterns or constellations of those concepts. The notion of morphology emphasises that there is a significance in examining specific patterns or structures of political concepts, a point that will be expanded on shortly. The *fourth* is that it focuses on the micro-level through an interpretive perspective that aims to uncover the detailed and nuanced patterns of actual thinking 'in the world'. This contrasts with macro approaches which view ideologies as grand narratives with totalising effects that tend to efface nuance (2013:117). The *fifth* sees 'ideologies as discursive competitions over the control of public political language', control which shapes political decisions and 'subsequent actions by and for collectivities' (2013:117). In other words, ideologies are not simply discursive; they have practical and material effects. The *sixth* feature is that this approach focuses on the 'everyday manifestations' of political thinking through careful and attentive engagement with political thinking, expression, and discourse in all its forms and varieties at all levels. The *seventh*, and final, feature is that ideology is not viewed as obscuring or masking or distorting political discourse; rather, ideologies are the 'actual modes of political thinking, whether expressed in the vernacular' or by political elites or by theorists (2013:118).

The notion of morphology places an emphasis on patterns and structure. For Freeden (2013:124), this opens up a way of seeing ideologies not as 'locked into an unyielding configuration' but rather as continuously changing and evolving through processes of contestation and competition, as well as renewal. This, again, provides another point of articulation with the *exchangespace* concept which, it will be recalled, is rooted in the idea that market-regulation relations are always dynamic rather than static. To help explain and make sense of this idea of ever-changing configurations of political concepts, Freeden introduces the distinction between core, adjacent, and peripheral concepts (2013:125). *Core* concepts are the most durable and change, if at all, at the slowest pace. They can be understood as essential or indispensable for maintaining the coherence and stability of an ideology (as a system of ideas). *Adjacent* concepts are less critical, and do not appear in all instances of the ideology, but nevertheless are important adjuncts to the core. They are very often part of an ideology's configuration of concepts but their positioning and the relationship between them is more susceptible to change. *Peripheral* concepts are more marginal and ephemeral and change at a much faster pace. They may disappear entirely, alter position, or even move closer to the core. Distinguishing these three types of concepts helps us to understand how ideologies typically have a blend of continuity and change, characterised by familiarity but rarely staying the same.

Freeden's approach provides a useful framework through which we might engage in the type of 'political mode of evaluation' that Loader and Sparks (2016) call for. They argue that Freeden's notion of ideology generates the outline for a research programme for such political evaluations, consisting of three key elements (Loader and Sparks 2016:325–326). First, an analysis that begins 'from the inside', in the sense of recovering and decoding the various actors' utterances and claims *on their own terms*. In other words, the aim is not to appraise or judge but rather to understand what people are saying and, following Skinner, what they are doing in saying it. Second, an evaluation that understands ideologies as group activities that are 'action-building'. There are multiple actors with diverse roles and based in varied agencies or institutions, all of whom contribute to ideological production, and the claims they make speak to specific groups' hopes and fears and mobilise support for different ways of responding to them. This notion of 'action-building' incidentally shares something in common with the Foucauldian governmentality analytic in which language is understood as an 'intellectual technology' which renders reality amenable to certain kinds of action (Rose et al 2006:89). Third, the evaluation also needs to proceed by appraising actors' claims in their social, cultural, and institutional contexts. It is the essence of political concepts that they are not free-floating but instead are socially anchored.

These understandings of ideology provide a way of engaging with, investigating, and making sense of the politics and political contestation of the drug question. The provocative claim being made, therefore, is that 'ideological politics is the appropriate arena for contesting and determining answers' to this question (Loader and Sparks 2016:318–319). In this sense, it allows us to redeem the concept of ideology as essential to the building of a better politics of drugs. The argument in this part of the book is that this 'better politics' is, in turn, a *sine qua non* for the development of radical and progressive drug law and policy reform. This turns on its head the conventional claim that it is politics and ideology that stand in the way of such reform. It is argued here that the entanglement of the drug question with ideological conflict is a phenomenon that needs to be understood rather than ignored. Freeden's work, as interpreted by Loader and Sparks, provides a concrete way of operationalising the concepts of politics and ideology in order to investigate this phenomenon in a rigorous empirical way.

The politics of drugs and drug control

Equipped with this understanding of politics and ideology, how can we begin to open up the 'black box' of the politics of drug control? Although it is commonplace—almost a cliché—to talk about the drug question as 'politicised' or 'political', exactly what that means is far less clear. As the previous section has started to suggest, to achieve critical clarity on this matter requires a focus on the nexus between the politics of the drug question and the wider sphere of political thinking. Drawing from Freeden, we know that it is impossible to step outside ideology and claim a non-ideological position on drugs. What we *can* do, as a step towards that elusive critical clarity, is to start to unpick what is at stake or what is involved in debates about drugs and drug control. Or, to put it another way, to ask where does all that 'heat' come from? What causes this heating up? How and why does it happen? As we will see, these are not straightforward questions to answer but asking them will undoubtedly move us closer to understanding what is going on.

To begin to engage with this challenge, I use three illustrative examples of aspects of the drug question which appear to be particularly potent in generating political heat. For each one, the aim is to provide only a brief sketch—a vignette—rather than a comprehensive analysis, in order just to illustrate how the political content of drug policy discourse can be brought more to the surface. The three vignettes are all on the theme of opium and opiates, partly to show how the politics of drug control is only loosely connected to the material nature of the substances themselves. The first revisits the nineteenth-century Opium Wars explored in Chapter 4, but from the perspective of a relatively recent incident. The second vignette looks at an aspect of the controversial heroin prescribing by Dr John Marks in England in the 1980s and early 1990s, an episode that at the time generated quite extraordinary political heat. The third examines the fentanyl crisis that has swept across parts of North America since 2013.

Vignette 1. Opium poppies

In the preface to historian Julia Lovell's outstanding book, *The Opium War*, she recounts an incident from November 2010, when UK Prime Minister David Cameron led a trade embassy to China (Lovell 2011:ix–xi). As Cameron and his large entourage arrived at a formal welcome ceremony

in Tiananmen Square in Beijing, they were allegedly asked by a Chinese
official to remove their Remembrance Day poppies. Online discussions
in China were angry, viewing the poppies as an insensitive reminder of
Britain's immoral imperial invasions in the nineteenth-century Opium
Wars. Lovell (2011:x) quotes one blogger asking rhetorically 'whose face is
the English prime minister slapping, when he insists so loftily on wearing
his poppy?'.

Cameron refused the request, of course, and a prime ministerial spokes-
person issued a statement emphasising the importance to Britain of com-
memorating her war dead. Newspapers in China and Britain expressed
some predictable outrage from each side, although responses more widely
were reportedly more nuanced. It later became less clear whether any official request to remove the poppies had actually ever been made. The 'poppy
controversy' soon passed but this curious diplomatic incident has some interesting things to tell us, from the perspective of the politics of drugs.

For historians, the echoes of the past sounded very loud. A trade mission to China, leading to a diplomatic incident shrouded in confusion and
misunderstandings, brought reminders of the Macartney embassy of 1793
and the Amherst embassy of 1816 (both of which were briefly discussed
in Chapter 4 as precursors to the first Opium War). Why, though, did the
wearing of poppies in Beijing in 2010—150 years after the end of the second
Opium War—cause such a set of responses? Here, we can see how in the
context of Sino-British relations, the drug question encodes, in a culturally
potent form, a series of concerns that are very clearly political and ideological, in the sense that Freeden uses those terms. Below, a couple of these
are briefly described.

The most striking aspect of the incident is that the poppy resonated so
strongly as a symbol in the context of official discussions about *trade* between Britain and China. Like Macartney and Amherst before him, David
Cameron arrived on Chinese shores in order to try to 'open up' China to
British trade. In a speech he gave on 10 November at Beida University in
Beijing, he began by describing how China was set to become the world's
biggest economy again at some point in the twenty-first century, noting this
was a position it had held in 18 of the previous 20 centuries. One passage in
his speech captured the core of his message:

> Britain is the country that argues most passionately for globalisation
> and free trade. Free trade is in our DNA. And we want trade with China. As
> much of it as we can get.

Now selling engineering products and financial services, rather than chests of opium, the British position was nevertheless not so different from two centuries before. The anger provoked in 2010 by the British party's poppy-wearing was partly driven by the place of the Opium Wars in China's cultural history and the *power* dynamic between the two countries. For China, the first Opium War marked the beginning of a 'century of humiliation' that lasted until the proclamation of the People's Republic of China in 1949 following the communist revolution. The symbol of the poppy, as a reminder of this humiliation, was perhaps not surprisingly felt by some Chinese to be a slap in the face by the 'lofty' British Prime Minister. The additional frisson in 2010, of course, was that the tables were now turned in terms of the relative power of the two countries. In the nineteenth century, the great imperial power of the British had forced the Chinese at gunpoint to accept the opium trade, whilst in the twenty-first century Britain was coming to Beijing to beg for trading agreements with a global economic superpower. These twin dynamics of trade and power remain closely connected to the politics of international drug policy.

The notion of humiliation is important and we see how this resonates at different levels, including in the vernacular of political discourse within the blogosphere. This points to how drug politics is often partly about international relations and the place of different nations within international society and that this does not solely apply to elite discourse. China's position in the world order has been troubled and contentious, from a Chinese perspective, for a very long time. Perhaps the clearest example of this is the notion of Unequal Treaties—that is, agreements made under conditions of coercion—which was rooted in the signing of the Treaty of Nanjing in 1842 at the end of the first Opium War but become a central theme of Sun Yat-sen's[1] dealings with foreign powers in the period after the end of the First World War until his death in 1925 (Wang 2003). The sharp sense of being treated as inferior by Western powers—and the absolute unacceptability of this—clearly remains strong even into the twenty-first century, and is deeply connected for the Chinese with the history of the opium trade and opium control.

---

[1] Sun Yat-sen was a political leader and philosopher in the tumultuous period of Chinese history in the first three decades of the twentieth century. He served as Provisional President of the Republic of China for the first two months of 1912 and later as leader of the Kuomintang (the Chinese National Party). See Schiffrin (1968).

The vignette points us then towards seeing how important trade, power, and international relations are to the politics of drugs. This plays out in different ways in different geographical contexts and it is essential to pay attention to these variations. Discourse about drug law reform will often resonate very differently in, for example, China, Afghanistan, or Colombia, compared to, say, the Netherlands, Spain, or Canada. The annual political dance in Vienna at the meeting of the UN Commission on Narcotic Drugs offers a small window into one strand of this complex aspect of drug politics (e.g. Fordham 2012). What the vignette illustrates is that this is not only about state actors and representatives but also 'everyday manifestations' of political thinking, in the sense described by Freeden (2013) in his account of ideology.

Vignette 2. Heroin reefers

As we briefly saw in Chapter 3, Dr John Marks was a consultant psychiatrist, working in Liverpool and some neighbouring towns at the sharp end of the heroin epidemic that had swept through parts of England and Scotland in the 1980s. Through his prescribing of injectable opiates, including heroin, he had become in just a few short years a highly controversial figure not only within the febrile local politics of responding to the drug problem in Merseyside but also nationally and internationally (see Seddon 2020b). But in 1989, he had a new idea. Given that many of the so-called 'new heroin users' of the time tended to start by smoking rather than injecting heroin, he began to think that prescribing injectables was not enough.

After exploring various ways of producing a smokable or inhalable form of heroin, local Liverpool-based pharmacist Jeremy Clitherow found a viable method, by dissolving heroin in chloroform and injecting the solution into a cigarette. As the chloroform rapidly evaporated, it left behind a green-tinged heroin-infused cigarette, which Marks and colleagues called 'heroin reefers' (Marks et al 1991). The same process was used to produce reefers containing methadone, cocaine, and dexamphetamine. The original idea was to use herbal cigarettes but some found these unpalatable. Clitherow's pharmacist colleagues were, however, not willing to supply tobacco cigarettes and these had to be provided by the client. Although there was no formal evaluation of the reefer experiment, it was claimed that local data showed a substantial reduction in the proportion of clients injecting and that it was therefore effective as a harm reduction measure (Marks and Palombella 1990).

The reefers Marks prescribed came to much wider public attention in December 1992 when the CBS documentary series *60 Minutes* aired a programme including a segment on Marks' work. In one part, presenter Ed Bradley spoke to Jeremy Clitherow in his pharmacy in Liverpool:

Ed (voiceover): And heroin isn't the only stuff to come in and out of here. Clitherow also sells prescriptions for cocaine and that is 100% pure free base cocaine. In other words, crack.
Ed (to Jeremy): So, in fact, when you are putting cocaine in here you are actually making crack cigarettes?
Jeremy: Yes.
Ed: In America that has a very negative connotation, but not for you?
Jeremy: Depends on which way you look at it. If they continue to buy on the street, whether it is heroin, methadone, crack, or whatever, sooner or later they will suffer from the merchandise they are buying. I want to bring them into contact with the system and let them get their drug of choice, if the physician agrees and prescribes it in a form which won't cause their health such awful deterioration.

The 'negative connotation' Ed Bradley alludes to has been extensively written about (e.g. Reinarman and Levine 1997, 2004). The mythologies about crack cocaine as uniquely addictive and destructive were pervasive in the United States in the 1980s and 1990s and became particularly controversial because of their racial dimension (crack use and trafficking being associated more with African Americans). The disparities in policing and sentencing between crack and powder cocaine underpinned what came to be seen as a major engine for racial injustice (see Sklansky 1995). As drug policy historians have repeatedly observed, *race* and racial politics have frequently been intertwined with the politics of drug control. Indeed, I have previously argued that this is encoded in the foundations of the drug concept and the origins of prohibition (Seddon 2016). This is important to understand as it tells us that part of what is at stake in the heated climate of drug policy debate is a wider discourse about race and difference. As Seth (2020) has recently shown in an important essay on the history of racism, there is an ongoing and unresolved debate amongst theorists and historians about whether contemporary racism is a product of Western modernity or else has a longer pre-modern history. As we have seen, the conceptual triangle of drug/drug problem/drug control is certainly a phenomenon of modernity shaped in part by imperial and colonial histories and it is this historical foundation that has bound the politics of race and drugs so tightly together for the last 150 years.

Another exchange in the *60 Minutes* programme is also illuminating:

Ed (voiceover): Addicts pick up their prescriptions twice a week from his neighbourhood pharmacy. And how does this affect his other customers?

Jeremy: The patient who comes in to pick up his prescription of heroin in the form of reefers would be indistinguishable from a patient who picks up any other medication. The prescription is ready and waiting and they pick it up just as they would pick up their aspirin or bandages.

Ed's question implies that the people coming to the pharmacy to collect heroin reefers— 'addicts', as he calls them—are likely to be disturbing in some way for other customers. Clitherow rejects the implication. The question points to another aspect of the politics of drugs that Marks' work stirred up. By focusing on making treatment as accessible as possible, by removing barriers like the requirement for supervised on-site consumption, and by developing innovations like heroin reefers to make his service as attractive as possible, he turned the conventional approach on its head. The latter could be characterised as having tight restrictions on access, imposing controls on client behaviour, and punishing infractions (see Bacon and Seddon 2020). One of the reasons Marks' unconventional ethos was so controversial, not just in the press but also with colleagues in the drug field, was that he stepped right over the line usually drawn between 'deserving' and 'undeserving' recipients of state-funded care and support. This distinction has a long history in the realm of social and welfare policy and an equally long one in the context of drug policy, where there has always been ambivalence about how deserving of help 'addicts' are. As historian Virginia Berridge (1979:77) notes, as far back as the nineteenth century the concept of addiction was a hybrid of 'disease *and* vice' (emphasis in original). This ambivalence remains an important force within the politics of drugs, and is linked to the wider politics of *welfare*. Prescribing heroin reefers on the NHS—partly justified by Marks because they would be more pleasurable for consumers than methadone syrup and therefore would keep users engaged with the service—was deeply challenging as a result.

Vignette 3. Fentanyl tablets

The story of human engagement with opium can be told in many ways. One obvious trajectory over the last 200 years has been the ever-increasing potency of opiates and opioids, from morphine in the nineteenth century, to heroin in the twentieth, and now to fentanyl in the twenty-first, a trajectory shaped in part by the emergence of laboratory chemistry and its later industrialisation (see Morris 2015). When morphine was first isolated in 1804, as the active alkaloid in the opium poppy, it was considered to be six times more potent than opium. Later that century, heroin was first synthesised and has been assessed to be up to five times more potent than morphine (Reichle et al 1962). Fentanyl, a synthetic opioid, is up to 100 times more powerful than morphine (Vardanyan and Hruby 2014) and there are several analogues of fentanyl that are even stronger (e.g. carfentanil is 100 times more powerful than fentanyl itself). At each step, this ratcheting up of potency has significantly impacted on the scale and nature of problems presented.

One of the most insightful observers of the North American drug situation, Dan Ciccarone, has argued that the United States has been experiencing a deep and prolonged opioid overdose crisis since 1999 (Ciccarone 2019, 2021). The first wave primarily involved prescription opioids like oxycodone and hydrocodone, whilst the second wave added a resurgent heroin problem to the mix. It is the third wave that has proved to be the most deadly, with the rapid spread of fentanyl (and analogues) since 2013 creating a serious crisis of drug-related deaths. As Pardo et al (2019) chart in extensive detail, the impact of fentanyl in those markets where it has achieved a foothold has been dramatic: quickly supplanting heroin as the dominant substance in circulation and significantly increasing rates of fatalities and non-fatal poisonings. Reuter et al (2021) speculate that we may be on the brink of a transformative moment or tipping point in which heroin could be replaced by fentanyl (and other synthetic opioids) in the global market, just as heroin previously replaced opium. They explore some of the consequences there may be of such a transformation, both for consumer markets and for the supply side in countries like Afghanistan.

The politics of the fentanyl crisis have been illuminating. At one level, it has been yet another version of the story of race and drugs. Reversing (and contrasting with) the representations of and responses to the crack problem, the majority of fentanyl consumers have been represented as white and the problem has largely been seen as a public health crisis.

The difference between the policing/enforcement response to the crack problem and the more health-oriented one to fentanyl has been widely ascribed to race (Johnston 2020). James and Jordan (2018) argue that in the context of the United States there has in fact been a double-erasure of the experience of black communities. On the one hand, the existence of any current opioid problem within those communities has been largely overlooked as the focus is almost exclusively on the white population. At the same time, the claim that the contemporary opioid crisis is novel and unprecedented ignores the heroin epidemics in the 1960s and 1970s that largely affected black communities in urban areas (and which were responded to in a considerably more punitive and less compassionate way than today's suburban 'white' drug problem).

But the politics of the opioid and fentanyl crisis are even more complex than this sadly familiar story of race and racism. Historian David Herzberg's (2020) book *White Market Drugs* excavates a critical fault line that has run throughout the history of the last two centuries of opioid use and along which periodic earthquakes have occurred. In some ways, this fault line is one of the most fundamental aspects of the politics of the drug question and Herzberg's insightful narrative skewers it more sharply perhaps than anyone has managed since David Courtwright's (1982) earlier classic *Dark Paradise*. Herzberg's focus is on the long history of addiction to legal pharmaceuticals in the United States—from morphine in the nineteenth century, to Quaaludes in the 1970s, to OxyContin in the 2000s—which he argues has been largely hidden from view, compared to the high visibility of the actually much smaller problem of addiction to illicit drugs. In the United Kingdom, dependence on pharmaceuticals has been similarly neglected, with the main exception of some feminist researchers who have pointed to the medicalisation of 'female problems' (e.g. Ettorre 1992). Herzberg argues that this relative invisibility has been accomplished by constructing clear distinctions between 'pharmaceuticals' and 'drugs' and between 'medicine' and 'vice'. Critically, he states that these distinctions are created rather than 'natural' (indeed, often the different labels are applied to substances that are chemically the same) and the boundaries between them change over time. This boundary-work is the 'subject of intense political conflict' (2020:3). The actors in this conflict include regulators (at both federal and state levels), consumers, politicians, doctors, pharmacists, professional associations, lawyers, activists, and, of course, the pharmaceutical industry. The fentanyl crisis is the latest instalment in this long narrative.

The politics of the fentanyl crisis involves a similarly broad cast of actors who are involved in coalitions, conflicts, and, above all, pursuing their own interests as they see them. Braithwaite and Drahos (2000) captured this, from a regulatory perspective, in their magisterial book *Global Business Regulation*. In one of their 13 case studies, they argue that the broad terrain of drug regulation—defined as the entire enterprise across 'drugs', intoxicants, and 'pharmaceuticals'—emerged historically from a progressive splitting into several separate regulatory regimes, with the international drug control system as simply one of these regulatory branches. Like Herzberg, they see the ever-changing contours of these regimes, and their boundaries and intersections, as the product of political contests between multiple actors operating within webs of influence. These contests are, of course, usually unequal, and the particular power and influence of the pharmaceutical industry is a critical element in the narrative, not only historically but still today. In a further twist on the story of this crisis, much of the imported fentanyl is believed to be produced in facilities in China, an issue that has been the subject of continuing US-China talks (Greenwood and Fashola 2021). In this way, the 'local' problem in North America is connected with a transnational issue that requires us to broaden our vision.

The political terrain of the drug question

These three vignettes have given a concise introduction to some of the major domains of the politics of drug control. In this section, this is developed a little further by drawing out some common themes. Again, the purpose here is not to present a comprehensive account but to give an overview of the political terrain occupied by drugs, as a means of starting to clarify what is at stake in debates about drug policy and drug law reform. Connecting this terrain with the theoretical account in Part I, this overview is set out in terms of the spheres of states, markets, and citizens, that is, in terms of market-regulation relations. These are presented separately but, of course, it is fundamental to the book's theoretical approach that these spheres are not simply deeply connected but should be understood as different aspects of the same thing. The political terrain within the drug control *exchangespace* is a complex system constituted by networks of ideas embedded in networks of people and networks of institutions, creating a web that spans across levels from local to global (Homer-Dixon et al 2013).

States

If we begin with states and their interactions with other states, we know from Part II of the book that the history of drug control from its creation at the start of the twentieth century has been built on relations between nations. As the first vignette illustrated, events at this level tend to unfold at a slow pace, reverberating across decades and sometimes even centuries. Lovell (2011:xi) claims, for example, that the Opium Wars have been 'haunting Sino-Western relations for almost two centuries'. This also shows how the forces shaping international drug control can be traced back to long before it was created. We might even say that international relations, conceived in a broad sense, is a major part of the background materials from which the drug control system was first forged. In the 2020s, the system continues to play out at this level, primarily on the stage of the United Nations.

Over the last two or three centuries, we have seen a repeated political template in which the interests of Western—often European—empires, often centring on trade, shape the 'play of power' within the *exchangespace* at this level. The Opium Wars explored in Chapter 4 offer one clear example but there are many others. The story, for example, of the coca leaf and cocaine in the Andean regions of Bolivia, Columbia, and Peru can be framed in this way. Historian Paul Gootenberg (2019) provides an outstanding historical synopsis to which interested readers are referred (see also Gootenberg 2009). In brief, he traces the story back to the conquest of the Incas by the Spanish in the sixteenth century and then maps the ways in which this eventually led to the American-driven 'war on cocaine' in the 1980s which proved so ruinously damaging to the region, and then on to the more recent counter-movements in Bolivia and Peru to reclaim the legitimate place of the coca leaf in Andean culture. The story is long and complex but it is impossible to understand without seeing it as embedded in a bigger narrative of international relations, revolving around power, empires, and geopolitics.

This is one way, also, of understanding the importance of race as one of the long arcs of development in the evolution of constructions of drugs and the drug problem. As the vignettes show, race (re-)emerges time and again in different guises and forms and never seems to leave the terrain of drug politics. We can probably fairly readily identify this in the context of issues like disproportionality in drug law enforcement and sentencing which has been repeatedly established as a significant driver of racial injustice (e.g. Shiner et al 2018). The Black Lives Matter social movement that emerged in 2013 illustrates how culturally and politically potent these concerns about

race and policing continue to be (Loader 2021), concerns which are inseparable from debates about drug law reform. Indeed, drug law reform non-
governmental organisations (NGOs) like Release, Transform, and the Drug
Policy Alliance (DPA) increasingly foreground race in their work. One of
the themes of this book is that contemporary concerns about race and drug
law enforcement are rooted in a much longer process of historical development that begins with empires and colonialism.

The colonial forces which are part of the origin story of international
drug prohibition have continued to exert a powerful influence. One place
that we see this effect today is in the way that drug law reformers, policy-
makers, and drug policy scholars continue to turn their gaze most readily
to Europe and North America, as if this is where the global heart of the
matter is still to be found. There is a degree of ignorance about what is going
on across the Global South (for an honourable exception, see Coomber
and South 2004) and a relative lack of interest in ideas and knowledge that
come from outside Northern universities. Why, for example, is there so
much focus in the research literature on studies of the regulation of commercialised cannabis markets in California or Colorado but so little on,
for instance, the reasons for the decline in Morocco of the cultivation of
the traditional *kif* cannabis variety? Why so much research on the fentanyl
crisis in North America but so little on addressing the 'other' opioid crisis
with tramadol that has swept across West Africa? Why so little attention
to thinking about how we might protect the rights of indigenous people in
places like Bolivia or India or Jamaica (where long-established cultural and
religious practices involve plants that are internationally controlled)? Why
is so much of the research done from within what Braithwaite (2021:32)
has called the 'imperial disciplines' of the Global North, like economics or
criminology, rather than interdisciplinary social science? The need to step
outside these Northern and Western frames of thinking is essential. This
is why drug law reform needs to be animated by a decolonising agenda, in
which Eurocentric and Western-centric perspectives on policy and knowledge production are decentred. A core theme of this book is that a major
part of how we should do this is by looking East to Asia and, in particular,
to China, which has a distinctive place in the past, present, and future of the
drug question that generally goes unrecognised.

Markets

Central to the theoretical discussions in Part I of the book was the understanding that drugs are commodities which are produced, distributed,

exchanged, and consumed in markets. Unsurprisingly, issues relating to markets and economics—trade, profit, commercialisation—run through the drug discourse. Current debates, for example, about liberalising cannabis markets (see Seddon and Floodgate 2020) are infused with concerns about whether corporate power can be adequately controlled, with multinational companies seeing enormous commercial opportunities opening up. In the United Kingdom, a new eco-system of cannabis lawyers, lobbyists, advocacy groups, and consultants has rapidly grown in the last few years in anticipation of regulatory change and the potential for profit-making (Gornall 2020). Concerns expressed by anti-reformers about 'Big Marijuana' potentially repeating the egregious behaviour of 'Big Tobacco' can generally be dismissed as hyperbolic propaganda but, nevertheless, point to an important aspect of the challenge for post-prohibition cannabis regulation. As we have seen, we can trace this economic dimension all the way back to the Opium Wars which economist Jeffrey Sachs (1999:91) once described as the 'first conflict of the modern capitalist era... fought to make the world safe for free trade in narcotics'.

According to political scientist Jonathan Kirshner (2003) 'money is politics' and this is profoundly true in the context of drugs. Drugs are consumable commodities which cease to exist after consumption. Money therefore serves a critical purpose as the means by which value is captured at different points in the supply chain. The distributive consequences that flow from different approaches to regulating those supply chains, and the value-capture that happens across them, are deeply political. We see multiple examples of this, from concerns about the impact of drug control interventions on poor coca leaf farmers in the Andean region (Dávalos and Dávolos 2020) to debates about the need for investment in social equity in the US states that have legalised cannabis markets (Kilmer and Neel 2020). Trying to disentangle regulation, markets, and politics from each other is simply an impossible task. This entanglement is what is described theoretically by the *exchangespace* concept.

The fentanyl vignette illustrated the deep significance of the legal pharmaceutical industry and its pursuit of profit to the drug question. But the drug trade also becomes enmeshed with legitimate businesses and the formal economy in other ways, directly through the mechanism of money. The laundering of the very large amounts of money generated by the trade necessitates the involvement of the institutions of the formal banking and financial systems. To give a well-known example, a decade ago one of the world's largest banks, HSBC, was implicated in laundering more than

US$800 million of proceeds from Mexican drug trafficking cartels, agreeing in 2012 to pay a fine of US$2 billion as part of a Deferred Prosecution Agreement (Hardouin 2017). The sheer scale of misconduct is astonishing but the critical point is that the financial interests in the drug trade are extremely dispersed and not just restricted to criminal economies. The ability of HSBC to evade prosecution was the product of a set of contested ideas about corporate conduct and responsibility, the relationship between governments and finance, the legitimate boundaries of criminal justice, and so on. And that terrain of contestation is inescapably political and, at the same time, tightly bound together with the (equally contested) debates about how we should regulate the international drug trade. The drugs-money-politics nexus is complex and entrenched (see van Duyne and Levi 2005).

Citizens

As the vignette about John Marks and heroin reefers nicely illustrated, the politics of drugs and the politics of welfare are often intertwined. In the most basic terms, this connection centres on the extent to which people who become addicted are responsible for their condition and, therefore, whether or not they are entitled to state help. Putting it even more bluntly, the argument runs like this: no one is forced to take heroin or crack for the first time, so why should society fund treatment services for those reckless or unwise people who end up addicted? As already noted, this is, of course, a particular twist on the old debate about the deserving and undeserving poor, a debate which is at heart about the parameters and limits of citizenship.

We can unpack this a little further. One element is about the concept of individual responsibility. What is the balance of responsibility for one's own fate? For a given individual how do we weigh the relative contributions of human agency and the constraints of social circumstances to the problems for which they seek the state's help? When those problems are related to addiction, the question of responsibility becomes even murkier, as the very concept involves the idea that an addicted person experiences a repeated 'loss of control' over their actions. Perhaps even more potent, in terms of generating political heat, is the matter of morality. What difference does it make to our calculus of responsibility that an individual is involved in criminality and that criminal acts (e.g. drug possession) are part and parcel of what they need help for?

In national contexts like the United Kingdom where drug treatment is provided by a state-run health service, these challenging questions of responsibility intersect with debates about resources and priorities. Is it right, for example, to spend money on prescribing methadone and providing counselling services to people addicted to heroin if we are at the same time having to ration expensive medication for cancer patients? This dilemma about priorities is in a sense the core of the deserving/undeserving dichotomy.

If, in the manner of Raymond Williams, we were to search for a cultural keyword that reveals something of how the politics of welfare and drugs coalesce around that dichotomy, it would be *dependency*. In a famous essay, Fraser and Gordon (1994) explore the concept in the context of political debates in the United States about welfare dependency. The political fear they analyse is the claim that by attempting to help the poor, in fact they become dependent on that support and lose the motivation to help themselves. They become locked into a life of existing on state support. It follows, so the argument goes, that generous welfare systems, despite their noble intentions, are actually counter-productive as mechanisms for addressing poverty. Such arguments form the terrain for heated ideological contestation about who 'deserves' help and what form that help should take. There is a parallel with drugs. Drug dependency is the problem but the political fear is that some forms of help—for example, indefinite prescribing of opiates like methadone—erode motivation to change and end up locking people into long-term state-funded dependency.

We can see, therefore, that this area of the politics of drugs is connected with several core elements of political ideologies (as systems of ideas), revolving in particular around understandings of what constitutes citizenship. What are the rights, obligations, and entitlements that accompany that citizenship? In what circumstances, if any, are they altered or eroded? With what consequences? And these are questions that are rightly considered to be of central importance in democratic deliberation, debate, and contestation, as they are partly about the appropriate scope and scale of the state itself.

Developing the theme of citizenship and the state, one of the longest-running strands of drug law reform discourse has centred on the question of civil liberties, that is, the freedoms that flow from the status of being a citizen. In the 1960s, this was a particularly powerful element within the reform movement (see Seddon 2020c). More recently, these issues have also been framed in the language of human rights (e.g. Bone 2020), which emphasises the broader idea of the universality of individual rights that accrue to all human beings regardless of citizenship. The fundamental question here is in what circumstances, and to what extent, should the state interfere in the private behaviour of citizens? Why should an individual's choice to alter their consciousness through consuming an intoxicant be a concern for the state at all?

These are fundamental matters. My aim here is not to adjudicate on these questions but just to sketch briefly what is at stake and give an illustration of how this manifests in debate and discourse on drug policy and drug law reform. Legal scholar Amber Marks (2019) provides a helpful analysis of the application of human rights law to cannabis consumption, which points us towards the key issues. She observes that much of the relevant case law is based on constitutional rights where the 'freedom to consume cannabis without State interference has been consistently situated within the right to privacy and associated personality rights, the objective of which is the protection of personal autonomy' (2019:218–219). The 'rights' question is then about the 'extent to which legal measures that interfere with autonomy ... can be justified as a proportionate means of achieving a legitimate objective' (2019:219). In several jurisdictions, the prohibition of personal cannabis consumption in private has been declared unconstitutional on this basis (e.g. a series of Supreme Court rulings in Mexico between 2015 and 2018, and rulings in 2018 by the Constitutional Courts in South Africa and Georgia). Strategic litigation has been a particularly effective reform strategy in Mexico, led over several years by México Unido Contra Delincuencia (MUCD), a Mexico-based campaigning NGO. Despite these successes in Mexico, South Africa, and elsewhere, the potential for rights-based litigation to serve as a tool for social change has been relatively underexplored in the context of drug law reform compared to some other policy domains. An interesting paper by Thornhill and Smirnova (2018) highlights the distinctive *political* impact of litigation through what they term its 'transformative, norm-producing' effects. There is considerable scope for litigation to be used more extensively as a politically-attuned mechanism for the advance of reform in the drug policy field.

These ideas of 'proportionality' and 'legitimate objectives' have technical definitions in public law and human rights jurisprudence (see Marks 2019:219–220; Ingram 2018). In effect, they involve the kind of weighing up of different interests that is the very stuff of politics and democratic debate. In the South African case, for example, the Constitutional Court explicitly asked whether the limits imposed on individuals in relation to cannabis were 'reasonable and justifiable in an open and democratic society based on human dignity, equality and freedom' (see Lubaale and Mavundla 2019).

The profoundly political nature of these questions of citizen-state relations and of individual rights and freedoms, which underpin thinking about drug control, could not be clearer.

Drug control is *politics*

Echoing Kirshner's claim that 'money is politics', it has been argued here that the drug question is so ineluctably political in nature that we can equally claim that 'drug control is politics'. This chapter has presented only a sketch of the terrain and is far from comprehensive but it should be clear that thinking about drugs is bound together with some of the most significant political ideas, from race to the welfare state to personal freedom. Indeed, following Loader and Sparks (2016:320), we might say that thinking about the drug question is deeply entangled with many of what they term the key 'concepts of modern political thought—order, authority, legitimacy, justice, democracy, citizenship, freedom, rights, obligation and so on'. In other words, far from politics in this field being about trivial matters drummed up by shallow populist politicians, the politics of drugs is, on the contrary, about profoundly important issues. (Criminologists with longer memories will note that Paul Rock (1977) said much of this many decades ago in his largely-forgotten edited collection *Drugs and Politics* but the fact that such a fine book is now scarcely remembered or cited perhaps makes the point most sharply that the politics of drugs and drug control has long been misunderstood.)

This is what is at stake when debates about drugs and drug control heat up. Indeed, this is precisely why there is often so much heat in this discourse. It is therefore imperative that we take the politics of drugs more seriously, that we challenge those who claim this is mere ideology, and that we bring our most powerful analytical tools to bear on the task. As has been shown in this chapter, a serious and sustained engagement with political science is essential, in order to ensure that we have the intellectual resources for this work. It is somewhat ironic that the rhetorical emphasis on science and evidence has often led to a focus on investigating relatively minor issues where the evidence is actually fairly settled (e.g. Heroin Assisted Treatment, which has repeatedly been shown to be effective but continues to be 'piloted' as if it is untested), whilst, at the same time, pretending that it is the political questions that are trivial or distracting. The argument in this chapter suggests that in fact the reverse is the case: it is the focus on science and evidence which has trivialised drug policy analysis whilst claiming to do the opposite. This is a provocative claim, of course, but if we persist with denying or downplaying the political nature of the drug question, we will continue to misrecognise and misunderstand what is happening in debates about drug policy and drug law reform. And this will not only condemn us to keep repeating the policy mistakes of the past but it will also limit the vocabulary we have available to articulate the case for change and reform.

Conclusion

This chapter has explored the question of what is at stake when drug laws and drug policy become a matter of political contestation. Rather than seeing the 'heating up' of debate as a problem to be avoided by 'scientific' researchers, it has tried to understand what this repeatedly observed phenomenon has to tell us sociologically, culturally, and politically. In doing so, it has drawn on a wide tradition of social science scholarship on ideologies, drawing in particular on Michael Freeden's contributions to this area, as well as the work of Loader and Sparks in the adjacent field of the politics of crime and security.

In a nutshell, the argument has been that political categories, ideas, and concepts are a ubiquitous feature of society, part of how we make sense of the world and find ways of living within it. It is therefore impossible to stand outside politics and take a non-ideological position in the social world. It follows that thinking about drugs and the drug question cannot evade or be separated from politics by claims to be following purely scientific or evidence-based positions. Using three brief policy vignettes as a starting point, the political terrain of drug control and drug law reform has been sketched out. It has been shown how thinking about drugs is entangled with a range of profoundly important political ideas. This guide or map helps us to make sense of precisely why debates about drugs are often so heated, as they are connected with questions that are the subject of deep ideological contestation. It also allows us to move beyond the simplistic, but common, claim that this heat is solely generated by moralising or populist politicians 'playing to the gallery'. Further, once these connections are made visible it becomes impossible to think of a depoliticised or apolitical way of talking about drugs. Indeed, it starts to become clear that appeals to science and evidence, and the denigration of political or ideological thinking, are actually themselves a form of political manoeuvre.

Developing this idea, how exactly might we understand the standard reformers' trope of 'evidence over ideology' as itself a political man-oeuvre? Drawing on Freeden, we can start by asking the Skinnerian question of what people are doing when they state this position. What is the 'action-building' objective of gathering support for this view? It appears that at least one goal is to place 'experts' and 'expertise' at the heart of policy-making. The impulse is to 'cool down' and depoliticise debates about the drug question and turn them into technical matters for experts. This was, in part, the original purpose of establishing the Advisory Council on the Misuse of Drugs on a statutory basis back in the early 1970s. As Loader and Sparks (2016:318) observe, this impulse has had parallels in the equally 'hot' field of crime and punishment. The idea of creating an autonomous body along the lines of an independent central bank to make policy decisions, or a scientific 'what works' clearing-house for evidence like NICE,[2] has had a strong appeal for some commentators who despair of what they see as the damaging dominance of a populist politics of crime. Loader and Sparks argue that the appeal of these types of technocratic governance is based, in part, on a claim that it is benefi-cial to strip out ideological contestation and conflict from the field and somehow insulate the policy process from politics.

The objection to this type of attempt at a technocratic insulation of policy is that it denies reality: to talk about crime and punishment (or drugs and drug control) is to engage with a whole set of wider political ideas about order, legitimacy, authority, and so on. It is simply impossible to reduce these down to questions about 'what works', as they are fundamentally pol-itical questions about the 'nature of the good society' (Loader 2010:83). And if we place these questions solely in the province of experts, then we undermine democratic politics itself by denying citizens the opportunity to participate in the democratic dialogue, debate, and disagreement that are an essential part of a healthy society. In other words, rather than trying to find ways to evade or remove politics, what we actually need is a way of developing a 'better politics' of drugs, that is, an 'inclusive and informed deliberative *politics*' of the drug question (Loader 2010:91, emphasis in ori-ginal). This will involve thinking through what public social science can

---

[2] The National Institute for Health and Care Excellence (NICE) is a public body origin-ally set up in 1999. Its purpose is to evaluate clinical effectiveness evidence in order to de-velop guidelines to inform decision-making about the commissioning of different treatment interventions.

be, and being imaginative about creating mechanisms for democratic deliberation, as a prelude to having societal conversations about drugs that are substantially different from those of the past. It is a challenge that is, of course, far from easy but outlining how this might start to be done is the task now of Chapter 7. As we will see, thinking democratically is a critical part of a strategy for meeting this challenge.

7
Democratic politics and drug law reform

Introduction

The argument developed in the previous chapter that the politics of drugs is something to be embraced and engaged with, rather than an obstacle to be overcome, leads us to a new question: how might a 'better politics' of drugs be achieved? Answering this, or beginning to, is the goal of this chapter. This is a challenging question, both intellectually and practically, and this chapter can only be a starting point in what needs to be a serious and thoroughgoing project. What the chapter aims to accomplish is to assemble some resources for building a new politics of drugs that can re-animate thinking about drug law and policy reform. As in previous chapters, the goal is ambitious and seeks to provide a basis for transformative rather than incremental change: it is a *new* politics that is sought, not yet another version of the old politics.

Part of the potential value for engaging with this question now, in the early 2020s, is that there is some evidence to suggest that we are at a moment of possibility for thinking differently about drugs and drug control. The accelerating spread of cannabis law reform over the last couple of decades continues and there are some grounds for believing that we may be approaching a tipping point for the fracturing of the global consensus on cannabis prohibition (see Seddon and Floodgate 2020). We must of course always be aware of the dangers of what Mike Savage (2009) has called 'epochalism' in social science—the tendency to diagnose indicators of social change too readily as harbingers of entirely new epochs or eras in society—but, at least for cannabis, we do seem to be *potentially* moving towards a new regulatory settlement (although it is far from certain that we will get there). In other spheres of drug policy, notably in relation to opiates, change is less apparent. Nevertheless, even there we might see the 2020s as

Rethinking Drug Laws. Toby Seddon, Oxford University Press. © Toby Seddon 2023.
DOI: 10.1093/oso/9780192846525.003.0007

offering at least the possibility of a watershed moment: if the calamitous and deadly opioid overdose crises of recent years are not enough to show how the policy status quo is failing, then we might ask what *would* it take?

An important preliminary matter is to ask what does a *better* politics of drugs mean? How do we define, evaluate, or measure this? After considering this, the chapter then proceeds by exploring two sets of interlinked questions. First, how can social scientists best intervene in societal debates and conversations about the drug question? In other words, how can social scientific knowledge be optimally used to shape social discourse and social action? This involves exploring and re-examining the much-discussed idea of 'public social science'. Second, through what deliberative and democratic mechanisms might we be able to build a new politics of drugs that could underpin transformative policy change? Distilling these questions into a single enquiry, and adapting from Loader and Sparks (2014:159), we might formulate the objective for this chapter as an exploration of how, in the context of the drug question, we might make 'intelligible and coherent' the idea of the production and dissemination of social science knowledge as a civic enterprise. The lesson from Chapter 6 is that this coherence will not come from the conventional route of trying to see social scientific evidence simply as an antidote to or replacement for the politicisation of policy. There needs to be a more thoroughgoing examination and consideration of what this knowledge or expertise actually is, what value it has, and how it can contribute to the advancement of policy on a question that must be recognised as inherently political. The final main section of the chapter looks at the international dimension of politics, reconnecting with the historical analysis in Part II of the book in order to recentre China in considerations of the global politics of drug law reform.

A *better* politics of drugs?

We can usefully begin answering the question of what a *better* politics of drugs might look like by trying to clarify what exactly is wrong with the current state of affairs. A conventional perspective would probably emphasise how the drug question generates a degree of political heat that obscures the legal, policy, and regulatory issues. In other words, it undermines the potential for rational and evidence-based debate about what should be done. There is of course considerable truth to this. Indeed, much has been written about 'drug war myths' and their pernicious impact on policy (e.g. Hart 2021) and this has become one of the tropes of drug law reform discourse. The plea is for policy to 'follow the science', unencumbered by the distortions of moralising politics.

But a somewhat different argument was made in the previous chapter. Rather than politics inhibiting rational policy-making, it was argued that there has been a persistent failure to recognise what is actually at stake in the politics of the drug question. It follows that trying to neutralise or evade the political, in favour of science or evidence, is a mistake. What is required is a different type of politics that can provide a more clear-sighted view of what is involved when societies seek to regulate supply chains for certain intoxicating substances and to control users of those substances. Once we start to see how the drug question is bound up not simply with trivial matters stirred up by vote-grubbing politicians and others but also with profoundly important questions of freedom, citizenship, equality, and rights, then the necessity of serious engagement with the political realm becomes very clear. It should be emphasised that this does not mean ignoring the undoubted pathologies of politics of the vote-grubbing kind but instead involves insisting that there is more going on than this and so much more to be said.

So what could be meant by a *better* politics? One dimension of this, as Loader and Sparks (2019) argue, is about process: creating space for more democratic deliberation of policy and policy options is itself intrinsic to a better politics. The challenge of democratising drug policy in this fashion is considered later in the chapter but here I want to focus on the other dimension, that is, outcomes. A starting point is to engage directly on the terrain of the political by attempting 'to offer a diagnosis and critique of the visions of order and governance embedded in actually existing practices of ... control' (Loader and Sparks 2014:163). In other words, those matters that I have suggested have tended to be obscured from view—freedom, citizenship, equality, rights, etc—can be made the explicit focus of analysis when evaluating alternative legal, regulatory, and policy options. We could ask of any new proposed intervention a series of questions based around these ideas. This in itself presents a markedly different approach to policy evaluation than is usually taken. A good example of the more conventional evaluative calculus is provided by MacCoun and Reuter (2011:63) who provide an elegant summary of a formula they suggest for assessing the impact of alternatives to prohibition:

Total drug-related harm = Harmfulness (average harm per dose) ×
Prevalence (number of users) × Intensity (number of doses per user).

For MacCoun and Reuter, the fundamental question to ask of any alternative policy is whether it will increase or decrease 'total drug-related harm'. Whilst it is true that their concept of 'harmfulness' could perhaps be made capacious enough to include negative impacts on freedom or rights or justice, this would be extremely difficult to calculate on a 'per dose' basis and, in any case, it is clear that this is not what MacCoun and Reuter envisage. They have in mind a more hard-headed instrumental form of reckoning (and this is, of course, absolutely vital too, as part of the drug policy research enterprise). The type of 'diagnosis and critique' proposed by Loader and Sparks may therefore offer an important new way of starting to define, evaluate, and (eventually) promote this elusive better politics of drugs. It remains, though, an approach which might tend to produce analyses that do not fully join the dots in engaging with the overarching question of the desired state of affairs—the 'nature of the good society', as Loader and Sparks (2014:161) put it—that we are trying to move towards. How could a more holistic political evaluation be made?

There are many different ways to answer that question but one of the most insightful and penetrating attempts to provide a framework for this kind of normative analysis has been developed over the course of 30 years by John Braithwaite, beginning with his groundbreaking book, *Not Just Deserts*, co-authored with political philosopher Philip Pettit (Braithwaite and Pettit 1990). I first encountered this book in the early 1990s as a graduate student studying criminology for the first time and trying to grasp the complexities of theories of legal punishment. But the book's scope and ambition is considerably broader than the canvas of criminal justice and Braithwaite has subsequently returned to further develop the ideas many times during the intervening decades (drawing in part on his co-author's continuing philosophical work on republicanism and freedom, e.g. Pettit 1997). Braithwaite's (2022) most recent book, *Macrocriminology and Freedom*, brings together much of his thinking on this question of what makes the 'good society' and is highly recommended for readers wishing to explore this further. The essence of his argument is that freedom—defined in a republican way as non-domination—should be the underpinning value and goal of governance. This is a social notion of freedom in the sense that it refers to the capacity to enjoy full citizenship in a society. Regulation and governance should therefore be directed to building freedom, tempering power, and reducing all forms of domination. Domination can include the impacts of poverty, injustice, racism, and so on, as well as more direct action by state agencies, institutions, and powerful private actors (e.g. corporations). Interestingly, he argues that the criminal law is by definition a form of domination and that criminalisation can only be justified if those inherent harms are outweighed by a positive impact in reducing domination. This has a particular resonance, of course, in the context of drug law reform.

It should be immediately clear how, in principle, Braithwaite's framework can be deployed for the type of normative analysis of drug law and policy that could help start to build a better politics of drugs. It is important though that when using the intellectual tools of philosophy for thinking about the normative and the political, we guard against politics becoming untethered from understandings of policy in action. Social scientists have tended to be reluctant to engage in normative analysis and there is even less work which tries to integrate this with explanatory accounts. Taking criminology as an example, this is why the contributions of Loader and Sparks that have been discussed in this part of the book are so important and yet stand out in the discipline as unusual. It perhaps also explains the varied responses to their initial contribution in the book *Public Criminology?* (Loader and Sparks 2010). Braithwaite, once again, offers a potential way forward here in the editorial manifesto for the journal *Regulation & Governance*:

> Regulation is a field where innovative moves are being made to integrate explanatory theory (ordered sets of propositions about the way the world is) and normative theory (ordered sets of propositions about the way the world ought to be). This means there is promise in crafting theory around concepts that are fertile simultaneously in normative and in explanatory theory—such as transparency, domination, procedural justice, and accountability. (Braithwaite et al 2007:4–5)

This is interesting in at least two (related) ways. First, it suggests that grounding the building of a better politics of drugs in normative concepts that can also do relevant explanatory work may be productive and important. The concept of freedom has the potential to be particularly fruitful here. I have previously argued (Seddon 2007, 2010) that there is a complex and deep historical relationship between 'drugs' (as a set of concerns about how we understand and regulate behaviours associated with a subset of intoxicating substances) and 'freedom' (as both an abstract ideal *and* a governmental concept that steers behaviour). Further exploring this relationship may prove to be a critical step in creating a new politics of drugs that can animate fresh thinking about law and policy reform. Second, the theoretical project in Part I of this book suggests some ways in which we might be able to start to do this. It will be recalled that the *exchangespace* concept provides a way to understand the complex constitutive relationship between drug markets and their regulation, moving beyond conventional control conceptions of market-regulation relations (in which regulation is conceived as an external control on already-existing markets). Central to *exchangespace* is what Hancher and Moran (1989/98:154) called the 'play of power', that is, the ways in which power shapes the competitive struggles, alliances, and interdependencies within that space, including who is excluded from it and who controls admission. This was visualised by imagining powerful actors as heavier objects distorting the flat sheet of the two-dimensional regulatory space, causing power and resources to accumulate in the larger depression caused by those objects. Domination, and freedom as non-domination, may have utility as conceptual tools which both aid understanding of how the 'play of power' within the *exchangespace* shapes what happens over time *and* serve as a normative yardstick for evaluating policy reform initiatives.

Part of building a better politics of drugs in these ways and along these lines envisages interaction between researchers and policy actors. This is of course not uncommon already and academics are increasingly encouraged and pressed to engage in 'policy engagement', 'knowledge exchange', and 'impact' work. This takes many forms and, indeed, there is a vast literature spanning across many fields which explores the different ways of doing this and the differential effectiveness of alternative approaches. Hoekstra et al (2020) provide an interesting and comprehensive 'review of reviews' which exhaustively maps what we know about 'what works' in research-policy partnerships. This type of work is invaluable but runs the risk of turning back towards approaches which assume that if only we can be sufficiently clear and rigorous in presenting evidence to policy actors, then better policy will inevitably follow (for a sophisticated version of this approach, see Garland 2021). As I have already argued, in the context of drug policy and drug law reform at least, this is a mistaken view as it misrecognises the political character of the drug question. A more fruitful way forward involves broadening out our vision somewhat, away from a narrowly instrumental perspective, towards a wider consideration of the relationships between, on the one hand, knowledge production, dissemination, and exchange and, on the other, ways of thinking and acting in the spheres of policy, practice, and civil society. These relationships are themselves all situated within political contexts, as is evident to any researcher who has ever engaged in policy-facing activity in 'heated' areas like drugs or crime. One important dimension of thinking this through in this broader way involves engaging with the debate on public social science to which we now turn in the next section.

Public social science and drug politics

Debates about what social science is, what it is for, and its value outside the academy, have a long history. How long a history this is, partly depends on how we define social science. There is, of course, a very long tradition of thinking about how human life is organised, how and why we co-operate, the causes and nature of conflict, the nature of justice, and so on. This can be traced back variously through diverse lineages of ancient Chinese, Indian, Islamic, and African thought, as well as the Western intellectual tradition. And no doubt much of this thinking has been motivated and driven by the desire to make human existence 'better' in some way or another.

The idea of 'social science' or of the 'social sciences' is more recent and, broadly speaking, is associated with the advent of modernity. Baker (1964) links the birth of the concept, at least in its Western guise, with the French Revolution and it was certainly part of the European intellectual landscape in the nineteenth century. By the twentieth century, many of these strands of social science were explicitly tied to programmes of social reform. In a criminological context, David Garland's (1985) first book *Punishment and Welfare* provides a specific historical example of this through a genealogical analysis of the formation of the modern welfare state in the early twentieth century and its connection to the new criminological science. Garland's genealogical approach places him in territory adjacent to Foucauldians, who have of course tended to see the connections between social science and social policy through the more jaundiced lens of knowledge-power relations. Foucault's (1977) own *Discipline and Punish* is probably the *locus classicus* of this genre and certainly the work most familiar to criminologists.

The purpose of alluding briefly to this history, and to some of the diversity of perspectives, is to underline that one of today's key reference points in these debates—Michael Burawoy's 2004 Presidential Address to the American Sociological Association—is a staging post in a much longer journey, rather than a point of origin. Nevertheless, Burawoy's reprise of the debate has become extremely influential over the last two decades, both as an explanation of what public sociology is and as a programmatic statement of what it should be (see also Burawoy 2004; Clawson et al 2007). It is fruitful to examine precisely what he argues.

At the heart of his argument is the connection he makes between public sociology and civil society, which he sees as allowing public sociology to serve the 'interests of humanity' by 'keeping at bay both state despotism and market tyranny' (Burawoy 2005:24). In other words, he locates public sociology in the non-state and non-market spaces of society. This is interesting theoretically from the perspective of this book's thesis. As will be recalled from Part I, the *exchangespace* concept explicitly seeks to transcend sharp demarcations between the spheres of state-market-society and instead create a theoretical lens that can 'see' all spheres at the same time and in their full interconnectedness. Burawoy, in contrast, claims as a virtue the potential for sociology to perform a type of standpointism on behalf of civil society. Some have been a little sceptical of such a grand claim being made for sociology rather than any other social science discipline (e.g. Braithwaite (2005:348) describes Burawoy as being 'charitable' to sociology) but perhaps the key weakness of the claim is its theoretically unsophisticated understanding of the interrelationships between states, markets, and civil society which does not really allow us to see how, in different contexts, all three spheres can be engaged with in order to serve the 'interests of humanity'. To see the market as the exclusive territory of economics and the state a terrain solely for occupation by political science is unnecessarily and unduly limiting intellectually.

Burawoy's central schema divides sociological knowledge into four types: policy, professional, critical, and public. He argues that these are mutually dependent forms of knowledge within the sociological enterprise and not separate strands of activity. His typology, in other words, is for analytical purposes rather than for dividing up the field or the work of individual sociologists. In very brief summary, he defines the types like this:

- *policy* sociology responds directly to questions or problems defined by policy clients;
- *professional* sociology is the mainstream disciplinary research and scholarship conducted in the academy;
- *critical* sociology focuses on questioning and critiquing the foundations and tenets of policy and professional sociology; and

- *public* sociology brings sociology into dialogue with wider society, catalysing discussion as well as participating in conversations that are already taking place.

We might carp about this typology—and, indeed, many sociologists have! — but Burawoy's interventions have proved highly productive in stimulating debate about this important set of questions concerning the relationships between social science knowledge and public discourse about the problems societies face (and how they should be solved). Two key points can be made here. The first has been best articulated by Braithwaite (2005), in his typically provocative and thought-provoking challenge to Burawoy. His central criticism is that Burawoy's schema is predicated on the foregrounding of a traditional disciplinary formation, namely, sociology, as key to unlocking the door to greater and more effective public engagement. Yet for Braithwaite this is a fundamental error as it is based on the false assumption that the way we have come to organise social science knowledge into particular disciplinary boxes (sociology, economics, political science, psychology, etc) is the optimal structure for the social sciences. He argues, on the contrary, that these boxes obstruct our ability to generate insights that cut across the categorical objects on which these disciplines focus. He calls instead for interdisciplinary social science organised around cross-cutting theoretical ideas, such as regulation, as the best way forward. The goal is to engage with the world as it is today, drawing in an open and pluralistic way on whatever intellectual resources best enable us to do this, and not to allow our insights to be shaped, restricted, or blocked by the organisation of knowledge that happened in the past when the modern disciplines originally emerged. This intellectual pluralism resonates powerfully with the theoretical approach developed in Part I of this book. It is particularly important when focusing on the drug question which has largely been dominated by medicine and psychiatry (when considering issues around health, addiction, and treatment) and by law and criminology (when considering drug control). The light shone from within these disciplinary boxes has illuminated particular questions (e.g. from law and criminology: should we legalise or decriminalise? what is the nature of the drug-crime link? how should we police drug markets?) whilst leaving others barely visible at all in the shadows (e.g. how should we regulate the cannabis trade in ways that are environmentally sustainable? how can we deliver post-prohibition transitional justice to communities that have been most harmed by drug prohibition?).

The second point concerns the idea of public sociology (or social science) stimulating and participating in conversations in wider society. This is clearly of critical importance and Burawoy has some interesting things to say on the matter. He begins with a useful definition of this aspect of public sociology:

> Public sociology brings sociology into a conversation with publics, understood as people who are themselves involved in conversation. It entails, therefore, a double conversation. (Burawoy 2005:7)

He suggests that a traditional form for this type of conversation involves, for example, scholars writing opinion pieces for newspapers. It is in that sense the one-way insertion of a voice into a societal conversation. A richer and more organic form for dialogue springs from ongoing relationships between academics and civil society groups (e.g. neighbourhood associations, human rights organisations, etc), where dialogue takes on more of the form of an ongoing 'process of mutual education' (2005:8). This organic type of dialogue, rooted in relationships and based on a shared commitment to learning, seems on the face of it to have more potential as a method for getting social science knowledge to circulate within discursive networks and communities outside the academy. Burawoy (2005:8) also suggests that academics could constitute themselves collectively as publics that act in the political arena. In other words, the British Society of Criminology or the Socio-Legal Studies Association or the International Society for the Study of Drug Policy could become prominent voices in public debate about drug policy.

The fact that the latter typically does not happen to any serious extent is interesting. Burawoy (2005:8) acknowledges that speaking on behalf of an academic disciplinary community is 'difficult and dangerous' and suggests, somewhat weakly, that 'we should be sure to arrive at public positions through open dialogue'. He immediately concedes the practical impossibility of this by noting that sociologists have 'different value commitments' and that public sociology can therefore 'as well support Christian Fundamentalism as it can Liberation Sociology or Communitarianism' (2005:8–9). For some critics of Burawoy, this simply highlights the futility of many aspects of his project. In an interesting paper, social movements researcher Alberto Arribas Lozano (2018) pinpoints this deliberate avoidance of 'choosing sides' as a fundamental weakness, recalling Howard Becker's (1967) famous article about side-taking (see also Hammersley

2001). He argues, first of all, that the very concept of public sociology is a local, specifically North American, one that has little or no resonance in many parts of the Global South. A sociologist in, for example, Colombia or South Africa, would simply not be able to conceive of a sociology that did not see public engagement as a constitutive element of a fundamentally emancipatory enterprise (2018:97–98). Simply put, in many places outside of Burawoy's North American bubble, the qualifier 'public' is redundant and there is no ambivalence about 'sides'. Lozano goes on to press an argument for collaborative practices of co-produced knowledge as the best way of pursuing the project of what he calls a 'decolonial social science' and a 'liberatory sociology' (2018:106). Lozano makes a persuasive argument but perhaps the clearest conclusion we can draw is that the explicit and transparent communication of a normative framework—whether Braithwaite's freedom as non-domination or an alternative idea—is an absolute necessity for building a better politics of drugs.

As we might by now expect, Loader and Sparks have also engaged productively with Burawoy's work, notably in their 2010 book *Public Criminology?* but in several other publications as well (e.g. Loader and Sparks 2011a). Rather than exhaustively setting out their position, I wish to focus here on one particularly pivotal concept they develop, the idea of the 'democratic under-labourer' (see Loader and Sparks 2010: ch 5; Loader and Sparks 2011b). The idea emerges from an evaluation of the respective virtues and vices of what they see as the dominant styles of public engagement within criminology: the scientific expert, policy advisor, observer-turned-player, social movement activist, and lonely prophet. The democratic under-labourer draws on the best features of these different styles and is conceived as a type of good-faith diplomat, shuttling between different camps and seeking to mediate difference. The under-labourer is driven by a commitment to producing reliable knowledge about crime and its control, to being curious about political and media constructions of crime and crime policy, and to recognising the values and normative judgements that underpin different positions in the field. We might think of the role as being one of engagement in public conversations in an area of academic expertise, with humility and open-mindedness, and driven by a desire to maximise mutual understanding whilst accepting that disagreements will remain. This is quite some distance away from the traditional conception of the academic as an elite expert advising on what is the 'best' policy or intervention.

If we think then of public social science as concerned at root with sharpening our sense of the public purpose of social science, then the discussion

above points to some of the key dimensions of this, notably the importance of rooting conversations in organic relationships, engaging in open
dialogue with diverse actors and being transparent about normative values.
Even if we retain a certain scepticism about whether public sociology will
prove to be a lasting idea outside North America, nevertheless this broader
concern for thinking about the public purpose of social science can still animate interesting and important work (e.g. Chatwin 2018). This all points, in
turn, to the centrality of democratic deliberation to our project of building
a better politics of drugs, a surprisingly thorny matter which is considered
in the next section.

Democratising drug politics

It was noted earlier in the chapter that *process* is inherently important within
politics and that finding or creating mechanisms for more democratic deliberation about drugs and drug control is itself a valuable and worthy goal.
In this section, this question of the democratisation of drug politics is explored, drawing (again) partly on the work of Loader and Sparks.

The idea that there is value in finding ways of giving citizens a greater
voice in drug policy debates is actually not as common in the field as might
be expected. An exception is the work of Alison Ritter and her colleagues at
the University of New South Wales, which provides a very useful consideration of the various ways in which deliberative spaces can be created as part
of drug policy-making processes (Lancaster et al 2018; Ritter et al 2018).
In her recent book, *Drug Policy*, Ritter (2022:120–136) revisits and extends
this work in the concluding chapter, primarily focusing on the notion of
participation and the best ways of achieving it. This is important but is arguably mainly a technical question. Here, I am more interested in the concept of democracy itself and the potential for democratic theory to provide
some intellectual resources for deepening our thinking about the politics of
drug law and policy reform.

In a collaborative project with political scientist Albert Dzur, Loader
and Sparks take as their starting point the observation that 'investigating
the ideals and institutions of democracy' is an 'underexploited resource' in
thinking about the reshaping of public policy (Dzur et al 2016:2–3). They
note the challenge this immediately poses to policy 'elitism' which assumes
that if we let 'experts' shape policy, outcomes will be better. The flip-side of
this elitism and its assumptions is a certain 'discomfort with democracy', a

phrase they borrow from Roberto Unger (Dzur et al 2016:4). In the drug field, a level of discomfort is perhaps understandable, as it is more populist approaches to drug politics that are often seen as barriers to reform. But this itself misrecognises—or, at best, simplifies—populism as a set of (regressive) outcomes rather than as a method or style of political communication that can be utilised in the service of diverse projects. Loader and Sparks (2017) suggest that the underpinning political logic of populism is built around three claims: speaking for 'the people … imagined and depicted as a homogeneous entity' (2017:100); viewing 'the people' as in opposition to 'elites' or 'the establishment'; believing in the enactment of the 'will of the people' as a direct form of popular sovereignty. Whilst it is perhaps easy to recognise reactionary or right-wing versions of populism—and British readers will immediately be reminded of the conduct of the Brexit debate— there can also be progressive populism which uses the same political logic and claims but in order to promote radical rather than reactionary goals.

An obvious example of progressive populism in the drug context is the case of coca leaf in Bolivia. Long part of indigenous Andean culture, coca growing became subject to increasingly heavy criminalisation from the early 1980s as part of international anti-cocaine efforts in the 'war on drugs'. In his outstanding book, anthropologist Thomas Grisaffi (2019) tells the story of how a social movement of Bolivian coca growers grew out of resistance to US-led militarised action in the name of cocaine prohibition. Coca-growing unions emerged in the 1980s and came to form an anti-imperialist indigenous political movement, eventually leading to the creation of the MAS Movement for Socialism political party in 1998. Evo Morales, who had been a leading figure in the coca-growing unions, became the leader of MAS and in 2006 was elected as President of Bolivia. Grisaffi argues that this social movement led in effect to a transformation of Bolivian democracy into what he terms a 'vernacular democracy' that was indigenous-led and grassroots-oriented. The Morales government demonstrated that this was not without tensions and difficulties but nevertheless offers an example of an alternative form of democracy that proved sustainable for a significant period of years.

The story of Bolivia is exceptionally interesting. It tells us, amongst other things, that any principled preference *for* expert-driven and *against* populist drug policy is only tenable from a Western-centric perspective. It may look that way in London or Los Angeles but it probably does not in La Paz. If we therefore accept that we should neither assume that it is self-evident that drug policy reform should be driven solely by elite expertise nor that populism inevitably erects barriers for progressive reform, then our challenge is to work through how to harness democracy in positive ways. For our purposes, as argued earlier, 'positive' is defined as related to action which increases freedom as non-domination.

In their collaborative work on democracy and penal policy, Dzur, Loader, and Sparks argue for three lines of analysis: critique, restraint, reconstruction (Dzur et al 2016:8–10). Each of these can usefully be applied in our consideration here of how to democratise the politics of drug control. Starting with *critique*, they argue for the analytical drawing on democratic ideals and practices in order to extend and broaden critiques of penal policy:

> To think democratically—rather than simply in crime control terms—about punishment is not just to revisit longstanding questions about the claims of retribution, deterrence, or rehabilitation as penal aims, or about the grounding of the sovereign right to punish in general. Rather, in our current contexts, it is also to seek to ask sharper questions about the collateral effects of the transformations of the carceral state upon political participation, the formation of civic identities and the associational life of impacted communities. (Dzur et al 2016:8)

For drug control, these 'sharper questions' include ones, for example, about the impact of local drug law enforcement practices on the associational life and political participation of young people from minority ethnic communities or about perceptions of political legitimacy amongst citizens who experience the relatively benign effects of prohibited drugs like cannabis compared to those of licensed (and often encouraged) intoxicants like alcohol. Other questions might include what the impact is on civic identities and civic engagement of major changes in national drug control policy (e.g. drug decriminalisation in Portugal in 2001 or cannabis legalisation in Uruguay in 2013). Some of these questions have been engaged with in a more direct way by the courts. For example, the 2018 decision by the South African Constitutional Court, briefly alluded to in the previous chapter, found that the prohibition of personal use of cannabis by adults in private was in violation of constitutional rights to privacy (Lubaale and Mavundla 2019). The Court explicitly framed the question before it as whether the limitation on privacy created by this prohibition was 'reasonable and justifiable in an open and democratic society based on human dignity, equality and freedom as required by section 36 of the Constitution'.[1] It concluded that it was not. The growing scholarship on the relationship between human rights laws and drug laws (e.g. Bone 2020) promises to provide some important elements for this type of critical analysis of drug control in relation to democratic ideals and concepts.

Turning to *restraint*, this line of analysis focuses on using democratic theory as a resource for thinking about how to restrain the reach of the coercive state. Again, human rights law offers one strand of thinking that may be productive here. Nevertheless, *legal* restraints on the state are not the end of the matter and represent only one form of restraint. There may be principled arguments for tempering state power that do not engage legal rights. Braithwaite (2019) explores some adjacent ideas in his characteristic creative and imaginative style. He argues that the notion of *tempering* power is a useful one that is distinct from ideas of limiting or controlling power as it is specifically about constraining arbitrary or unchecked power (Braithwaite 2019:531). In other words, tempering power is about ensuring that power is exercised in ways that include appropriate checks, balances, and accountability mechanisms. In short, properly tempered power is democratic. He explores this idea in a couple of quite different contexts—first, through his collaborative research on the people power movement in East Timor in the late 1990s (Braithwaite et al 2012) and, second, in an analysis of the failures to regulate corporate power which led to the 2008 global financial crisis— but there are several important lessons we can draw for our concern with democratising the ways in which societies approach the drug question.

Underpinning his argument is the idea that the evaluative yardstick or guiding principle for tempering power is to ensure that the exercise of power operates to 'maximize freedom' defined as non-domination (Braithwaite 2019:532). Drawing on his two sets of examples, he crafts some hypotheses about how to temper power in freedom-maximising ways (2019:591–594). These include the importance of explicitly requiring power to be tethered to accountability mechanisms, of ensuring regulation is responsive and attuned to local context, and of creating forms of hybrid governance with multiple branches of power. Applied to the drug question, they provide ways of thinking about several aspects of the legal and policy challenge, for example, how to restrain local drug law enforcement and how to moderate

---

[1] *Minister of Justice and Constitutional Development & Others v Prince; National Director of Public Prosecutions & Others v Rubin; National Director of Public Prosecutions & Others v Acton & Others* [2018] ZACC 30 (*Prince 2* Constitutional Court decision) para 59.

and control corporate power in supply chains (e.g. within a legal cannabis industry). One of the most important and useful aspects of these ideas is that Braithwaite develops them not only from research on tempering military or political power but also research on restraining economic power within markets. This gives them a particularly powerful resonance within the *exchangespace* theoretical framework which incorporates the ideas of power, networks, and hybrid governance that Braithwaite explores.

Lastly, *reconstruction* focuses analysis on thinking through and attempting to build new ideas for how democratic societies might respond to the drug question. For Dzur et al (2016:9), this is partly about recognising the two main political alternatives—populism versus expert-driven technocracy—as in fact 'twin pathologies of our contemporary antipolitical malaise', both of which undermine rather than develop democracy. They argue that there is a need to find innovative ways of building in democratic participation through 'deliberative practices whose aim is to promote civic reintegration, emphasize mutual accountability for penal decisions, and foster proper recognition that those whom we punish are co-citizens' (Dzur et al 2016:10).

In a recently-published essay, Loader and Sparks (2022) argue for the relevance here of ideas derived from the American pragmatist tradition of John Dewey and, in particular, Dorf and Sabel's (1998) notion of 'democratic experimentalism'. This is also an important point of reference for Braithwaite (e.g. Braithwaite 2019). Loader and Sparks (2019:116) suggest that the purpose of this approach is 'not to discover better policies that can be inserted into, or developed by, existing institutions, but instead to make and imagine, and experiment with, institutional arrangements that foster and sustain extended democratic participation in determining how crime and security questions are addressed and resolved'. Substituting 'drugs' for 'crime and security', we can see that in 'thinking democratically' about our approach to the drug question, we need to find new ways of facilitating public participation, debate, and discussion. In a spirit of experimentalism, we must be prepared to be innovative in doing this, to try things out, and to learn what works best.

Through these three moments of critique, restraint, and reconstruction, it is possible to see an outline of how democratic theory can move us far beyond seeing democratising drug policy in simple and narrow terms as just being about increasing the amount of public participation or discussion in the policy-making process (valuable though that is). Instead, 'thinking democratically' about the drug question is about understanding why this question is so politically potent and therefore how our collective discussions about reform are also about the nature of the 'good society' and how we might create it. Public social science that is interdisciplinary is a critical component in this endeavour. In the next section, this argument is further extended by looking at these questions from a world-system rather than nation-state perspective.

A cosmopolitan politics of drugs

We saw very clearly in Part II of the book how the initial conditions for global prohibition were set in a framework of international trade and international relations. It was argued that this transnational dimension is hard-wired into the drug control system. Much of the discussion about public social science and deliberative democratic approaches, however, is often framed in terms of nation-states. Whilst this is important, it misses a major part of what is distinctive about the drug question and the historical development of prohibition.

If we widen out our vision to encompass politics at a global scale, we first have to recognise how the world has been changing across recent decades. The nations that are now shaping the future of the globe are no longer European (with the exception of the largest European nation, Russia) and the hegemony of the twentieth century's superpower, the United States, is fading. As Braithwaite (2021:33) observes, in the 2020s, the centres of power lie to the East: China as the world's dominant economic power, the wider Asian region with its fast-growing populous countries like India, Pakistan, and Indonesia, and the rich countries of the Middle East like Saudi Arabia, the United Arab Emirates, and Qatar. Any serious politics of drug control, understood as a global system, needs to grasp these fundamental shifts in global power, and move away from continuing to see what happens in Europe and North America as the epicentre of events. This, of course, has been one of the major themes of this book, that is, the need to recentre China and Asia within our analyses of the past, present, and future of drug law and policy. What might this mean for this chapter's challenge of thinking about how we can build a better politics of drugs?

Not for the first time, John Braithwaite offers some particularly acute insights that provide a helpful starting point. In an essay directly responding to Loader and Sparks on the need for a public criminology, he argues, somewhat provocatively, for the need for a more cosmopolitan vision that can see the potential for stepping outside of the North Atlantic bubble of democratic under-labouring and being willing to engage more directly with, for example, China. In building this argument he draws on Peter Drahos' (2021) astonishing heterodox book *Survival Governance* which argues that, contrary to conventional (Western) wisdom, humanity's greatest hope of averting the planetary ecological crisis may lie with countries in East Asia and especially China. The nub of his argument is that the crisis has cascaded to a point where the standard price and other market-oriented mechanisms that Western governments tend to reach for are too slow to keep pace with the shifts now taking place in earth systems and that much more muscular top-down state levers need to be pulled. For Braithwaite (2021:28), one of the key lessons from Drahos is that staying inside the 'North-Atlantic policy machines' is likely to lead to failure.

How might we translate this bold argument about planetary survival into the context of thinking about the politics of transforming drug policy? Braithwaite (2021:31) acknowledges that part of his purpose in responding to Loader and Sparks by calling for 'authoritarian under-labouring' is to provoke and stimulate 'thinking in a more fundamentally critical way' about the whole project of public criminology. He begins by refusing neat distinctions between great powers that are 'democratic' and those that are 'authoritarian', pulling no punches as he does so:

> Yes, China puts Muslim Uighurs into re-education camps in massive numbers. But the United States has maintained detention of Muslims without trial in Guantanamo Bay for two decades; their British and other Western allies barely whimpered when their own citizens were detained there without trial, nor when the West detained much larger numbers without trial in Abu Graib and many other prisons in Iraq and Afghanistan, including the one that incubated Islamic State and its leaders, and actively participated in extraordinary rendition of suspected terrorists so they could be tortured by the most authoritarian regimes in the world, such as that of Gadaffi's Libya. (Braithwaite 2021:32)

Rather than essentialising, for example, China as one thing and the United States as another, he suggests we need a more sophisticated understanding which recognises that all great powers a) are authoritarian to some degree; b) operate within the global capitalist system; and c) rely to varying extents on state intervention to achieve their goals. In the 2020s, it is more accurate and more helpful, he argues, to see ourselves as living in an era of variegated forms of capitalism, with variation visible both between and within nations (2021:33). For Braithwaite, two important points follow from this. First, democracy itself cannot be seen as an unquestionable ideal. What he terms 'domination by democracy' is entirely possible (e.g. Americans repeatedly voting for presidents who continue detention without trial at Guantanamo Bay). He argues that non-domination is the higher-order ideal, over and above democracy. Second, civic republican under-labouring, oriented around the goal of maximising freedom as non-domination, is therefore a broader and better strategy than democratic under-labouring (2021:35). Braithwaite goes on to critique the capacity of what he terms the 'imperial disciplines' of the Global North to provide the intellectual resources for doing this, arguing that a discipline like criminology, for example, is 'not only pathologically Northern, it is also pathologically national; the greater part of it is a conglomerate of different Northern national policy sciences about crime' (2021:36). The overall conclusion he draws is that rather than 'public criminology' or 'public sociology', what is needed is interdisciplinary social science, with a cosmopolitan vision and a commitment to civic republican values. In his view, this provides a stronger foundation for productive dialogue between academics and wider society that has some chance of changing the world for the better. Braithwaite's own exemplary career spanning many decades provides a real-world illustration of how this is possible.

We can develop this idea a little further by engaging with sociologist Robert Fine's influential historical and theoretical work on cosmopolitanism. In his 2007 book, Fine sets out an account of what he terms 'cosmopolitan social theory'. He presents a rich and complex argument that repays attention by anyone interested in modernity and the human condition, in the very broadest senses. Here, I draw strategically on Fine's account by focusing on those elements with most relevance to the discussion in this chapter of the project of building a better politics of drugs. Four key points can be made. First, it is made very clear that cosmopolitanism is an idea with Kantian roots which cannot be reduced to the modern notion of globalisation. Its fundamental premise is about the *universality of humanity*, rather than about our levels of global connectedness. Second, cosmopolitanism calls for an analysis that goes beyond the limitations of nation-state boundaries. It sees the world through a *transnational* lens. Third, like Braithwaite, Fine also points to the need for social science to transcend traditional disciplinary boundaries, through an *interdisciplinary* ethos.

Fourth, cosmopolitanism is primarily a 'way of thinking' or, more prosaically, a *methodology*, rather than either a description of, or prescription for, the world.

As a way of thinking, Fine's cosmopolitan consciousness or outlook suggests how important it is to nurture collaborative forms of knowledge production, bringing together scholars from different disciplines and from all corners of the world, in order to underpin a cosmopolitan interdisciplinary social science oriented to understanding human beings and human societies (Braithwaite 2021:36). These knowledge networks need also to connect with transnational networks of NGOs, advocates, campaigners, intergovernmental agencies, and others, as a means of forging new understandings of the problems we collectively face as well as new ideas about how to solve them. This transnational approach does not mean effacing the importance of localised knowledge production or research-policy partnerships but rather points to the value of connecting together the global and the local. As Braithwaite (2021:36–38) argues, this all highlights the limitations of the type of 'democratic under-labouring' outlined by Loader and Sparks.

What this cosmopolitan vision—as envisaged by Braithwaite and Fine—may mean for the politics of the drug question is potentially highly challenging. In one sense, ever since the creation of the international drug control system at the beginning of the twentieth century, the regulatory vision has been transnational and delivered through international institutional arrangements (first, under the auspices of the League of Nations and, later, the United Nations). Yet it has at the same time tended to be distinctly Western-centric in its outlook. As we saw in Part II, the centrality of China and Asia within the origin story of today's global control system has been consistently downplayed and obscured not only in policy and political discourse but also in the research literature. The fact that the very concept of a 'drug' was the product of a set of historical processes shaped by the then pre-eminent Western imperial powers, with 'foreign' plants like opium (and, soon after, coca and cannabis) prohibited whilst other intoxicants like alcohol were not, tells us that the historical foundations of global drug prohibition were built on the terrain of a distinctive political settlement (Seddon 2016). But in almost all research, policy and political discussions and debate, the drug concept is assumed to be self-evident, neutral, and scientific. A cosmopolitan 'way of thinking' would question and deconstruct this false self-evidence.

These foundational matters are vitally important—they highlight how the drug question is political 'all the way down'—but what would a cosmopolitan vision also help us see if we were embarking on the more immediate project of building a better politics of drugs in the 2020s? If we briefly take David Courtwright's (2001) 'little three' intoxicants—opium, coca, and cannabis—we can start to get an indication of where it might take us. Looking, first, at opium, the biggest problem we have today is the overdose crisis which takes different forms in different regions (fentanyl and analogues in the United States, heroin in Europe, etc). From a cosmopolitan perspective, it is hard to see how this can be properly addressed by policy-makers without engaging with geopolitical concerns across the vast region that historian Peter Frankopan (2015) describes as linking East and West. Whether it is opium poppy cultivation in the context of the troubled politics of Afghanistan or the production of fentanyl in facilities in China, solutions will not be found without stepping outside a Western frame of reference. Finding better ways of regulating the globalised and economically powerful pharmaceutical industry is also essential and will require recognition of China's continuing rise in the sector. For coca, second, the example of Bolivia was briefly discussed earlier in the chapter but there is a wider manifestation of this issue across the Andean region. The question of how to respect the place of the coca leaf in indigenous culture in that region in the context of Western-driven anticocainism is, again, a deeply complex and difficult political matter. But if it is ignored, it is difficult to see how a global cocaine regulation system can avoid perpetuating injustices in Latin America. Lastly, for cannabis, as the most-consumed prohibited drug in the world, perhaps on the cusp in the next few decades of becoming part of a new global industry, there is a profoundly important set of political questions to engage with concerning how that industry can be made environmentally sustainable (see Seddon and Floodgate 2020). A cosmopolitan politics of cannabis regulation places the planetary ecological crisis centre-stage and understands that regulation must be forged in the full understanding that we now live in the Anthropocene epoch. This entails a globalised transnational approach. Focusing simply on whether particular regulatory models in North America are 'effective' (typically defined in parochial nation-state or even local terms) will not suffice if we are to take seriously the threat to humanity's survival presented by the climate crisis.

Conclusion

An obvious and entirely reasonable question to ask at the end of a pair of chapters on the politics of drugs is Lenin's famous injunction: what is to be done? Here, I want to draw together the argument that has been developed about finding more productive ways of engaging with the political dimensions of the issue, in order to show how this opens up some different lines of flight towards alternative futures. Some of these lines are analytical, some are practical, and all have the potential to help us rethink and reshape our approach.

Focusing, first of all, on the analytical, one of the purposes of re-orienting our perspectives on the politics of the drug question is to open up a critical space for the serious analysis of the political dimensions of the problem. By framing politics as a distraction from evidence-based policy development, it is arguable that some reformers have inadvertently undermined this critical task. The need for drug control and drug policy to be subjected to penetrating class-based analyses, for example, has rarely been adequately met. Similarly, the intertwined politics of race and drugs has tended to be engaged with at the level of manifestations of injustice (e.g. racial disproportionality in policing) rather than through critical analysis that exposes the deep connections between drugs, race, colonialism, and modern capitalism. All of these political concerns can only be properly brought to the surface if we reject superficial and misguided calls for the removal of politics and ideology from discourse on drug policy and drug law reform. Indeed, the redeeming of the concept of ideology is perhaps the single most important analytical step forward in the building of a better politics of drugs.

Sticking with the analytical dimension, by understanding the drug question as inherently political, and as connected with many of the core ideas and concepts of modern political thought, it moves the politics of drugs and drug control into a more mainstream space. In effect, it presses us to discuss drugs in the broader context of thinking about the 'good society', about how we wish to live, and about how we govern ourselves. This, in turn, pushes normative thinking to the forefront. In other words, rather than being reluctant to engage with questions about how the world *should* be, we need to do this with as much seriousness and intellectual rigour as we do with the more conventional social science questions about how the world *is*. It will be recalled from Part I, that the *exchangespace* concept drives theoretically the insight that thinking about what state of affairs we are trying to steer ourselves towards is essential. By seeing market-regulation relations as complex adaptive systems, the challenge for policy reform shifts *away* from the design of optimal rule systems and rule-enforcement strategies and *towards* the crafting of ways of steering the flow of events in desired directions. And that, in turn, necessitates thinking seriously about what those directions are. It has been argued in this part of the book that the guiding star should be the republican goal of maximising freedom as non-domination. This places political thinking and political discourse at the very heart of regulatory strategy and practice.

If politics is central to drug policy, what have we learned about how we might start to develop new practical forms of political engagement with the drug question? There is an important set of what we could term 'technical' solutions that are focused on creating institutional arrangements within which deliberative practices—that is, practices which centre collective discussion as the underpinning for decision-making—can flourish. These include innovative ideas such as citizens' councils or assemblies, and citizens' juries, as well as more routine commitments to ad hoc public consultation and state-citizen dialogue. Deliberative democracy has become a vibrant area within political science in recent decades and there is much to learn here. The Handbook edited by Bächtiger et al (2018) provides a rich and detailed mapping of the field, which stresses deliberation as a reform movement within local, national, and global governance. Making connections between deliberation in this broad sense and the drug law and policy reform movement may prove critical to the forging of a better politics of drugs. As Braithwaite (2022:1) suggests, it is not really possible to be serious about 'expanding freedom without engaging with social movement struggles'. This is an important point, as the emphasis I have placed on democracy and deliberation should not be mistaken for a desire to downplay the extent to which the politics of drugs is bound up with questions of power, domination, and injustice. It will never be enough for us all just to talk more.

This should remind us, finally, that one important voice often muted in dialogue and discussions about drugs and drug control is that of those people who take (controlled) drugs and are subject to the various forms of behavioural regulation that constitute prohibition. Here, there may be something to learn from the experiments created by Michel Foucault and others in the 1970s in relation to the question of prison conditions. The Groupe d'Information sur les Prisons (GIP), which operated from December 1970 to February 1973, focused on bringing to the surface, and making visible, the intolerable realities of experiences of imprisonment (see Thompson and Zurn 2021). One of the distinctive features of the GIP was that it did not follow the conventional path of either carrying out research studies or making reform proposals, rather it aimed simply to amplify the voices of prisoners speaking directly of their own experiences of incarceration. We could point also to a radical tradition in the field of mental health politics which has sought over the last half-century to centre the perspectives of 'survivors' of the psychiatric system. Nikolas Rose's (2019) thought-provoking book, *Our Psychiatric Future*, is particularly insightful on this. He argues that psychiatry is an inherently and intensely political science, and that genuinely transforming psychiatric power will require the proper recognition of the voices of the recipients of professional psychiatric practice. Perhaps the overarching lesson is that anti-politics in all its forms—whether technocratic or populist—involves a silencing of those at the sharp end of social control and that our quest for a better politics of drugs must begin by acknowledging this. The cosmopolitan version of this lesson highlights how the volume of these voices is also systematically raised or lowered depending on what part of the world they emanate from. The noisiest, inevitably, are in the Global North and this too must be addressed. In the final chapter, we return to these questions in the context of one of the book's central concerns: what are the implications for the drug law reform project of the fact that we are now living in a world where the centre of global power has moved eastwards to China?

8
Conclusion
Rethinking reform

Introduction

On 1 April 2019, the Chinese government announced in Beijing that it would ban all variants of fentanyl, fulfilling a promise that Xi Jinping had made the previous year to Donald Trump as part of China-US trade talks. The historical echoes sounded deep with irony. In the nineteenth century, Britain, then the world's great power, had twice waged war on China to force her to accept imports of opium grown in British-controlled India, and China had suffered enormously as a result. In 2019, the twentieth century's great power, the United States, was on its knees in the face of a deadly opioid crisis fuelled by fentanyl and other opioids manufactured largely in China and India. American calls for tighter regulatory controls on fentanyl sounded like the mirror image of the Chinese pleas for tougher action against opium in the meetings in Shanghai back in February 1909. With China now emerging as the twenty-first century's global superpower, things had turned full circle but this time with roles (and power) reversed between East and West.

In this small announcement, we can see illuminated, all at once, 200 years of global history. And in this sudden brightness we can also see right into the heart of this book's thesis, a thesis we can summarise in three core propositions.

Proposition 1: The history of drug control is a geopolitical story about trade, with China at the centre.

Proposition 2: This story only makes full sense in the context of the bigger narrative of the emergence and evolution of global colonial capitalism in the modern world.

Rethinking Drug Laws. Toby Seddon, Oxford University Press. © Toby Seddon 2023.
DOI: 10.1093/oso/9780192846525.003.0008

Proposition 3:   It is a regulatory story about the setting and policing of boundaries between licit and illicit trade.

Or, in a short form of six keywords: China, power, colonialism, capitalism, trade, law.

In this short concluding chapter, I aim to do just two things. First, to summarise the three main parts of the book, focusing on drawing out what is new about the perspectives on the theory, history, and politics of drug control that each part, respectively, presents. The claim made, across all three of those domains, is that the arguments in the book constitute fundamentally new ways of knowing such that we might think of the book as attempting to effect a paradigm shift. Second, to address readers who may at this point be thinking 'fine ... but so what?', by setting out what I see as the implications for research, policy development, and law reform. This is the book's 'call to action' for those engaged in the drug law reform enterprise, whether as thinkers, researchers, campaigners, advocates, or indeed legislators and policy-makers.

Paradigm shift: theory, history, politics

The concept of a paradigm shift in knowledge is primarily associated with Thomas Kuhn and his famous short book *The Structure of Scientific Revolutions*, first published in 1962 after a long gestation (see Reisch 2016). His central concept of a paradigm is notoriously slippery (Hacking 2016). Indeed, at a 1965 meeting in London, chaired by Karl Popper and at which Kuhn gave a paper, Margaret Masterman (1969) famously claimed to have identified 21 different usages of 'paradigm' in *Structure* and Kuhn (1969) himself conceded it was confused. Nevertheless, many scholars have honed in on the idea of a paradigm as a model or exemplar, that is, as a set of shared examples used by scientists within a field that together constitute a distinctive framework of understanding or way of knowing. A paradigm, in other words, provides a scientist with a map to identify what questions to ask and what methods to pursue when engaging with a puzzle or problem. It is a guide to how to proceed.

In his introductory essay to the fiftieth-anniversary edition of *Structure*, Ian Hacking (2012:xi) noted that in the half-century since the publication of Kuhn's little book, the idea of a 'paradigm shift' had become so common as to be now almost banal. But we can get an insight into what Kuhn himself meant from some of the metaphors he uses in *Structure*. Moving to a new paradigm was like: a religious conversion; living in a different world; or viewing the world through different glasses. As Lorraine Daston (2020:412) puts it, for Kuhn a paradigm shift is a 'reinterpretation of the world' that is 'fundamental and irreversible'. It is not just a new theory or a new perspective, it is a point of discontinuity at which a new map is created for a new world (see Winther 2020). So how far does this book match up to this Kuhnian notion?

Theory

In Part I of the book, the goal was to develop some new intellectual resources to help understand what drug laws and drug control are and how they function. The motivation for this task was the view that existing theoretical understandings—as articulated in the conventional conceptual language of prohibition/legalisation, criminalisation/decriminalisation, and so on—were of limited utility for the task of deepening critical thinking about drug law reform.

The starting point was two simple linked ideas:

1. Drug control can be understood as a form of market regulation.
2. There is much to be learned from market regulation in other sectors.

From the first idea, a striking insight emerged: drug prohibition is not an absence of regulation (the idea of drugs as circulating in 'unregulated' criminal markets) but rather a specific type of regulatory regime. From the second idea, another important insight flowed: the necessity for drawing on cross-disciplinary and cross-sectoral insights into market regulation.

The next step was to think about the relationship between markets and regulation. Following Shearing (1993), a distinction was made between a *control* perspective (regulation as external controls on pre-existing markets, required only when market forces fail to deliver public goods) and a *constitutive* conception (regulation as constitutive of the markets it seeks to control). It was argued that a constitutive perspective foregrounds the notion that markets cannot and do not precede, or exist outside of, regulation. In other words, markets and regulation are inseparable phenomena. Pushing this idea further led to a fundamental new insight: that we can best understand this inseparability by viewing markets and regulation not as distinct spheres but rather as two sides of the same coin. The new concept of *exchangespace* was introduced to capture this insight, defined as the regulatory space within which economic exchange occurs. Part of its novelty is the refusal to make bright-line definitions of what behaviour and which actors count as 'regulatory' and which as 'economic'.

A specification of *exchangespace* was developed, emphasising its multi-dimensional character, and drawing on insights from diverse disciplines (including economics, sociology, politics, law, and regulation studies). At the heart of this specification were the three connected ideas that *exchangespace* is a *complex* social system that is *networked* and polycentric, and which is always situated in a *political* context shaped by power. The value of drawing on theoretical work that has engaged with these ideas—complex systems science, network analysis, political economy—was explored.

One of the major analytical shifts driven by *exchangespace* was then examined: the foregrounding of time as a critical variable. By moving from thinking about static rule-systems to complex adaptive networks, we start to see flow and flux as core characteristics. This, in turn, means that understanding how and why change happens—from the short term to the *longue durée*—becomes a central analytical task. This is necessary both when looking backwards in historical time and when thinking forwards to future reform. It is imperative therefore to be able to explain and understand patterns of change over time. In exploring this question theoretically, this part of the book identified some core concepts for making sense of regulatory trajectories, including ideas of initial conditions, path dependence, the significance of 'crises', and network structures.

In summary, it was argued in Part I of the book that the *exchangespace* concept is an analytical game-changer, that is, a theoretical tool that can generate novel and transformative insights about drug control, drug laws, and drug law reform. It provides a new vocabulary for talking about what those things are and how they function. And with that new language, new ways of seeing the world also emerge, as do new possibilities for intervening in it.

History

In the second part of the book, the focus turned to attempting to understand the nineteenth-century origins of today's international drug control system. It is a foundational idea of complexity thinking that complex systems are highly sensitive to 'initial conditions'. The *exchangespace* concept therefore gives a theoretical importance to recovering the historical origins of drug control, as key to understanding subsequent regulatory trajectories.

The conventional 'origin story' for global drug prohibition is that it was forged in the early twentieth century, driven largely by the United States, and that post-1945 this became the American-led 'War on Drugs'. Like all such stories, this is partly true but Part II of the book attempted to provide a different perspective by shifting the analytical gaze from West to East and recentring China and Asia in the story. Part of the rationale for this shift was recent work on global history, notably by Peter Frankopan (2015), which has developed a radical re-assessment of world history by arguing that the dominance of Europe and the West over the last 500 years has actually been a temporary shift in power and that this historical 'blip' is coming to an end now with the rise (again) of China in the twenty-first century.

For our story, this took us back to the early nineteenth century and an examination of relations between China and the British Empire. The two conflicts (1839–1842 and 1856–1860) in the middle of that century known as the 'Opium Wars' were explored in some detail, as pivotal moments in Sino-British relations. This analysis showed how some of the foundations for the twentieth-century international drug control system were in fact built much earlier than is usually assumed and were not American-driven. Perhaps the most fundamental insight from this historical re-assessment was the way that opium control in the nineteenth century was forged through a military contestation of the boundaries between legal and illegal trade. We also saw how by the time of the second Opium War, both the military action and the post-conflict diplomacy in the 1860s were now multinational affairs. This has become a feature of drug control ever since.

The focus then moved on to the first decade of the twentieth century. This is a period that is often overlooked, in the hurry to get to the two big drug policy landmarks of the time: the 1912 Opium Convention agreed at The Hague and the establishment in 1920 of international drug control under the auspices of the newly-created League of Nations. Whilst those two landmarks are, of course, of enormous significance, it was argued that the Shanghai meetings in early 1909 are critical to the story as they make visible the connections between the nineteenth and twentieth centuries. Instead of seeing Shanghai simply as a rehearsal for the meetings at The Hague between 1911 and 1914, this part of the book showed how the discussions there highlighted that it was the opium situation in China, and the legacies of the Opium Wars, that drove the creation of the first iteration of international drug prohibition in 1920. The centrality of China—rather than America—also pointed to the importance of taking account of the impact of the fall of the Qing dynasty in the 1911 revolution, an event that is largely absent from most accounts of the origin of prohibition but which arguably is one of the most significant moments in the story.

The initial conditions from which today's prohibition emerged were identified then as trade and power in an international context. More specifically, the historical analysis showed that the central driving forces in the early evolution of drug control were international trade and commerce, economic regulation, European colonial power, and the modernisation of China. This is a very different origin story from the one that is usually told and has radical implications for how to consider the possibilities for reform today.

Politics

In Part III, this question of how we should understand the 'play of power' that underpins theoretical and historical perspectives on drug control was directly addressed. It was argued, first of all, that the common complaint from drug law reformers that drug policy is politicised rather than evidence-based is based on a narrow understanding of the political. Rather than lamenting this state of affairs, we need to try to *understand* why there is so often so much political 'heat' around the drug question. Serious engagement with political science is essential, built on embracing instead of denying the intertwining of drugs and politics. One of the fundamental lessons from political scientists is that ideology—in the sense of political ideas and concepts—is a ubiquitous feature of societies, representing one of the ways in which human beings make sense of the social world. It cannot be avoided through appeals to science or evidence. In other words, we need to take the politics of drugs seriously.

Using some specific examples, the analysis in this part of the book identified first how thinking about drugs and drug control is bound up with some deeply important political ideas, from personal freedom to welfare to citizenship to race. This tells us why it is such a heated area. In this sense, the standard claim that 'politicising' drugs is a shallow or trivial response to the issues is the wrong way round. The politics of drugs is profoundly significant and it is in fact claims that it is possible or desirable to base drug policy solely on 'the science' which are a trivialisation of what is at stake. Indeed, it was argued further that appeals to expertise, and corresponding attempts to downplay or remove the political, are potentially quite damaging. When it is understood that the drug question is inherently political, prioritising expert views over the opportunity for democratic dialogue and discussion becomes a strategy that will forever fall short.

The challenge then is not to ignore or deny politics but instead to find ways of developing a 'better politics' of drugs, that is, one that is inclusive and informed. Can we find, in other words, ways to have more productive and fruitful societal conversations about the drug question? This challenge was explored in several directions. A starting point was to emphasise the necessity of rigorous examination of normative issues and values. This is something that social scientists often baulk at but which is essential. Serious thinking, and open discussion, about what we are trying to achieve—for example, maximising freedom, tempering power, reducing domination—has to be a first step in any collective process of considering future change or reform. Without clarity on values or goals, conversations are inevitably unanchored and susceptible to buffeting by different interests.

It was then argued that to build on this foundation of transparent discussions about the normative questions requires thinking about new forms of political engagement with the drug question. This is partly about articulating the relationships between knowledge production, societal conversations, and policy change, sometimes captured in the idea of 'public social science', but also involves exploring concrete tools for democratic deliberation and revisiting the terrain of social movement politics. The notion of 'thinking democratically' about drugs was also examined, referring to the idea that it is important to consider the impact of different approaches to the drug question on political participation and citizenship identities, that is, to think of drug control as itself having democratic effects. Lastly, the importance of a cosmopolitan vision which decentres and looks beyond the Global North was argued to be critical. The book's central theme about the necessity of recentring China and Asia in our analysis was revisited in this context.

Research and policy futures

At this point in the book, we reach the stage of needing to address the 'so what?' question that the late Roger Matthews (2009), channelling Elliott

Currie, once asked so sharply of criminologists. Readers who have got this far will know, first of all, that the book's argument is not really a criminological one (although I hope criminologists will find it interesting and illuminating). This is an important starting point. One way of reading the book is to see it as an extended argument for a revised practice of social science, moving away from the strict positioning of research within any of the traditional North Atlantic disciplinary silos—criminology, sociology, economics, etc—and towards a more pluralistic and cosmopolitan interdisciplinary social science. It has used the organising concept of regulation to provide coherence to this disciplinary boundary-crossing, based on the simple idea that the regulation of drugs can be usefully conceived 'as a practice that can be enriched from what we know about the regulation of all manner of things, and therefore by regulatory theory' (Braithwaite 2022:xvi). This has been the foundational idea for much of my work over the last decade (e.g. Seddon 2013, 2014, 2016, 2020a; Bacon and Seddon 2020; Seddon and Floodgate 2020).

One of the advances made in this book, in terms of theory and methods, has been to provide a sharper set of conceptual tools for this research, by focusing on market-regulation relations and developing the concept of *exchangespace*. There is much *theoretical* work to be done in further developing *exchangespace*, especially through further exploration of the disciplinary and intellectual building blocks from which it was assembled. There are, for example, many further insights from the field of economic sociology that could be used to deepen and extend the concept. The field of complex systems science similarly offers many potential avenues for strengthening the theoretical foundations of the concept. There is undoubtedly a space here for a programme of collaborative cross-disciplinary theoretical projects, to extend, challenge, and develop the work set out in Part I. In terms of *methodological* advances, the *exchangespace* concept is potentially generative of multiple new research approaches. An obvious area is through harnessing the various techniques of computational social science, particularly for the detailed description and analysis of network behaviour. Further methodological innovation could come from marrying this together with qualitative enquiry and ethnographic approaches. An advanced quantitative approach that is also open to the rich and deep insights of qualitative methods offers an exciting future direction for research that seeks to understand the different aspects of how drug regulation works and how it could be made to work better.

Perhaps the most significant implication of the book is linked to one of its core goals: to rethink the 'pathologically Northern' perspectives (Braithwaite 2021:36) that still prevail in drug policy analysis. We have seen historically how shifts in global power have always shaped trajectories of the drug problem and of international drug control, from the British-driven Opium Wars in the nineteenth century to the American-led 'War on Drugs' in the post-1945 period. This suggests a new but fundamental question that needs to be asked now: as the centre of global power shifts from Washington to Beijing and the American Century gives way to the Asian Century, what are the implications for the project of drug law reform which until this point has been viewed almost exclusively from a North Atlantic perspective?

We certainly know that the world geopolitical map is being redrawn and that one of the fundamental drivers is what President Xi Jinping in 2017 called the 'project of the century': the Belt and Road Initiative (BRI) (see Hillman 2020). This is important in the general sense already noted that shifts in global power tend to influence and shape the trajectory of international drug control. But the BRI is also significant in a more specific way, as its purpose is to transform connectivity—in trade, transport, and information—across Eurasia, radiating out from China, in order to re-configure the place of China and the wider region in the global economy. When we also understand the drug phenomenon as constituted by a set of transnational supply chains and drug control as a particular form of market regulation, then the BRI becomes even more directly relevant. Yet you will struggle to find serious attention being paid to the BRI in the drug policy field.

This lacuna is in many respects completely understandable. It is hard to see Asia as a focal point for reform when we know that, for example, it remains in the 2020s the region in the world where the death penalty is most heavily used for drug offences (Larasati and Girelli 2021). But this is a form of myopia that is precisely shaped by Western-centrism. Why, after all, the concern about the death penalty in Asia but amnesic silence about the place of European colonialism in the very creation of that penal model of drug control?

One way to think critically about this is by using some of the ideas and concepts of colonial theory. Gurminder Bhambra (2021) has argued that the field of international political economy needs to develop an under-standing of how the origins of modern capitalism are deeply entangled with histories of colonialism. She calls for a reorientation of our framework for the analysis of the global economic order so that it can include proper consideration of the historical importance of colonial relations. This insight helps us to contextualise the historical analysis in Part II of the book, which showed the deep connections between Western imperial projects and the nineteenth-century foundations of drug prohibition. Prohibition is, in other words, a product of these wider processes that contributed to the making of the modern world and has been profoundly shaped by colonialism. If we are to unpick—theoretically, historically, politically—the various threads that make up the fabric of today's international drug control system, we therefore need to approach this enterprise as a decolonising project. And this requires the rejection of research and policy vistas that are centred only by a Western gaze.

So what might a decolonising project to rethink drug control and drug law reform in the Asian Century look like? One way forward may be to draw on Peter Drahos' (2021) exceptional book, *Survival Governance*, which explores a China-led scenario for saving the planet from climate catastrophe in the twenty-first century (the 'Chinese Century', as the book's subtitle has it). As he acknowledges, on the face of it, it is an unlikely scenario but over the course of 200 or so pages of argument—framed, like this book, by the organising concept of regulation—he develops a compelling thesis which may perhaps provide an initial way into rethinking approaches to the drug question.

There are three key steps to his argument that are relevant to thinking about new policy futures for drug control. The first is to understand that the climate change challenge for the planet is fundamentally about how we organise and govern world capitalism. As we have seen across all three parts of this book, the question of how we should regulate drugs is similarly also at its heart a question of how we should regulate capitalism. The second step is to acknowledge that whilst world capitalism was under US leadership in the post-1945 period, by the 2020s the United States has been joined, and probably surpassed, by China. This means that for the steering of the trajectory of the system of world capitalism in the twenty-first century, more now 'rests on the planning and decisions of China than of any other capitalist state' (Drahos 2021:224). In other words, whatever China's stance on drug control, its economic planning is going to have an enormous impact. The third step is to see that whilst there may be several reasons to be concerned about China's pre-eminence on the world stage, it also offers some potential benefits. Regulatory action that requires very strong, rapid, and directive state intervention is likely to be more possible if led by the Chinese government. Centralised authoritarian control may be what is needed to change course and turn the tanker around. This is the nub of Drahos' heterodox argument.

A more concrete way we can see how this perspective might start to generate some new ideas about drug law and policy reform is to return to the BRI. As Drahos (2021:16) emphasises, the BRI represents a unique opportunity to build 'global circuits of transport infrastructure, trade and finance' that could transform connectivity in the coming decades. He also notes the lesson from the history of the ancient Silk Roads that these circuits will also buzz with cultural flows and the exchange of 'changing ideas about the world system' (2021:18). In the context of his thesis, this presents unprecedented opportunities to move away from economies built on fossil fuels and to create what he calls a new bio-digital energy paradigm. Some may be sceptical about the likelihood of Drahos' environmental vision being realised but it is certainly the case that for some time to come China is going to drive the transformation of economic infrastructure that cannot fail to reshape some of the patterns of global drug supply and their regulation. Understanding this, there is an opportunity to attempt to engage with China to guide what directions this reshaping goes in. There may be equivalent scepticism about how productive this is likely to be but, if we accept that the global drug problem is a market regulation challenge, then to ignore the way China's BRI is reshaping the world's economic landscape is deeply misguided. I would go further and argue that if we cannot see how to engage positively with China on this, then the fault lies largely with the distortions created by our Western-centric vision. How, for example, can we hope to develop new approaches to regulating the world heroin market if we ignore the shared border area between China and Afghanistan which was once an important thoroughfare for the ancient trading routes of the Silk Road (Dai 1966) and has recently become a renewed focus for Chinese involvement in Afghanistan's affairs (Swanström and Tucker 2019; see also Mohapatra 2007)? Western powers, especially the United States and the United Kingdom, certainly bear a very heavy political and ethical responsibility for many of the problems being experienced in Afghanistan in the 2020s, but this should not blind us to the potential space for China to drive a different future for the country and the region which may, in turn, reshape the world heroin market.

The final 'call to action' is in many respects the most fundamental and the most important. As was argued in Part III of the book, reforming the way we deal with the drug question will have to proceed on the basis of a full-throated and unapologetic engagement with politics and values. This applies equally to research, law reform, and policy development. There must be clarity and transparency about our goals and principles and about what we are trying to achieve. This orientation towards goals rather than rules is also fundamental to the constitutive underpinnings of *exchangespace* that were explored in Part I. As was discussed in the previous chapter, John Braithwaite (2022) makes a powerful case that a republican vision of building freedom, tempering power, and reducing domination of all kinds should be the objectives for regulation and governance. I largely agree but the issues are difficult and it is probably wise to remain open to persuasion that there may sometimes be other goals or priorities. In my view, the most important moves are to acknowledge the necessity of political engagement and to be open and transparent about normative thinking. Reformist rhetoric about purely 'evidence-based policy' or 'following the science' must be abandoned.

Readers will note that I have not arrived here at a detailed proposal for a programme of reform. This has been deliberate. My purpose with this book has been to change the way we think about drug law and policy, to produce a new map for a (potential) new world, and this means stepping outside the usual parameters of policy discourse. It should be clear by now, for example, that I do not think the fundamental debate is about whether we should turn the criminal law on or off for the control of markets in particular psychoactive substances. To frame the matter in this way is facile. Regulatory futures need to be conceived as decentring the influence of old stars (the regulatory state, law and rules, the West) and following new ones more closely (regulatory space, principles and goals, the East). As should also be clear, the language of regulation should not be confused with technocracy or any denial of the importance of power and politics. Quite the contrary. What will ultimately be essential in new approaches to the drug question is a full engagement with the diverse social and cultural contexts in which the regulation of psychoactive trade is situated. One of the great insights from Braithwaite's (2022:624–628) magisterial *Macrocriminology and Freedom* is that institutions matter for regulation and that the best strategies build on what is already there and already working. In other words, bottom-up solutions hold more promise than top-down structures or regimes (however carefully designed). This is the place to look for a better regulatory future, rather than any grand blueprint for global drug control written by someone like me.

Conclusion

In April 2016, I was in New York for a meeting of the International Society for the Study of Drug Policy (ISSDP) on cannabis policy in the Americas. At the end of the first day, I was due to meet up with some colleagues for dinner. I was a little early, so decided to have a drink in the bar of my hotel before setting off for the restaurant. I sat at a stool at the bar and after five minutes became aware of a man taking the stool next to me. He ordered a beer and asked me if I had been at the cannabis conference. I said yes and he inquired what my interest was. I explained I was an academic researcher and then asked him the same question, expecting that he was either an academic or a policy wonk. His reply took me completely by surprise: he was a businessman, attending the meeting to help him decide whether cannabis was an industry worth investing in or not.

This was a revelatory moment for me. I realised two things: that the world was changing fast with cannabis rapidly becoming big business in North America; and that cannabis law reform was as much about commerce and capitalism as it was about the familiar 'progressive' tropes of civil rights and personal freedom. On the flight home to the United Kingdom a couple of days later, I began to hatch some ideas for a project which eventually led to a book on cannabis regulation (Seddon and Floodgate 2020) and some archival research on drug law reform activism in the 1960s (Seddon 2020c). But in many ways this revelatory moment shaped the heart of this book as well. Its central premise, after all, is that drug laws and policy are a form of market regulation and that the drug law reform enterprise therefore needs to be understood as a business regulation problem. I have attempted in the three substantive parts of the book to make sense of this intellectual project and policy challenge in theoretical, historical, and political registers, based on the overarching idea that regulatory theory holds the key to effecting a paradigm shift. Whether this new paradigm will fly and, if it does, whether it will make a difference to the world, is uncertain, but I have no doubt at all that the research and policy status quo is long past its sell-by date. A change is surely going to come.

References

Aaronson, E. (2019) 'The Strange Career of the Transnational Legal Order of Cannabis Prohibition' *UC Irvine Journal of International, Transnational, and Comparative Law* 4 78–96.

Abel, E. (1980) *Marihuana: The First Twelve Thousand Years.* New York: Plenum Press.

Amicelle, A., Côté-Boucher, K., Dupont, B., Mulone, M., Shearing, C., and Tanner, S. (2017) 'Criminology in the Face of Flows: Reflections on Contemporary Policing and Security' *Global Crime* 18(3) 165–175.

August, V. (2022) 'Network Concepts in Social Theory: Foucault and Cybernetics' *European Journal of Social Theory* 25(2) 271–291.

Ayres, I. and Braithwaite, J. (1992) *Responsive Regulation: Transcending the Deregulation Debate.* Oxford: Oxford University Press.

Bächtiger, A., Dryzek, J., Mansbridge, J., and Warren, M. (eds) (2018) *The Oxford Handbook of Deliberative Democracy.* Oxford: Oxford University Press.

Bacon, M. and Seddon, T. (2020) 'Controlling Drug Users: Forms of Power and Behavioural Regulation in Drug Treatment Services' *British Journal of Criminology* 60(2) 403–421.

Baker, K.M. (1964) 'The Early History of the Term "Social Science"' *Annals of Science* 20(3) 211–226.

Barabási, A.-L. (2016) *Network Science.* Cambridge: Cambridge University Press.

Barop, H. (2015) 'Building the "Opium Evil" Consensus—The International Opium Commission of Shanghai' *Journal of Modern European History* 13(1) 115–137.

Becker, H. (1963) *Outsiders: Studies in the Sociology of Deviance.* New York: Free Press.

Becker, H. (1967) 'Whose Side Are We On?' *Social Problems* 14(3) 239–247.

Beckert, J. and Dewey, M. (2017) 'Introduction: The Social Organization of Illegal Markets' in: J. Beckert and M. Dewey (eds) *The Architecture of Illegal Markets: Towards an Economic Sociology of Illegality in the Economy.* Oxford: Oxford University Press, 1–34.

Beckert, J. and Wehinger, F. (2013) 'In the Shadow: Illegal Markets and Economic Sociology' *Socio-Economic Review* 11 5–30.

Beeching, J. (1975) *The Chinese Opium Wars.* London: Hutchinson.

Bennear, L. and Wiener, J. (2019) *Adaptive Regulation: Instrument Choice for Policy Learning over Time.* Harvard Kennedy School Working Paper.

Berg, J. and Shearing, C. (2021) 'Criminology: Some Lines of Flight' *Journal of Criminology* 54(1) 21–33.

Berridge, V. (1977) 'Opium Eating and Life Insurance' *British Journal of Addiction* 72 371–377.

Berridge, V. (1979) 'Morality and Medical Science: Concepts of Narcotic Addiction in Britain, 1820–1926' *Annals of Science* 36(1) 67–85.

Berridge, V. (1980) 'The Making of the Rolleston Report, 1908–1926' *Journal of Drug Issues* 10(1) 7–28.

Berridge, V. and Edwards, G. (1981) *Opium and the People: Opiate Use in Nineteenth-Century England.* London: Allen Lane.

Bewley-Taylor, D. (1999) *The United States and International Drug Control, 1909–1997.* London: Continuum.

Bewley-Taylor, D. and Jelsma, M. (2011) *Fifty Years of the 1961 Single Convention on Narcotic Drugs: A Reinterpretation.* Series on Legislative Reform of Drug Policies No. 12. Amsterdam: Transnational Institute.

Bewley-Taylor, D., Blickman, T., and Jelsma, M. (2014) *The Rise and Decline of Cannabis Prohibition: The History of Cannabis in the UN Drug Control System and Options for Reform.* Amsterdam: Transnational Institute.

Bhambra, G. (2021) 'Colonial Global Economy: Towards a Theoretical Reorientation of Political Economy' *Review of International Political Economy* 28(2) 307–322.

Bichler, G., Malm, A., and Cooper, T. (2017) 'Drug Supply Networks: A Systematic Review of the Organizational Structure of Illicit Drug Trade' *Crime Science* 6 Article 2.

Bigo, D. (2017) 'International Flows, Political Order and Social Change: (In)Security, By-Product of the Will of Order over Change' *Global Crime* 18(3) 303–321.

Black, J. (2002) 'Critical Reflections on Regulation' *Australian Journal of Legal Philosophy* 27 1–36.

Bone, M. (2020) *Human Rights and Drug Control: A New Perspective.* London: Routledge.

Bourgois, P. (2018) 'Decolonising Drug Studies in an Era of Predatory Accumulation' *Third World Quarterly* 39(2) 385–398.

Bracken, G. (2019) 'Treaty Ports in China: Their Genesis, Development, and Influence' *Journal of Urban History* 45(1) 168–176.

Braithwaite, J. (2003) 'What's Wrong with the Sociology of Punishment?' *Theoretical Criminology* 7(1) 5–28.

Braithwaite, J. (2005) 'For Public Social Science' *British Journal of Sociology* 56(3) 345–353.

Braithwaite, J. (2008) *Regulatory Capitalism: How It Works, Ideas for Making It Work Better.* Cheltenham: Edward Elgar.

Braithwaite, J. (2014) 'In Praise of Tents: Regulatory Studies and Transformative Social Science' *Annual Review of Law & Social Science* 10(1) 1–17.

Braithwaite, J. (2019) 'Tempered Power, Variegated Capitalism, Law and Society' *Buffalo Law Review* 67(3) 527–594.

Braithwaite, J. (2020a) 'Crime as a Cascade Phenomenon' *International Journal of Comparative and Applied Criminal Justice* 44(3) 137–169.

Braithwaite, J. (2020b) 'Meta Governance of Path Dependencies: Regulation, Welfare, and Markets' *The ANNALS of the American Academy of Political and Social Science* 691 30–49.

Braithwaite, J. (2021) 'Authoritarian Under-labouring?' in: T. Daems and S. Pleysier (eds) *Criminology and Democratic Politics.* London: Routledge, 25–41.

Braithwaite, J. (2022) *Macrocriminology and Freedom.* Canberra: ANU Press.

Braithwaite, J. and Drahos, P. (2000) *Global Business Regulation*. Cambridge: Cambridge University Press.

Braithwaite, J. and Pettit, P. (1990) *Not Just Deserts: A Republican Theory of Criminal Justice*. Oxford: Clarendon Press.

Braithwaite, J., Coglianese, C., and Levi-Faur, D. (2007) 'Can Regulation and Governance Make a Difference?' *Regulation & Governance* 1 1–7.

Braithwaite, J., Charlesworth, H., and Soares, A. (2012) *Networked Governance of Freedom and Tyranny: Peace in Timor-Leste*. Canberra: ANU Press.

Bruun, K., Pan, L., and Rexed, I. (1975) *The Gentlemen's Club: International Control of Drugs and Alcohol*. Chicago: University of Chicago Press.

Burawoy, M. (2004) 'Public Sociologies: Contradictions, Dilemmas, and Possibilities' *Social Forces* 82(4) 1603–1618.

Burawoy, M. (2005) 'For Public Sociology' *American Sociological Review* 70(1) 4–28.

Burris, S., Drahos, P., and Shearing, C. (2005) 'Nodal Governance' *Australian Journal of Legal Philosophy* 30 30–58.

Burris, S., Kempa, M., and Shearing, C. (2008) 'Changes in Governance: A Cross-Disciplinary Review of Current Scholarship' *Akron Law Review* 41(1) 1–66.

Buzan, B., Wæver, O., and de Wilde, J. (1998) *Security: A New Framework for Analysis*. London: Lynne Rienner.

Callon, M., Meadel, C., and Rabeharisoa, V. (2002) 'The Economy of Qualities' *Economy and Society* 31(2) 194–217.

Campbell, D. and Klaes, M. (2005) 'The Principle of Institutional Direction: Coase's Regulatory Critique of Intervention' *Cambridge Journal of Economics* 29(2) 263–288.

Castells, M. (1996) *The Rise of the Network Society*. Oxford: Blackwell.

Castells, M. (1997) *The Power of Identity*. Oxford: Blackwell.

Castells, M. (1998) *End of Millennium*. Oxford: Blackwell.

Chatwin, C. (2018) *Towards More Effective Global Drug Policies*. London: Palgrave.

Chouvy, P.-A. (2020) 'Le *kif*, l'avenir du Rif? Variété de pays, terroir, labellisation, atouts d'une future légalisation' *Belgeo: Revue Belge de Géographie* 1.

Ciccarone D. (2019) 'The Triple Wave Epidemic: Supply and Demand Drivers of the US Opioid Overdose Crisis' *International Journal of Drug Policy* 71 183–188.

Ciccarone, D. (2021) 'The Rise of Illicit Fentanyls, Stimulants and the Fourth Wave of the Opioid Overdose Crisis' *Current Opinion in Psychiatry* 34(4) 344–350.

Clarke, M. (2000) *Regulation: The Social Control of Business between Law and Politics*. London: Macmillan.

Clawson, D., Zussman, R., Misra, J., Gerstel, N., Stokes, R., Anderton, D., and Burawoy, M. (eds) (2007) *Public Sociology: Fifteen Eminent Sociologists Debate Politics and the Profession in the Twenty-first Century*. Los Angeles: University of California Press.

Coase, R. (1960) 'The Problem of Social Cost' *Journal of Law and Economics* 3 1–44.

Cohen, S. (1981) 'Footprints on the Sand: A Further Report on Criminology and the Sociology of Deviance in Britain' in: M. Fitzgerald, G. McLennan, and J. Pawson (eds) *Crime & Society: Readings in History and Theory*. London: Routledge, 220–247.

Collins, J. (2018) 'Empire, War, Decolonization and the Birth of the Illicit Opium Trade in Burma 1800–1961' in: J. Windle, J. Morrison, A. Winter, and A. Silke (eds) *Historical Perspectives on Organised Crime and Terrorism*. London: Routledge, 169–187.

Collins, J. (2022) *Legalising the Drug Wars: A Regulatory History of UN Drug Control*. Cambridge: Cambridge University Press.

Coomber, R. and South, N. (eds) (2004) *Drug Use and Cultural Contexts 'Beyond the West'*. London: Free Association.

Coriat, B. and Weinstein, O. (2010) 'The Market, Institutions and Transactions' in: M. Harvey (ed) *Markets, Rules and Institutions of Exchange*. Manchester: Manchester University Press, 32–61.

Courtwright, D. (1982) *Dark Paradise: A History of Opiate Addiction in America*. Cambridge, MA: Harvard University Press.

Courtwright, D. (2001) *Forces of Habit: Drugs and the Making of the Modern World*. Cambridge, MA: Harvard University Press.

Courtwright, D. (2005) 'Mr ATOD's Wild Ride: What Do Alcohol, Tobacco, and Other Drugs Have in Common?' *Social History of Alcohol and Drugs* 20 105–124.

Crick, E. (2012) 'Drugs as an Existential Threat: An Analysis of the International Securitization of Drugs' *International Journal of Drug Policy* 23(5) 407–414.

Crouch, C. (1986) 'Sharing Public Space: States and Organised Interests in Western Europe' in: J. Hall (ed) *States in History*. Oxford: Blackwell, 177–210.

Dai, S.-Y. (1966) 'China and Afghanistan' *The China Quarterly* 25 213–221.

Daniels, C., Aluso, A., Burke-Shyne, N., Koram, K., Rajagopalan, S., Robinson, I., Shelly, S., Shirley-Beavan, S., and Tandon, T. (2021) 'Decolonizing Drug Policy' *Harm Reduction Journal* 18 Article 120.

d'Aspremont, J. and Zhang, B. (2021) 'China and International Law: Two Tales of an Encounter' *Leiden Journal of International Law* 34(4) 899–914.

Daston, L. (2020) 'Thomas S. Kuhn, *The Structure of Scientific Revolutions* (1962)' *Public Culture* 32(2) 405–413.

Dávalos, E. and Dávolos, L. (2020) 'Social Investment and Smallholder Coca Cultivation in Colombia' *Journal of Development Studies* 56(6) 1118–1140.

Decorte, T., Pardal, M., Queirolo, R., Boidi, M., Aviles, C., and Franquero, O. (2017) 'Regulating Cannabis Social Clubs: A Comparative Analysis of Legal and Self-Regulatory Practices in Spain, Belgium and Uruguay' *International Journal of Drug Policy* 43 44–56.

Demaret, I., Quertemont, E., Litran, G., Magoga, C., Deblire, C. Dubois, N., De Roubaix, J., Charlier, C., Lemaitre, A., and Ansseau, M. (2015) 'Efficacy of Heroin-Assisted Treatment in Belgium: A Randomised Controlled Trial' *European Addiction Research* 21 179–187.

Deming, S. (2011) 'The Economic Importance of Indian Opium and Trade with China on Britain's Economy, 1843–1890' *Economics Working Papers* 25.

Dikötter, F., Laamann, L., and Xun, Z. (2004) *Narcotic Culture: A History of Drugs in China*. Chicago: University of Chicago Press.

Dorf, M. and Sabel, C. (1998) 'A Constitution of Democratic Experimentalism' *Columbia Law Review* 98(2) 267–473.

Downs, J. (1968) 'American Merchants and the China Opium Trade, 1800–1840' *Business History Review* 42(4) 418–442.

Drahos, P. (ed) (2017) *Regulatory Theory: Foundations and Applications*. Canberra: ANU Press.

Drahos, P. (2021) *Survival Governance: Energy and Climate in the Chinese Century*. Oxford: Oxford University Press.

Dzur, A., Loader, I., and Sparks, R. (2016) 'Punishment and Democratic Theory: Resources for a Better Penal Politics' in: A. Dzur, I. Loader, and R. Sparks (eds) *Democratic Theory and Mass Incarceration*. Oxford: Oxford University Press, 1–17.

Eastwood, N., Fox, E., and Rosmarin, A. (2016) *A Quiet Revolution: Drug Decriminalisation Across the Globe*. London: Release.

EMCDDA (European Monitoring Centre for Drugs and Drug Addiction) (2017) *Changes in Europe's Cannabis Resin Market*. Lisbon: EMCDDA.

Esherick, J. (2012) 'Reconsidering 1911: Lessons of a Sudden Revolution' *Journal of Modern Chinese History* 6(1) 1–14.

Ettorre, E. (1992) *Women and Substance Use*. London: Palgrave.

Ewald, F. (1991) 'Insurance and Risk' in: G. Burchell, C. Gordon, and P. Miller (eds) *The Foucault Effect: Studies in Governmentality*. Chicago: University of Chicago Press, 197–210.

Eyffinger, A. (2019) 'The Three Hague Opium Conferences (1911–1914)' in: A. Eyffinger (ed) *T.M.C Asser (1838–1913)*. Leiden: Brill, 1687–1712.

Farrall, S. (2021) *Building Complex Temporal Explanations of Crime: History, Institutions and Agency*. London: Palgrave.

Fay, P. (1975) *The Opium War: 1840–1842*. Chapel Hill: University of North Carolina Press.

Feuerwerker, A. (1980) 'Economic Trends in the Late Ch'ing Empire, 1870–1911' in: J. Fairbank and K. Liu (eds) *The Cambridge History of China*. Cambridge: Cambridge University Press, 1–69.

Fine, R. (2007) *Cosmopolitanism*. London: Routledge.

Fligstein, N. (2001) *The Architecture of Markets: An Economic Sociology of Twenty-First-Century Capitalist Societies*. Princeton: Princeton University Press.

Fogel, J. (2006) 'Opium and China Revisited: How Sophisticated was Qing Thinking in Matters of Drug Control?' *China Review International* 13(1) 43–51.

Fordham, A. (2012) '55th Session of the CND—Not Quite Déjà Vu' *Drugs and Alcohol Today* 12(3).

Foucault, M. (1977) *Discipline and Punish: The Birth of the Prison*. London: Allen Lane.

Foucault, M. (1984) 'Nietzsche, Genealogy, History' in: P. Rabinow (ed) *The Foucault Reader*. New York: Pantheon, 76–100.

Foucault, M. (1991a) 'Politics and the Study of Discourse' in: G. Burchell, C. Gordon, and P. Miller (eds) *The Foucault Effect: Studies in Governmentality*. Chicago: University of Chicago Press, 53–72.

Foucault, M. (1991b) 'Questions of Method' in: G. Burchell, C. Gordon, and P. Miller (eds) *The Foucault Effect: Studies in Governmentality*. Chicago: University of Chicago Press, 73–86.

Foucault, M. (2008) *The Birth of Biopolitics: Lectures at the Collège de France, 1978–1979*. London: Palgrave.

Foucault, M. (2019) *Penal Theories and Institutions: Lectures at the Collège de France, 1971–1972*. London: Palgrave.

Frankopan, P. (2015) *The Silk Roads: A New History of the World*. London: Bloomsbury.

Frankopan, P. (2018) *The New Silk Roads: The Present and Future of the World*. London: Bloomsbury.

Fraser, N. and Gordon, L. (1994) 'A Genealogy of *Dependency*: Tracing a Keyword of the U.S. Welfare State' *Signs: Journal of Women in Culture and Society* 19(2) 309–336.

Freeden, M. (1996) *Ideologies and Political Theory: A Conceptual Approach*. Oxford: Oxford University Press.

Freeden, M. (2013) 'The Morphological Analysis of Ideology' in: M. Freeden, L. Sargent, and M. Stears (eds) *The Oxford Handbook of Political Ideologies*. Oxford: Oxford University Press, 115–137.

Gane, N. (2018) 'Foucault's History of Neoliberalism' in: L. Downing (ed) *After Foucault: Culture, Theory and Criticism in the 21st Century*. Cambridge: Cambridge University Press, 46–60.

Gao, H. (2020) *Creating the Opium War: British Imperial attitudes towards China, 1792–1840*. Manchester: Manchester University Press.

Garland, D. (1985) *Punishment and Welfare: A History of Penal Strategies*. Aldershot: Gower.

Garland, D. (2021) 'What's Wrong with Penal Populism? Politics, the Public, and Criminological Expertise' *Asian Journal of Criminology* 16 257–277.

Garnsey, E. (1998) 'The Genesis of the High Technology Milieu: A Study in Complexity' *International Journal of Urban and Regional Research* 22(3) 363–377.

Gereffi, G., Humphrey, J., and Sturgeon, T. (2005) 'The Governance of Global Value Chains' *Review of International Political Economy* 12(1) 78–104.

Gerring, J. (1997) 'Ideology: A Definitional Analysis' *Political Research Quarterly* 50(4) 957–994.

Gilpin, R. (2001) *Global Political Economy: Understanding the International Economic Order*. Princeton: Princeton University Press.

Goodman, J., Sherratt, A., and Lovejoy, P. (eds) (1995) *Consuming Habits: Drugs in History and Anthropology*. London: Routledge.

Gootenberg, P. (2009) *Andean Cocaine: The Making of a Global Drug*. Chapel Hill: University of North Carolina Press.

Gootenberg, P. (2019) 'Coca and Cocaine in Latin American History' in: *Oxford Research Encyclopedia of Latin American History*. Oxford: Oxford University Press.

Gornall, J. (2020) 'Big Cannabis in the UK: Is Industry Support for Wider Patient Access Motivated by Promises of Recreational Market Worth Billions?' *BMJ* 368:m1002 doi:10.1136/bmj.m1002

Granovetter, M. (1985) 'Economic Action and Social Structure: The Problem of Embeddedness' *American Journal of Sociology* 91(3) 481–510.

Greenwood, L. and Fashola, K. (2021) *Illicit Fentanyl from China: An Evolving Global Operation*. Washington, DC: US-China Economic and Security Review Commission.

Grisaffi, T. (2019) *Coca Yes, Cocaine No: How Bolivia's Coca Growers Reshaped Democracy*. Durham, NC: Duke University Press.

Hacking, I. (2012) 'Introductory Essay' in: T. Kuhn *The Structure of Scientific Revolutions: 50th Anniversary Edition*. Chicago: University of Chicago Press, vii–xxxvii.

Hacking, I. (2016) 'Paradigms' in: R. Richards and L. Daston (eds) *Kuhn's Structure of Scientific Revolutions at Fifty: Reflections on a Science Classic*. Chicago: University of Chicago Press, 96–114.

Hall, S., Critcher, C., Jefferson, T., Clarke, J., and Roberts, B. (1978) *Policing the Crisis: Mugging, the State, and Law and Order*. London: Macmillan.

Hammersley, M. (2001) 'Whose Side was Becker on? Questioning Political and Epistemological Radicalism' *Qualitative Research* 1(1) 91–110.

Hancher, L. and Moran, M. (1989/1998) 'Organizing Regulatory Space' in: R. Baldwin, C. Scott, and C. Hood (eds) *A Reader on Regulation*. Oxford: Oxford University Press, 148–172.

Harcourt, B. (2011) *The Illusion of Free Markets: Punishment and the Myth of Natural Order*. Cambridge, MA: Harvard University Press.

Hardouin, P. (2017) 'Too Big to Fail, Too Big to Jail: Restoring Liability a Lesson from HSBC Case' *Journal of Financial Crime* 24(4) 513–519.

Hart, C. (2021) *Drug Use for Grown-Ups: Chasing Liberty in the Land of Fear*. London: Penguin.

Hartnoll, R., Mitcheson, M., Battersby, A., Brown, G., Ellis, M., Fleming, P., and Hedley, N. (1980) 'Evaluation of Heroin Maintenance in Controlled Trial' *Archives of General Psychiatry* 37 877–884.

Harvey, M. (2010) 'Introduction: Putting Markets in their Place' in: M. Harvey (ed) *Markets, Rules and Institutions of Exchange*. Manchester: Manchester University Press, 1–31.

Harvey, M. and Randles, S. (2010) 'Markets, the Organisation of Exchanges and "Instituted Economic Process": An Analytical Perspective' in: M. Harvey (ed) *Markets, Rules and Institutions of Exchange*. Manchester: Manchester University Press, 62–81.

Henderson, J. (2005) 'Global Production Networks, Competition, Regulation and Poverty Reduction: Policy Implications' *Centre on Regulation and Competition Working Paper No 115*. Manchester: University of Manchester.

Herzberg, D. (2020) *White Market Drugs: Big Pharma and the Hidden History of Addiction in America*. Chicago: University of Chicago Press.

Hickman, T. (2000) 'Drugs and Race in American Culture: Orientalism in the Turn-of-the-Century Discourse of Narcotic Addiction' *American Studies* 41(1) 71–91.

Hillman, J. (2020) *The Emperor's New Road: China and the Project of the Century*. New Haven: Yale University Press.

Hiromasa, I. (1986) 'Wu Lanxiu and Society in Guangzhou on the Eve of the Opium War' *Modern China* 12(1) 103–115.

Hiromasa, I. (2004) *Shindai ahen seisaku shi no kenkyu* [Studies in the history of Qing policy toward Opium]. Kyoto: Kyoto University Press.

Hoekstra, F., Mrklas, K., Khan, M., McKay, R., Vis-Dunbar, M., Sibley, K., Nguyen, T., Graham, I., SCI Guiding Principles Consensus Panel, and Gainforth, H. (2020) 'A Review of Reviews on Principles, Strategies, Outcomes and Impacts of Research Partnerships Approaches: A First Step in Synthesising the Research Partnership Literature' *Health Research Policy and Systems* 18 1–23.

Holley, C. and Shearing, C. (2017) 'A Nodal Perspective of Governance: Advances in Nodal Governance Thinking' in: P. Drahos (ed) *Regulatory Theory: Foundations and Applications*. Canberra: ANU Press, 163–180.

Holley, C., Mutongwizo, T., and Shearing, C. (2020) 'Conceptualizing Policing and Security: New Harmscapes, the Anthropocene, and Technology' *Annual Review of Criminology* 3 341–358.

Homer-Dixon, T., Maynard, J., Mildenberger, M., Milkoreit, M., Mock, S., Quilley, S., Schroder, T., and Thagard, P. (2013) 'A Complex Systems Approach to the Study of Ideology: Cognitive-Affective Structures and the Dynamics of Belief Systems' *Journal of Social and Political Psychology* 1(1) 337–363.

Hughes, C. (2017) 'Portuguese Drug Policy' in: R. Colson and H. Bergeron (eds) *European Drug Policies: The Ways of Reform*. London: Routledge, 164–181.

Hughes, C. and Stevens, A. (2010) 'What Can We Learn from the Portuguese Decriminalization of Illicit Drugs?' *British Journal of Criminology* 50(6) 999–1022.

Inglis, B. (1976) *The Opium War*. London: Hodder & Staughton.

Ingram, K. (2018) *Drugs and Human Rights: A Constitutional Approach. Is It an Abuse of Human Rights to Place Medically Useful Drugs into Schedule 1 of the Misuse of Drugs Regulation 2001?* PhD Thesis. University of Manchester.

James, K. and Jordan, A. (2018) 'The Opioid Crisis in Black Communities' *Journal of Law, Medicine & Ethics* 46 404–421.

Jansseune, L., Pardal, M., Decorte, T., and Franquero, O. (2019) 'Revisiting the Birthplace of the Cannabis Social Club Model and the Role Played by Cannabis Social Club Federations' *Journal of Drug Issues* 49(2) 338–354.

Johnson, J. (2010) 'The Future of the Social Sciences and Humanities in the Science of Complex Systems' *Innovation: The European Journal of Social Science Research* 23(2) 115–134.

Johnston, G. (2020) 'The Kids Are All White: Examining Race and Representation in News Media Coverage of Opioid Overdose Deaths in Canada' *Sociological Inquiry* 90(1) 123–146.

Joseph, R. (1975) 'The Economic Significance of *Cannabis sativa* in the Moroccan Rif' in: V. Rubin (ed) *Cannabis and Culture*. The Hague: Mouton, 185–194.

Kammersgaard, T. (2020) 'Being "in place", being "out of place": Problematising Marginalised Drug Users in Two Cities' *International Journal of Drug Policy* 75 102589.

Kaufman, A. (2010) 'The "Century of Humiliation", Then and Now: Chinese Perceptions of the International Order' *Pacific Focus* 25(1) 1–33.

Kaufman, A. (2013) 'In Pursuit of Equality and Respect: China's Diplomacy and the League of Nations' *Modern China* 40(6) 605–638.

Kelleher, J. and Tierney, B. (2018) *Data Science*. Cambridge, MA: The MIT Press.

Kilmer, B. and Neel, E. (2020) 'Being Thoughtful about Cannabis Legalization and Social Equity' *World Psychiatry* 19(2) 194–195.

Kingsberg, M. (2011) 'Abstinent Nation, Addicted Empire: Opium and Japan in the Meiji Period' *Social History of Alcohol and Drugs* 25 88–106.

Kirby, W. (1997) 'The Internationalization of China: Foreign Relations at Home and Abroad in the Republican Era' *The China Quarterly* 150 433–458.

Kirshner, J. (2003) 'Money is Politics' *Review of International Political Economy* 10(4) 645–660.

Kozma, L. (2011) 'Cannabis Prohibition in Egypt, 1880–1939: From Local Ban to League of Nations Diplomacy' *Middle Eastern Studies* 47(3) 443–460.

Kuhn, T. (1962) *The Structure of Scientific Revolutions*. Chicago: University of Chicago Press.

Kuhn, T. (1969) 'Reflections on My Critics' in: I. Lakatos and A. Musgrave (eds) *Criticism and the Growth of Knowledge*. Cambridge: Cambridge University Press, 231–278.

Kushner, H. (2006) 'Taking Biology Seriously: The Next Task for Historians of Addiction?' *Bulletin of the History of Medicine* 80(1) 115–143.

Kushner, H. (2010) 'Toward a Cultural Biology of Addiction' *BioSocieties* 5 8–24.

Lancaster, K., Ritter, A., and Diprose, R. (2018) 'Recasting Participation in Drug Policy' *Contemporary Drug Problems* 45(4) 351–365.

Larasati, A. and Girelli, G. (2021) *The Death Penalty for Drug Offences: Global Overview 2020*. London: Harm Reduction International.

Levi-Faur, D. (2013) 'The Odyssey of the Regulatory State: From a "Thin" Monomorphic Concept to a "Thick" and Polymorphic Concept' *Law & Policy* 35(1–2) 29–50.

Levi-Faur, D. (2014) 'The Welfare State: A Regulatory Perspective' *Public Administration* 92(3) 599–614.

Lindesmith, A. (1965) *The Addict and the Law*. Bloomington: Indiana University Press.

Lines, R. (2017) *Drug Control and Human Rights in International Law*. Cambridge: Cambridge University Press.

Loader, I. (2010) 'Is It NICE? The Appeal, Limits and Promise of Translating a Health Innovation into Criminal Justice' *Current Legal Problems* 63(1) 72–91.

Loader, I. (2021) *Recognition and Redemption: Visions of Safety and Justice in Black Lives Matter* (6 May 2021). Available at SSRN: https://ssrn.com/abstract=3840 766 or https://dx.doi.org/10.2139/ssrn.3840766.

Loader, I. and Sparks, R. (2010) *Public Criminology?* London: Routledge.

Loader, I. and Sparks, R. (2011a) 'Braithwaite, Criminology and the Debate on Public Social Science' in: S. Parmentier, L. Walgrave, I. Aertsen, J. Maesschalck, and L. Paoli (eds) *The Sparking Discipline of Criminology: John Braithwaite and the Construction of Critical Social Science and Social Justice*. Leuven: Leuven University Press, 85–114.

Loader, I. and Sparks, R. (2011b) 'Criminology's Public Roles: A Drama in Six Acts' in: M. Bosworth and C. Hoyle (eds) *What is Criminology?* Oxford: Oxford University Press, 17–34.

Loader, I. and Sparks, R. (2014) 'The *Question* of Public Criminology: Seeking Resources of Hope for a Better Politics of Crime' *International Annals of Criminology* 52(1–2) 155–177.

Loader, I. and Sparks, R. (2016) 'Ideologies and Crime: Political Ideas and the Dynamics of Crime Control' *Global Crime* 17(3-4) 314–330.

Loader, I. and Sparks, R. (2017) 'Penal Populism and Epistemic Crime Control' in: A. Liebling, S. Maruna, and L. McAra (eds) *Oxford Handbook of Criminology.* 6th Edition. Oxford: Oxford University Press, 98–115.

Loader, I. and Sparks, R. (2019) 'Democratic Experimentalism and the Futures of Crime Control' in: P. Carlen and L. França (eds) *Justice Alternatives.* London: Routledge, 105–120.

Loader, I. and Sparks, R. (2022) 'Reasonable Hopes: Social Theory, Critique and Reconstruction in Contemporary Criminology' in: A. Liebling, J. Shapland, R. Sparks, and J. Tankebe (eds) *Crime, Justice and Order: Essays in Honour of A.E. Bottoms.* Oxford: Oxford University Press, 100–128.

Lovell, J. (2011) *The Opium War.* London: Macmillan.

Lowes, P. (1966) *The Genesis of International Narcotics Control.* Geneva: University of Geneva.

Lozano, A. (2018) 'Reframing the Public Sociology Debate: Towards Collaborative and Decolonial Praxis' *Current Sociology* 66(1) 92–109.

Lubaale, E.C. and Mavundla, S.D. (2019) 'Decriminalisation of Cannabis for Personal Use in South Africa' *African Human Rights Law Journal* 19 819–842.

Lunze, K., Lernet, O., Andreeva, V., and Hariga, F. (2018) 'Compulsory Treatment of Drug Use in Southeast Asian Countries' *International Journal of Drug Policy* 59 10–15.

McAllister, W. (2000) *Drug Diplomacy in the Twentieth Century: An International History.* London: Routledge.

MacCoun, R. and Reuter, P. (2011) 'Assessing Drug Prohibition and Its Alternatives: A Guide for Agnostics' *Annual Review of Law & Social Science* 7 61–78.

McLean, S. and Rose, N. (2021) 'Drug Overdose Deaths, Addiction Neuroscience and the Challenges of Translation' *Wellcome Open Research* 5:215 https://doi.org/10.12688/wellcomeopenres.16265.2

McMahon, M. and West, W.G. (1992) 'Interview with Rosa del Olmo' *Journal of Human Justice* 4(1) 97–116.

Madancy, J. (2000) 'Poppies, Patriotism, and the Public Sphere: Nationalism and State Leadership in the Anti-Opium Crusade in Fujian, 1906-1916' in: T. Brook and B. Wakabayashi (eds) *Opium Regimes: China, Britain, and Japan, 1839-1952.* Los Angeles: University of California Press, 228–247.

Mahoney, J. (2000) 'Path Dependence in Historical Sociology' *Theory and Society* 29(4) 507–548.

Mao, H. (2016) *The Qing Empire and the Opium War: The Collapse of the Heavenly Dynasty.* Cambridge: Cambridge University Press.

Marks, A. (2019) 'Defining "Personal Consumption" in Drug Legislation and Spanish Cannabis Clubs' *International and Comparative Law Quarterly* 68 193–223.

Marks, J. (1987) 'The Paradox of Prohibition' *Mersey Drugs Journal* 1 6–7.

Marks, J. (1990) 'The Paradox of Prohibition' in: J. Hando and J. Carless (eds) *Controlled Availability: Wisdom or Disaster?* NDARC Monograph No 10. Sydney: University of New South Wales, 7–10.

Marks, J. and Palombella, A. (1990) 'Prescribing Smokable Drugs' *The Lancet* 335(8693) 864,

Marks, J., Palombella, A., and Newcomber, R. (1991) 'The Smoking Option' *Druglink* May/June 10–11.

Martin, J. (2014) *Drugs on the Dark Net: How Cryptomarkets Are Transforming the Global Trade in Illegal Drugs*. London: Palgrave.

Martin, J., Munksgaard, R., Coomber, R., Demant, J., and Barratt, M. (2020) 'Selling Drugs on Darkweb Cryptomarkets: Differentiated Pathways, Risks and Rewards' *British Journal of Criminology* 60(3) 559–578.

Masterman, M. (1969) 'The Nature of a Paradigm' in: I. Lakatos and A. Musgrave (eds) *Criticism and the Growth of Knowledge*. Cambridge: Cambridge University Press, 59–90.

Matthews, R. (2009) 'Beyond "So What?" Criminology' *Theoretical Criminology* 13(3) 341–362.

May, C. (2017) *Transnational Crime and the Developing World*. Washington, DC: Global Financial Integrity.

Maynard, J. (2013) 'A Map of the Field of Ideological Analysis' *Journal of Political Ideologies* 18(3) 299–327.

Melancon, G. (1999) 'Honour in Opium? The British Declaration of War on China, 1839–1840' *The International History Review* 21(4) 855–874.

Melancon, G. (2003) *Britain's China Policy and the Opium Crisis: Balancing Drugs, Violence and National Honor, 1833–1840*. Aldershot: Ashgate.

Mills, J. (2003) *Cannabis Britannica: Empire, Trade and Prohibition 1800–1928*. Oxford: Oxford University Press.

Mitter, R. (2005) 'Modernity, Internationalization, and War in the History of Modern China' *The Historical Journal* 48(2) 523–543.

Mitter, R. (2021) 'The World China Wants: How Power Will—and Won't—Reshape Chinese Ambitions' *Foreign Affairs* 100(1) 161–175.

Mohapatra, N.K. (2007) 'Political and Security Challenges in Central Asia: The Drug Trafficking Dimension' *International Studies* 44(2) 157–174.

Morris, P. (2015) *The Matter Factory: A History of the Chemistry Laboratory*. London: Reaktion Books.

Morse, H.B. (1910) *The Period of Conflict, 1834–1860*. New York: Longmans.

Motono, E. (2000) *Conflict and Cooperation in Sino-British Business, 1860–1911: The Impact of the Pro-British Commercial Network in Shanghai*. London: Palgrave.

Musto, D. (1972) 'The Marihuana Tax Act of 1937' *Archives of General Psychiatry* 26 101–108.

Musto, D. (1973) *The American Disease: Origins of Narcotic Control*. New Haven: Yale University Press.

Nadelmann, E. (1990) 'Global Prohibition Norms: The Evolution of Norms in International Society' *International Organization* 44(4) 479–526.

Newman, R.K. (1989) 'India and the Anglo-Chinese Opium Agreements, 1907–14' *Modern Asian Studies* 23(3) 525–560.

Pardal, M. (2018) 'The Belgian Cannabis Social Club Landscape' *Drugs and Alcohol Today* 18(2) 80–89.

Pardal, M. (ed) (2023) *The Cannabis Social Club*. London: Routledge.

Pardal, M., Decorte, T., Bone, M., Parés, O., and Johansson, J. (2022) 'Mapping Cannabis Social Clubs in Europe' *European Journal of Criminology* 19(5) 1016–1039.

Parker, H., Bakx, K., and Newcomber, R. (1988) *Living with Heroin: The Impact of a Drugs 'Epidemic' on an English Community*. Milton Keynes: Open University Press.

Pardo, B., Taylor, J., Caulkins, J., Kilmer, B., Reuter, P., and Stein, B. (2019) *The Future of Fentanyl and other Synthetic Opioids*. Santa Monica: RAND.

Parssinen, T. and Kerner, K. (1981) 'An Historical Fable for Our Time: The Illicit Traffic in Morphine in the Early Twentieth Century' *Journal of Drug Issues* 11 45–60.

Pettit, P. (1997) *Republicanism: A Theory of Freedom and Government*. Oxford: Oxford University Press.

Pigou, A. (1920) *The Economics of Welfare*. London: Macmillan.

Porter, R. (1996) 'The History of the "Drugs Problem"' *Criminal Justice Matters* 24(1) 3–5.

Potter, G. and Chatwin, C. (2018) 'Not Particularly Special: Critiquing 'NPS' as a Category of Drugs' *Drugs: Education, Prevention and Policy* 25(4) 329–336.

Pound, R. (1910) 'Law in Books and Law in Action' *American Law Review* 44(1) 12–36.

Queirolo, R., Boidi, M., and Cruz, J. (2016) 'Cannabis Clubs in Uruguay: The Challenges of Regulation' *International Journal of Drug Policy* 34 41–48.

Reichle, C., Smith, G., Gravenstein, J., Macris, S., and Beecher, H. (1962) 'Comparative Analgesic Potency of Heroin and Morphine in Postoperative Patients' *Journal of Pharmacology and Experimental Therapeutics* 136(1) 43–46.

Reinarman, C. and Levine, H. (eds) (1997) *Crack in America: Demon Drugs and Social Justice*. Los Angeles: University of California Press.

Reinarman, C. and Levine, H. (2004) 'Crack in the Rearview Mirror: Deconstructing Drug War Mythology' *Social Justice* 31(1–2) 182–199.

Reins, T. (1981) *China and the International Politics of Opium, 1900–1937: The Impact of Reform, Revenue, and the Unequal Treaties*. PhD Thesis. Claremont Graduate School.

Reins, T. (1991) 'Reform, Nationalism and Internationalism: The Opium Suppression Movement in China and the Anglo-American Influence, 1900–1908' *Modern Asian Studies* 25(1) 101–142.

Reisch, G. (2016) 'Aristotle in the Cold War: On the Origins of Thomas Kuhn's *Structure of Scientific Revolutions*' in: R. Richards and L. Daston (eds) *Kuhn's Structure of Scientific Revolutions at Fifty: Reflections on a Science Classic*. Chicago: University of Chicago Press, 12–30.

Reuter, P., Pardo, B., and Taylor, J. (2021) 'Imagining a Fentanyl Future: Some Consequences of Synthetic Opioids Replacing Heroin' *International Journal of Drug Policy* 94 103086.

Rittel, H. and Webber, M. (1973) 'Dilemmas in a General Theory of Planning' *Policy Sciences* 4(2) 155–169.

Ritter, A. (2022) *Drug Policy*. London: Routledge.

Ritter, A., Lancaster, K., and Diprose, R. (2018) 'Improving Drug Policy: The Potential of Broader Democratic Participation' *International Journal of Drug Policy* 55 1–7.

Rock, P. (ed) (1977) *Drugs and Politics*. London: Routledge.

Rolles, S., Murkin, G., Powell, M., Kushlick, D., Saunter, N., and Slater, J. (2016) *The Alternative World Drug Report*. 2nd Edition. Bristol: Transform.

Root, H. (2020) *Network Origins of the Global Economy: East vs West in a Complex Systems Perspective*. Cambridge: Cambridge University Press.

Rose, N. (2019) *Our Psychiatric Future: The Politics of Mental Health*. Cambridge: Polity.

Rose, N., O'Malley, P., and Valverde, M. (2006) 'Governmentality' *Annual Review of Law and Social Science* 2 83–104.

Russo, E. (2007) 'History of Cannabis and Its Preparations in Saga, Science, and Sobriquet' *Chemistry & Biodiversity* 4(8) 1614–1648.

Sachs, J. (1999) 'Twentieth-Century Political Economy: A Brief History of Global Capitalism' *Oxford Review of Economic Policy* 15(4) 90–101.

Savage, M. (2009) 'Against Epochalism: An Analysis of Conceptions of Change in British Sociology' *Cultural Sociology* 3(2) 217–238.

Schelling, T. (1978) *Micromotives and Macrobehavior*. New York: Norton.

Schiffrin, H. (1968) *Sun Yat-sen and the Origins of the Chinese Revolution*. Los Angeles: University of California Press.

Scott, C. (2001) 'Analysing Regulatory Space: Fragmented Resources and Institutional Design' *Public Law* 283–305.

Seddon, T. (2007) 'Drugs and Freedom' *Addiction Research & Theory* 15(4) 333–342.

Seddon, T. (2010) *A History of Drugs: Drugs and Freedom in the Liberal Age*. London: Routledge.

Seddon, T. (2013) 'Regulating Health: Transcending Disciplinary Boundaries' *Health Care Analysis* 21 43–53.

Seddon, T. (2014) 'Drug Policy and Global Regulatory Capitalism: The Case of New Psychoactive Substances (NPS)' *International Journal of Drug Policy* 25(5) 1019–1024.

Seddon, T. (2016) 'Inventing Drugs: A Genealogy of a Regulatory Concept' *Journal of Law & Society* 43(3) 393–415.

Seddon, T. (2020a) 'Markets, Regulation and Drug Law Reform: Towards a Constitutive Approach' *Social & Legal Studies* 29(3) 313–333.

Seddon, T. (2020b) 'Prescribing Heroin: John Marks, the Merseyside Clinics, and Lessons from History' *International Journal of Drug Policy* 78 102730.

Seddon, T. (2020c) 'Immoral in Principle, Unworkable in Practice: Cannabis Law Reform, the Beatles and the Wootton Report' *British Journal of Criminology* 60(6) 1567–1584.

Seddon, T. and Floodgate, W. (2020) *Regulating Cannabis: A Global Review and Future Directions*. London: Palgrave.

Seth, V. (2020) 'The Origins of Racism: A Critique of the History of Ideas' *History and Theory* 59(3) 343–368.

Sewell, W. (2005) *Logics of History: Social Theory and Social Transformations.* Chicago: University of Chicago Press.

Shamir, R. and Hacker, D. (2011) 'Colonialism's Civilizing Mission: The Case of the Indian Hemp Drug Commission' *Law & Social Inquiry* 26(2) 435–461.

Shearing, C. (1993) 'A Constitutive Conception of Regulation' in: P. Grabosky and J. Braithwaite (eds) *Business Regulation and Australia's Future.* Canberra: Australian Institute of Criminology, 67–79.

Shearing, C. and Froestad, J. (2010) 'Nodal Governance and the Zwelethemba Model' in: H. Quirk, T. Seddon, and G. Smith (eds) *Regulation and Criminal Justice: Innovations in Policy and Research.* Cambridge: Cambridge University Press, 103–133.

Shiner, M., Carre, Z., Delsol, R., and Eastwood, N. (2018) *The Colour of Injustice: 'Race', Drugs and Law Enforcement in England and Wales.* London: Release.

Shortis, P., Aldridge, J., and Barratt, M. (2020) 'Drug Cryptomarket Futures: Structure, Function and Evolution in Response to Law Enforcement Actions' in: D. Bewley-Taylor and K. Tinasti (eds) *Research Handbook on International Drug Policy.* Cheltenham: Edward Elgar, 355–380.

Siegel, R. (1989). *Intoxication: Life in Pursuit of Artificial Paradise.* New York: Dutton.

Sinclair, D. (1997) 'Self-Regulation Versus Command and Control? Beyond False Dichotomies' *Law & Policy* 19(4) 529–559.

Sklansky, D. (1995) 'Cocaine, Race, and Equal Protection' *Stanford Law Review* 47(6) 1283–1322.

Smail, D.L. (2008) *On Deep History and the Brain.* Los Angeles: University of California Press.

Smith, J. (1994) *The Spanish-American War 1895–1902: Conflict in the Caribbean and the Pacific.* London: Routledge.

Strang, J., Metrebian, N., Lintzeris, N., Potts, L., Carnwath, T., Mayet, S., Williams, H., Zador, D., Evers, R., Groshkova, T., Charles, V., Martin, A., and Forzisi, L. (2010) 'Supervised Injectable Heroin or Injectable Methadone Versus Optimised Oral Methadone as Treatment for Chronic Heroin Addicts in England after Persistent Failure in Orthodox Treatment (RIOTT): A Randomised Trial' *The Lancet* 375(9729) 1885–1895.

Strang, J., Groshkova, T., Uchtenhagen, A., van den Brink, W., Haasen, C., Schechter, M., Lintzeris, N., Bell, J., Pirona, A., Oviedo-Joekes, E., Simon, R., and Metrebian, N. (2015) 'Heroin on Trial: Systematic Review and Meta-Analysis of Randomised Trials of Diamorphine-Prescribing as Treatment for Refractory Heroin Addiction' *British Journal of Psychiatry* 207(1) 5–14.

Strange, S. (1970) 'International Economics and International Relations: A Case of Mutual Neglect' *International Affairs* 46(2) 304–315.

Su, Z. (2020) 'China and the Origin of International Opium Commission' *Social History of Alcohol and Drugs* 34(2) 233–239.

Swanström, N. and Tucker, J. (2019) 'China in Afghanistan—A New Force in the War in Afghanistan?' in: A. Awotona (ed) *Rebuilding Afghanistan in Times of Crisis*. London: Routledge, 156–173.

Tadros, V. (2011) 'Harm, Sovereignty, and Prohibition' *Legal Theory* 17(1) 35–65.

Taylor, A. (1967) 'American Confrontation with Opium Traffic in the Philippines' *Pacific Historical Review* 36(3) 307–324.

Taylor, L. (1971) *Deviance and Society*. London: Joseph.

Thomas, C. (2003) 'Disciplining Globalization: International Law, Illegal Trade, and the Case of Narcotics' *Michigan Journal of International Law* 24(2) 549–576.

Thompson, K. and Zurn, P. (eds) (2021) *Intolerable: Writings from Michel Foucault and the Prisons Information Group (1970–1980)*. Minneapolis: University of Minnesota Press.

Thornhill, C. and Smirnova, M. (2018) 'Litigation and Political Transformation: The Case of Russia' *Theory and Society* 47 559–593.

Tooze, A. (2014) *The Deluge: The Great War and the Remaking of the Global Order*. London: Allen Lane.

Trocki, C. (1999) *Opium, Empire and the Global Political Economy: A Study of the Asian Opium Trade 1750–1950*. London: Routledge.

United Nations Office on Drugs and Crime (UNODC) (2020a) *World Drug Report 2020*. Vienna: United Nations.

United Nations Office on Drugs and Crime (UNODC) (2020b) *In Focus: Trafficking over the Darknet—World Drug Report 2020*. Vienna: United Nations.

Urry, J. (2005) 'The Complexity Turn' *Theory, Culture & Society* 22(5) 1–14.

van Duyne, P. and Levi, M. (2005) *Drugs and Money: Managing the Drug Trade and Crime-Money in Europe*. London: Routledge.

Vardanyan, R. and Hruby, V. (2014) 'Fentanyl-related Compounds and Derivatives: Current Status and Future Prospects for Pharmaceutical Applications' *Future Medicinal Chemistry* 6 (4) 385–412.

von Bertalanffy, L. (1968) *General System Theory: Foundations, Development, Applications*. New York: George Braziller.

Wagner, R. (2020) *Macroeconomics as Systems Theory: Transcending the Micro-Macro Dichotomy*. New York: Palgrave Macmillan.

Warf, B. (2014) 'High Points: An Historical Geography of Cannabis' *Geographical Review* 104(4) 414–438.

Wang, D. (2003) 'The Discourse of Unequal Treaties in Modern China' *Pacific Affairs* 76(3) 399–425.

Watts, D. and Strogatz, S. (1998) 'Collective Dynamics of "Small-World" Networks' *Nature* 393 440–442.

Wertz, D. (2013) 'Idealism, Imperialism, and Internationalism: Opium Politics in the Colonial Philippines, 1898–1925' *Modern Asian Studies* 47(2) 467–499.

Windle, J. (2013a) 'How the East Influenced Drug Prohibition' *The International History Review* 35(5) 1185–1199.

Windle, J. (2013b) 'Harms Caused by China's 1906–17 Opium Suppression Intervention' *International Journal of Drug Policy* 24(5) 498–505.

Winther, R. (2020) *When Maps Become the World*. Chicago: University of Chicago Press.

Wong, J. (1998) *Deadly Dreams: Opium, Imperialism, and the Arrow War (1856–1860) in China*. Cambridge: Cambridge University Press.

Zheng, Y. (2003) 'The Social Life of Opium in China, 1483–1999' *Modern Asian Studies* 37(1) 1–39.

Zheng, Y. (2018) *Ten Lessons in Modern Chinese History*. Manchester: Manchester University Press.

Index